AFRICA THROUGH AN ECONOMIC LENS

AFRICA

THROUGH AN

ECONOMIC LENS

Amadou Sy

BROOKINGS INSTITUTION PRESS
Washington, D.C.

The Brookings Institution is a private nonprofit organization devoted to research, education, and publication on important issues of domestic and foreign policy. Its principal purpose is to bring the highest quality independent research and analysis to bear on current and emerging policy problems. Interpretations or conclusions in Brookings publications should be understood to be solely those of the authors.

Library of Congress Cataloging-in-Publication data are available.

ISBN 978-0-8157-3473-4 (pbk. : alk. paper)
ISBN 978-0-8157-3474-1 (ebook)

9 8 7 6 5 4 3 2 1

Typeset in Sabon

Composition by Westchester Publishing Services

CONTENTS

	Preface	vii
1	**Introduction: A Vision for Africa**	1
2	**Examining the Africa We Have**	8
3	**Maintaining the Momentum**	26
4	**Sharing the Benefits**	53
5	**Financing Africa's Development**	62
6	**Big Risks and Big Opportunities**	97
7	**Africa's Partners**	147
8	**Delivering on the Vision: Making It Happen**	226
9	**Conclusion**	241
	References	245
	Index	261

PREFACE

This book draws on my experience as director at the Africa Growth Initiative (AGI), a part of the Global Economy and Development (GED) division at the Brookings Institution. Through conferences, seminars, meetings, blog posts, papers, briefings, and editorial comment, AGI scholars examine the problems of the countries of Africa and seek to encourage policies that could lead to sustainable and inclusive growth on the continent. The scholars think ahead, focusing on broad issues of importance to Africa rather than simply reacting to a specific crisis.

When I joined Brookings in 2013, the GED's outstanding communications team was led by Mao-Lin Shen, who encouraged me to write weekly blogs on African issues. I was thrilled by the opportunity to finally have an open platform to test my ideas and help push the African agenda in Washington, D.C.

After more than three years of writing on African issues, I could see that the weekly blogs were telling a narrative that needed to be heard more widely if it was to affect Africa's future. The writings used a lens that is often overlooked when thinking about Africa: the economic lens. For instance, when the U.S. media focused on the Ebola outbreak, I felt that learning about the economic impact of the crisis would help all stakeholders.

As I prepared to move on from my directorship of AGI (I am now a nonresident senior fellow there), Kemal Derviş, vice president of GED, urged me to write a book about the continent. I revisited the blogs, conference proceedings, and working papers I had worked on during my time at Brookings (these are all available on the institution's web page—www.brookings.edu/project/africa-growth-initiative/—and I am thrilled to see that the conversation continues with a new and dynamic team at GED). *Africa through an Economic Lens* is the result of that exercise, with the addition of new writing about how Africa can move forward in the future.

I am particularly grateful to Christina Golubski and Zenia Lewis for editing and helping me organize the background material for this book, as well as Rabah Arezki for reviewing it. I would also like to thank Brahima Coulibaly and the late Mwengi Kimenyi, the current and former directors of AGI, as well as my former colleagues there—Omid Abrishamchian, Bryce Campbell, Amy Copley, Temesgen Deressa, Armand Dieng, Otito Greg-Obi, Aki Nemoto, Jessica Pugliese, Kristina Server, Jacqueline Sharkey, Eyerusalem Siba, Mariama Sow, Tor Syvrud, Valeriya Ten, and Andrew Westbury—for their collaboration. I learned a lot from many experts, but I could always count on my colleagues at GED—director Homi Kharas, Amar Bhattacharya, Laurence Chandy, Soumya Chattopadhyay, Karim Foda, Jeffrey Gutman, Joshua Meltzer, Eswar Prasad, Ernesto Talvi, Guillermo Vuletin, and Rebecca Winthrop—to help me test and refine my ideas. I would like to gratefully acknowledge the program support provided by the Bill & Melinda Gates Foundation. Brookings recognizes that the value it provides is in its commitment to quality, independence, and impact. Activities supported by its donors reflect this commitment. Thank you to William Finan and Janet Walker at Brookings Institution Press, and to John Donohue at Westchester Publishing Services. Last but not least, I dedicate this book to my late father, Dr. Amadou Yoro Sy, who passed away in 2017, and to my family for their unconditional support.

1

Introduction: A Vision for Africa

Policymakers and political commentators in the United States typically look at the continent of Africa in four ways, or through four lenses:

1. Security experts focus on security risks and the strategy to combat terrorism and related risks in Africa, such as U.S. involvement in solving the crisis in Africa's Great Lakes region, U.S. advisers assisting in the Sahel in the fight against Boko Haram and the Lord's Resistance Army, or U.S. participation along the coast of Somalia and in the Gulf of Guinea in the fight against piracy.
2. Humanitarian aid experts focus on addressing situations such as those in South Sudan and the Central African Republic and epidemics such as the Ebola virus that struck first in West Africa. Other types of aid experts look at ways to address longer-term issues, such as improving health and education.
3. China experts focus on that country's growing role in Africa and what it means for the United States.
4. Oil and other natural resource specialists focus on exploration and exploitation of such assets.

Of course, all these issues are interdependent and have important consequences for growth and development.

Before joining the Africa Growth Initiative (AGI), I had spent the previous fifteen years working in Washington on issues related to banking, capital markets, and macroeconomics in Africa and other emerging markets. The experience has allowed me to understand in depth the different perceptions of Africa and ways the continent's development is viewed. The breadth of issues facing Africa is quite large. At seminars, remarks from panelists and questions from the audience would trigger even more questions that I felt weren't being answered.

The private sector makes most of the investments in information and communication technology on the continent, whereas governments focus more on transportation and energy. I, along with other AGI scholars, thought seriously about how the private sector could better achieve development objectives and partnerships with governments and other stakeholders—for example, in filling Africa's infrastructure gap. What will be the next wave of private sector investment now that almost every African has a cell phone? How can foreign direct investment that builds an offshore oil platform—oil is an enclave sector—benefit the country and its people beyond the expected oil revenues?

We examined how to get more and better financing for development in Africa. Within this theme, we looked at external financing—private capital, official development assistance, and remittances—that flowed to Africa during 1990–2012, how the relative role of each component has changed, and the opportunities and risks associated with each one. We also went beyond averages and focused on how policies should be different for different countries or groups of countries. For instance, the role of official development assistance has decreased in sub-Saharan Africa, but countries with fragile central governments are still heavily dependent on it. Foreign direct investment has increased a lot but most goes to resource-rich countries. I wrote extensively on financing infrastructure in Africa, examining the role of the private sector, official development financing, China, and African governments in funding major infrastructure projects. My colleagues and I also looked at reducing the infrastructure gap through efficiency gains, most of which can be attained through better governance.

We were also thinking of going one step deeper than the national level to assess the challenges that rapid urbanization will create in the Africa of tomorrow and how to address them. We considered how big data can play a role in circumventing existing challenges in the availability of reliable data to guide policy analysis. For instance, we used mobile phone usage data in Senegal to see how the opening of a toll highway is changing how people commute to work, and in particular how the toll highway is affecting subsections of the Dakar urban metropolitan area. We strived to better understand the growth traps and opportunities for Africa's dominant economies (South Africa and Nigeria). In addition, our work examined the role of the United States as a central partner to African stakeholders, not only governments but also the private sector and civil society. Despite the wide variety of issues, the constant was that our economic approach complemented the different voices in the conversation about Africa in Washington.

This book covers many of the issues that I focused on in my work with the Brookings Institution, specifically as they fit into the vision for Africa. Many on the continent itself, through its regional bodies and political leadership, civil society groups and private sector, have gone to great lengths to envision the Africa of the future. The African Union created Agenda 2063, which takes the input from its member states to detail a comprehensive plan for the development of the entire continent. This book examines the vision Africa has for itself and looks at where Africa currently stands in terms of economic growth and stability. It delves into the state of Africa's economic growth and stability, and my recommendations for ensuring that Africa continues to deliver on its anticipated vision—in making progress, maintaining momentum, overcoming challenges, and sharing the benefits as it achieves growth. Lastly, the book examines the efforts and status of Africa's partners in realizing the vision.

THE VISION FOR AFRICA

The African Union's Agenda 2063 framework document spells out its vision for "an integrated, prosperous and peaceful Africa, driven by its own citizens and representing a dynamic force in the international arena."[1] With a vision for Africa fifty years into the future, the African Union certainly cannot be faulted for short-term thinking.

The framework was developed through consultations with a wide range of stakeholders, including "youth, women, Civil Society Organizations, the Diaspora, African Think Tanks and Research Institutions, Government planners, Private Sector, the African media, inter-faith leaders, the Forum for Former African Heads of State and Government, African Islands States and others."[2] The seven aspirations that make up Agenda 2063 are the following:

> 1. A prosperous Africa based on inclusive growth and sustainable development; 2. An integrated continent, politically united, based on the ideals of Pan Africanism and the vision of Africa's Renaissance; 3. An Africa of good governance, respect for human rights, justice and the rule of law; 4. A peaceful and secure Africa; 5. An Africa with a strong cultural identity, common heritage, values and ethics; 6. An Africa whose development is people-driven, relying on the potential of African people, especially its women and youth, and caring for children; and 7. Africa as a strong, united, resilient and influential global player and partner.

The framework of the agenda then goes into great detail as to how to attain these seven aspirations with priority areas and targets. The entire document examines development objectives such as education, health, agriculture, and infrastructure. It specifies the importance of economic transformation, value addition, and shared growth, and it highlights the importance of women and youth in this vision.

The document has specific ideas and numbers for its economic growth objectives, like growing GDP at rates of 7 percent or more, ensuring that 90 percent of Africa's agricultural exports are processed locally, and having a manufacturing sector that absorbs half of all new entrants into the job market.

The specifics of this vision are lofty, if somewhat utopian, and this book does not attempt to give solutions for how to achieve them. How-

1 African Union Commission (2015).
2 African Union Commission (2015).

ever, I do discuss some of the ways that Africa can work to deliver on this broader vision for a prosperous and integrated continent, through maintaining the existing momentum, managing risks, seizing opportunities, wise financing, and of course, sharing the benefits to create "the Africa we want."

A PERSONAL NOTE

I left Senegal when I was eighteen years old, about twenty-six years after its independence in 1960. The Senegalese were considered lucky because we had managed to have a peaceful transition in 1981 when President Léopold Sédar Senghor resigned and President Abdou Diouf took over. Military coups were the norm across the continent; we feared attacks by mercenaries armed by Muammar Qaddafi; neighboring Guinea-Bissau and Cape Verde fought Portugal for independence a decade earlier; apartheid was still the law in South Africa; Mobutu Sese Seko was ruling Zaire; Angola was war stricken; Namibia was not an independent state; and Bob Geldof and Band Aid were singing "Do They Know It's Christmas?" to raise funds for famine relief in Ethiopia. When I graduated from high school, a few friends received scholarships to study in the Soviet Union and communist China, and I remember meeting them during the summer break with a flurry of questions about what life was like in the two countries.

Most African economies, including my country's, were undergoing difficult structural adjustment as the postindependence episode of economic growth came to a screeching halt and reversed in 1980, in the aftermath of the oil crises of the 1970s. I remember civil servants being let go and a tense situation when sacked policemen decided to march to the presidential palace in Dakar, where an armed military was waiting for them. Thankfully, dialogue prevailed that day.

Since the 1980s, Africa has improved its economic and institutional governance; the population is growing; Human Development Index indicators, such as those on infant and maternal mortality, have improved a lot; and large cities are growing even larger. But what strikes me the most today is the confidence of the youth in taking their destiny into their own hands, how technologically savvy they are, how urbanized they have become, how aware they are of what goes on in the rest of the world, and how entrepreneurial they are, even politically—the youth played an instrumental role in the 2007 and 2012 presidential elections in Senegal. My generation was much more dependent on the public sector for almost everything—getting a phone, getting an education, getting a scholarship, getting a job—and often we had to be politically aligned with those in power to get them. Unfortunately, jobs are still scarce and some Senegalese youth take incredibly high risks to immigrate to Europe by boat. This, to me, is a stark reminder that we are not there yet.

LOOKING AHEAD

A more peaceful and prosperous Africa is in everyone's interest. In a sense, such an Africa is a global public good because it would translate into more trade and investment, more jobs, and more security for all. Now is an excellent time to step up our efforts to reach this goal because Africa is at a crossroads, and if the right path is taken, it could take us closer to reaching the continent's growth and human development objectives. Take economic growth, for instance. It took a little over twenty years for per capita income in sub-Saharan Africa to recover and surpass its 1980 level, in 2003. Since then, per capita income has been growing at a rapid and sustainable pace of about 3 percent per year thanks not only to a more favorable external environment but also to better economic and political governance.

However, these aggregate figures mask that some countries have grown poorer than they were at independence in the 1960s. For most of these countries, conflicts have had severe negative effects on per capita income. In others, the deterioration of terms of trade (the prices of their exports relative to the price of their imports) reversed the gains of the years immediately after independence. Even within countries, income disparities across regions can be high, fueling internal conflicts such as in Nigeria. The Ebola crisis in West Africa served as a stark reminder that underinvestment in health infrastructure bears heavy human and economic costs.

It is therefore important that policymakers not only continue improving economic and political governance but accelerate the pace of reforms, including structural transformation. As a banker recently said, when it comes to Africa, it is no longer a matter of "why Africa?" but "how Africa?"

This book is, therefore, focused on realizing this idea of "how Africa." Using research and policy analysis based on my time with the Brookings Institution, I examine the vision for Africa—as established by its policymaking institutions like the African Union and by its private sector, civil society, women, and youth. I look at the continent's progress in delivering on this vision, specifically its ability and progress in maintaining momentum, sharing the growth benefits, and financing its development. The risks and opportunities that are a part of this vision and the partners—country, institutional, and private sector—that are working with Africa in achieving its vision are also covered.

2

Examining the Africa We Have

As is often discussed, the *Economist* went from labeling Africa on its cover as the "hopeless continent" in the early years of the twenty-first century to showing an "Africa rising" a little more than a decade later (*Economist*, 2000, 2011). At the end of 2016, Jeffery Gettleman published an article questioning not only the sustainability but the reality of the "Africa rising" narrative, which had persisted because of the dramatic economic growth the continent has undergone in recent years. Citing Ethiopia's unrest, South Sudan's civil war, and the region's high unemployment rates, Gettleman intimated that the narrative around the continent should really be "Africa reeling."

Despite these low points in Africa's recent history, though, many countries on the continent continue to truly rise. Regional integration is reimagining how African countries interact and creating immense opportunities for poor, landlocked countries in particular. The Human Development Index demonstrates social and economic progress, as does the Ibrahim Index of African Governance of the Mo Ibrahim Foundation, which highlights steps countries are taking toward democracy and good governance. In spite of pockets of violence, Africa has become much more peaceful. A 2017 World Bank report, *Africa's Pulse*, even distinguishes between "established" and "improved" African economies in contrast to economies "stuck in the middle," "slipping," and "falling behind" (pp. 19–21). Cherry-picking some of the continent's steps backward does not undo the Africa rising narrative but rather takes us sixteen years back to the then-popular "hopeless continent" narrative—a fruitless one.

Whether describing Africa as "hopeless," "rising," or "reeling," no one can deny that African countries have made substantial gains. So many countries are quickly rising to the top. GDP in Côte d'Ivoire, Ethiopia (in spite of the regrettable flashes of internal violence), Kenya (ironically, Gettleman's article is a "Memo from Nairobi"), and Senegal is expected to grow at more than 5 percent in the next few years (International Monetary Fund, 2016). Yet, not surprisingly, oil exporters such as Nigeria and Angola will continue to suffer from the lack of diversification of their sources of revenues, and South Africa—a middle-income country—is struggling from self-inflicted wounds. But even within these countries, some regions and sectors will fare better than others.

Africans are past the debate of whether their countries are hopeless, rising, or reeling. What they want to see is resilient, sustainable, and inclusive growth, and the debate they are interested in is about the actual policies that will generate such outcomes. That is why youth in Burkina Faso took to the streets in the capital, Ouagadougou, to resist attacks against democracy. That is what many Congolese in the Democratic Republic of the Congo have been fighting for.

Africans are asking themselves one question: What's next? That is the debate they want to have. What the economic shocks to the continent are doing is separating countries into two groups—and the backsliding of a few does not mean an avalanche for all.

A COMPLEX NARRATIVE OF A CONTINENT IN FLUX

After more than a decade of relatively strong economic progress, sub-Saharan Africa's aggregate GDP growth is slowing as external shocks threaten recent advances. According to the International Monetary Fund's *Regional Economic Outlook* for sub-Saharan Africa for 2017, the continent grew at an average rate of 5.5 percent between 2000 and 2015. The regionwide growth rate in 2015 was 3.4 percent, the lowest level in about fifteen years, and in 2016 the region's growth rate fell to 1.4 percent on average, which is the lowest it has been in more than twenty years.[1] This was due in part to a commodity slump, with the price of oil falling from $108 to $47 per barrel between June 2014 and January 2015. Many oil economies were in recession in 2016, and countries with a heavy reliance on natural resources were also struggling.

In 2017, oil prices remained relatively low. Adding to this was a slowdown in China's economic growth, worries over higher U.S. interest rates, climate effects from El Niño threatening agricultural production, and serious conflict in parts of the continent. The signs of growth behind the region's economic promise seem to be in peril. Though, as discussed, this story line has swung before. The hopeless story, in numbers, is one of a continent beset by stalled growth. For example, deteriorating terms of trade after the oil shocks in the 1970s hurt commodity-dependent African countries. In 2015, the region's terms-of-trade deterioration was estimated at 18.3 percent in aggregate, though for oil exporters it was 40 percent (World Bank, 2015a, p. 30).

African countries are also plagued by fragile institutions. In the 1970s and 1980s, news was dominated by coups, civil wars, and rising strongmen. The twin blows of anemic economic growth and poor institutions set back human development and trapped far too many in poverty.

The story shifted from the mid-1990s onward. This was thanks in part to rebuilt political institutions, foreign assistance tied to macroeconomic and fiscal reforms, debt reduction or forgiveness, work to advance the UN Millennium Development Goals, and the fading of colonial vestiges after the Cold War. Another boost came from national reform and accountability measures as well as successful campaign efforts by in-country civil society activists.

Also fueling the rosier scenario was a concerted effort to tackle the region's infrastructure gap and a pivot by China to support trade and investment rather than simply use checkbook diplomacy. Foreigners and

1 International Monetary Fund (2017b). Growth was expected to recover modestly to 2.6 percent in 2017 driven by one-off factors in Nigeria, Angola, and South Africa, the three largest economies.

Africans began focusing on the following positive trends: the region's youth population bulge, which constitutes a dividend if young workers can develop skills to compete; growing digital dividends, such as those earned by M-Pesa, a highly successful mobile payment initiative; the rising middle class and its members' enormous potential as consumers; and rapid urbanization. In addition to these positive trends, regional integration efforts have improved. A continental free trade agreement has been signed. Human development improved hand in hand with economic growth, with the child mortality rate falling two and a half times faster between 2000 and 2015 than between 1985 and 2000.

Yet despite all this, the pendulum is swinging back, as Chinese policymakers have reacted to their economic slowdown by reducing China's reliance on domestic investment and curbing their appetite for imported commodities.

Within the region, threats include cross-border violence in the Sahel, around the Lake Chad basin, in the Gulf of Guinea where piracy is rampant, and in eastern Democratic Republic of the Congo where violence is still a concern. Although peaceful elections are on the rise, some leaders have learned quickly how to win elections but not how to improve institutions. Fragile countries with poor institutions and security and humanitarian situations that require UN or regional peacekeeping operations continue to dampen prospects. The situation is particularly deplorable in South Sudan, and dark clouds still loom above the Democratic Republic of the Congo, the Central African Republic, and Burundi.

Missed in the binary of a hopeless versus a rosy narrative are large disparities among countries in terms of political and economic governance. Commodity exporters like oil-rich Nigeria and Angola and copper-rich Zambia have been particularly hard hit. Conflict-affected countries such as the Central African Republic, Guinea, and Guinea Bissau are yet to recover. Others, like Mozambique, Ghana, and South Africa, still suffer from self-inflicted wounds. Mozambique's indebtedness was found to have been grossly underestimated as the scale of government-guaranteed debt emerged. Ghana's fiscal position deteriorated after the 2012 general election, and South Africa is experiencing anemic growth because of faulty decisionmaking and energy disruptions. Many countries are vulnerable to higher external refinancing costs as their currencies fall relative to the U.S. dollar. In the first six months of 2016, Nigeria's naira fell by 29 percent against the U.S. dollar.

While boom times seem to be over for oil-exporting countries, prospects look hopeful for several other countries, including Kenya, a commodity importer. Though labeled fragile, Côte d'Ivoire has revived growth from a low base and energized its agricultural production, becoming the world's largest cashew nut producer (on top of already being the largest cocoa producer). Ethiopia, using a Chinese-inspired growth model, has grown rapidly.

Tailored sector-specific opportunities may help some economies pull out of the slump. For example, the retail sector remains attractive in the wealthier suburbs of Lagos and Nairobi where shopping malls are popping up. Cement production in many countries, including Ethiopia, is expanding. Energy generation, especially from renewable sources such as solar, hydropower, and geothermal, also holds potential. A transport corridor (the Northern Corridor) linking five East African countries should boost trade, while plans for highways in West Africa will better connect cities there. Digital payment systems are expanding rapidly, particularly in fragile countries.

A consensus is emerging among African policymakers about what needs to be done, driven in part by global commitments linked to the UN Sustainable Development Goals (which replaced the Millennium Development Goals), climate plans agreed at the 2015 Paris Conference of Parties, and the 2015 Addis Ababa Action Agenda of the Third International Conference on Financing for Development agreed on by the international community.

While sound macroeconomic policies remain essential, economic diversification is more important now than ever, especially for commodity exporters. For instance, according to the Organization of Petroleum Exporting Countries, oil exports represent 90 and 95 percent, respectively, of total exports from Nigeria and Angola. Diversification must also involve stepped-up public investment, including for infrastructure. This has been achieved through the issuance of Eurobonds, which increased from $200 million in 2006 to $1.6 billion in 2015 (Mbu, 2016). Nevertheless, countries will need to rely more on safer domestic financing sources and improve the quality of public spending.

Another priority is to connect to global and regional value chains in agroprocessing and light manufacturing. As part of this, structural transformation and infrastructure improvements are essential. Better stewardship of the region's primary commodities matters too, since new discoveries are being made and the resulting revenues will need to be managed for current and future generations.

With the region's population expected to exceed 1.2 billion by 2025, due in part to a youth bulge, finding jobs for youth and women is vital. Governments, together with the private and the nonprofit sectors, should work together to adapt education systems so that they equip students to compete for the jobs of the future. All stakeholders should do more to support small businesses and young entrepreneurs. Achieving "pro-poor" growth across the continent may require taking a page from the Asian model of improved agriculture productivity and greater support for light manufacturing.

The potential offered by technology to boost job growth merits attention too. The manufacturing sector is being transformed as automation and robots make some low-skilled jobs obsolete. The services sector—one of Africa's main engines of growth—is dominated by the informal sector, which is often plagued by low productivity. To really take off, services need support from African policymakers, including incentives for technological upgrades and funding for worker training.

Ultimately, national policymakers with a sense of urgency and the drive to implement concrete strategies will be crucial to realizing the region's promise. They are forging ahead in some countries, even if the path is not smooth. Getting lagging countries on board is the biggest challenge. Doing so requires a mix of domestic policies and global governance reforms. For now, it may be the domestic actors who hold the most potential to be the main agents of change.

STRUCTURAL TRANSFORMATION OF AFRICAN ECONOMIES

To better understand what is happening on the continent, I analyze data-demonstrated trends of convergence and divergence with respect to structural transformation, as well as the rebasing of GDP, which several countries undertook, and how this affects structural transformation.

Convergence or Divergence

A major theme of policymaker discussions has been convergence—the rapid approach of average incomes in low- and middle-income countries toward those in advanced economies—and its sustainability. This issue is particularly interesting to examine in the sub-Saharan African context, specifically to understand what has been holding the region back, how Africa might reach the rapid convergence seen by other emerging economies, and if and how convergence might be sustained.

As most know, despite the "growth miracles" (countries with 7 percent or more GDP growth for twenty-five years or more), on the continent, sub-Saharan Africa still has a long way to go. Africa's economic growth started much later and has progressed much more slowly than the rest of the developing world; thus, its per capita income gap with advanced economies still remains quite large. In fact, African economies still have not even converged with other emerging economies (see figure 2-1).

In addition to slow growth, Africa faces many challenges: conflict-ridden countries still have declining income per capita, and inequality is rampant. While Africa's poverty rate is dropping, its share in global pov-

FIGURE 2-1 Sub-Saharan Africa and Other Emerging Economies

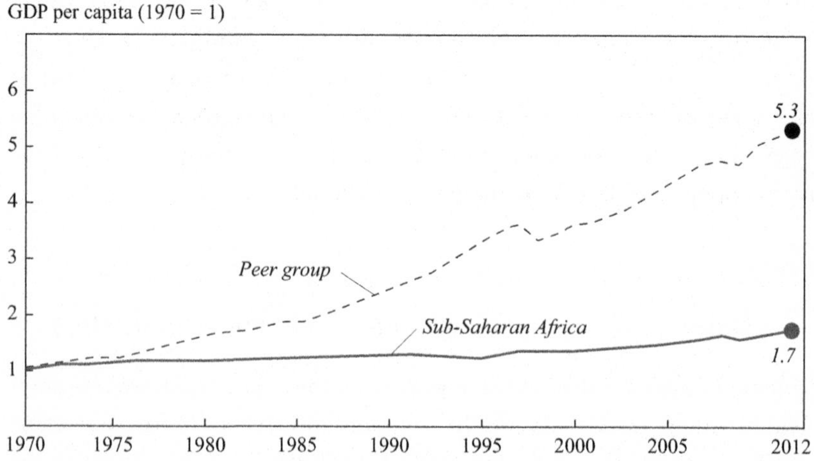

Source: African Center for Economic Transformation (2014). Earlier transformer countries are Brazil, Chile, Indonesia, Malaysia, Singapore, South Korea, Thailand, and Vietnam.

erty is not. In 1990, 56 percent of Africans lived on less than $1.25 a day, meaning that they represented 15 percent of those in poverty worldwide. Over the next twenty years, the region's poverty rate dropped to 48 percent, but its share of global poverty doubled. At this rate, many predict that by 2030 Africa's poverty rate will fall to 24 percent but represent 82 percent of the world's poor (Chandy, Penciakova, and Ledlie, 2013).

Of the utmost importance for convergence, though, is structural transformation in the region. If sub-Saharan Africa can reduce its reliance on unproductive and volatile sectors, it will build a foundation on which economic growth—and convergence—can be sustained.

Current African Economies: Agriculture, Natural Resources, and Services

Currently, African economies are characterized by a reliance on natural resources, agriculture, and a budding services sector. Natural resources are, and will likely continue to be, major drivers of Africa's economic growth: about twenty African countries derived more than 25 percent of their total goods exports in 2000–11 from them. Unfortunately, this dependence on natural resources accompanies financial volatility, rent-seeking behavior, and a loss of competitiveness, among many other challenges—making a turn away from natural resources necessary for long-term, sustainable growth. Similarly, most African economies depend heavily on the low-yield agriculture sector—the least productive sector and the one with the lowest income and consumption levels.

Labor has been moving out of the agriculture sector and into the services sector. From 2000 to 2010, the agriculture labor force share fell by about 10 percent, while services grew by 8 percent (McMillan and Harttgen, 2014). While much of the movement into the services industry has been into productive areas such as telecommunications and banking, most service sector jobs in sub-Saharan Africa are informal. Although informal activities offer earning opportunities to many people, they are often unstable, and it is far from clear that they can be an engine of sustainable and inclusive high economic growth. In addition, growth in the services sector overall has historically not shown the economic returns that industry has. If policymakers can enhance productivity in the services sector, then growth could take off even more rapidly, but until then, the highly productive manufacturing sector will be the key to Africa's convergence.

The Missing Piece: African Industry

Industrialization in Africa is low: manufacturing—the driver of growth in Asia—employs less than 8 percent of the workforce and makes up only 10 percent of GDP on the continent (Rodrik, 2014). In comparison to the 8 percent growth in the services sector from 2000 to 2010, manufacturing saw only 2 percent growth (McMillan and Harttgen, 2014). In addition, the region's manufacturing sector is dominated mostly by small and informal (and thus less productive) firms. Research has shown that industry was key to the explosive and continued growth in Asia and Europe, and without concentration on or support of the manufacturing sector, African economies are not likely to replicate those convergence dynamics (Rodrik, 2014). Thus, Africa's slow pace of industrialization means that, in addition to its late start and past sluggish growth, the region has another obstacle on its way toward convergence.

There is hope, however; there are already hints that structural transformation might be happening. The 2013 rebasing of Nigeria's economy revealed some important new trends. There, the contribution from oil and gas to GDP fell by 18 percent, and the contribution from agriculture fell by 13 percent. At the same time, telecommunications' and manufacturing's contributions rose.

Achieving a successful economic transformation will help capitalize on improved growth fundamentals and achieve high and sustained per capita growth rates. However, for such a process to yield lasting benefits, it is crucial to better understand the ongoing structural changes taking place in Africa. This is an important task for economists studying Africa, and in addition to achieving a "data revolution" (Center for Global Development and the African Population and Health Research Center, 2014), both meta-analysis and case study methods can be useful complements to the current body of research concerning the continent (Chandy, Penciakova, and Ledlie, 2013; McMillan and Harttgen, 2014; Rodrik, 2014).

Rebasing GDP: Evidence of Structural Transformation?

Rebasing GDP—revising the methods and base data used to calculate GDP—has become a growing trend among African countries in recent years. The process, which provides a clearer picture of an economy's size and structure, has implications for a wide array of economic stakeholders: for instance, updated figures allow governments to better evaluate their fiscal positions and potential revenue bases while providing investors with more accurate information on which to base their investment decisions. (See the Kenya National Bureau of Statistics [2014] report on the Revised National Accounts for a more detailed analysis of these implications.) In 2014 alone, Kenya, Nigeria, Tanzania, Uganda, and Zambia completed rebasing exercises, which led to significant revaluations of their GDPs: Nigeria's 2013 GDP nearly doubled, Tanzania's grew by a third, Kenya's and Zambia's increased by a quarter, and Uganda's rose by 13 percent.

Below I focus on how these GDP revisions have generated more accurate data, enabling fine-grained research into the following questions: How has the structure of African economies changed over the last decade? How have different sectors grown and contracted? Answering these questions is important to ensuring that Africa's economic growth remains sustainable, becomes more inclusive, and supports efforts to reduce poverty. In fact, in a recent paper on economic growth and convergence, I stress the need to better understand the ongoing structural changes taking place in Africa and call on relevant authorities to implement national statistical development strategies to enhance analysis on these transformations (Sy, 2014a). Africa's GDP rebasing exercises are useful steps in this direction and yield practical information to advance economic research. Some major gaps in African economic data still exist and have led to calls for a "data revolution" in Africa (see Center for Global Development and the African Population and Health Research Center, 2014; Jerven, 2013).

What Do These Boosts in GDP Signify?

Nigeria's rebasing, which lifted its GDP from $270 billion to $510 billion in 2013, revealed not only that its economy surpassed South Africa's, to become the largest in Africa, but that its share of sub-Saharan

African GDP grew from 21.3 percent to 31.7 percent (see table 2-1). Kenya's revised 2013 GDP of $55.2 billion augmented its per capita income from $994 to $1,269, allowing Kenya to be recategorized from a low-income to a lower-middle-income country according to World Bank metrics (Sy, 2015a). Effects have implications outside borders: The East African Community (EAC) grew its regional economy by nearly a fifth (from $110.3 billion to $134.9 billion) following the rebasing of three of its five member countries in 2014. These substantial boosts in GDP raise the profile of these countries as attractive investment destinations and can help improve investor confidence in the region.

Importantly, these sudden increases in GDP did not make these countries richer overnight. In fact, the sudden expansion of GDP has no immediate impact on the vast majority of the countries' citizens—poverty rates remain high, and performance in social development indicators has not changed. Instead, the revised GDPs show that, before rebasing, calculations relied on outdated figures (related to the overall price structure of a country's economy) and no longer accurately represented the size or composition of the economy. Revised GDPs take into account formerly omitted economic activities performed by informal businesses and recent booms in several sectors, such as information and communication technology, telecommunications, banking, and real estate. Updating the base figures for these calculations and incorporating previously overlooked sectors provides a much more precise assessment of the economies' sizes and sectoral contributions to GDP.

Drivers of Sustainable Growth

The revised GDP series for Kenya, Nigeria, Tanzania, Uganda, and Zambia highlight an important trend that generally aligns with findings from the World Bank and others—that the services sector is the single largest component of African economies (accounting for half or more of total GDP) and that the manufacturing and agriculture sectors remain essentially unchanged or have shrunk. Fueled by Africa's vast and growing labor resources, services sectors across the continent have expanded in recent years, but this growth may have been largely based on low-productivity activities that are unlikely to spur accelerated growth.

TABLE 2-1 GDP, before and after Rebasing in 2013

	Kenya (2013)	**Nigeria (2013)**	**Tanzania (2013)**	**Uganda (2013/14)**	**Zambia (2010)**[a]
Change in base year	From 2001 to 2009	From 1990 to 2010	From 2001 to 2007	From 2002 to 2009/10	From 1994 to 2010
GDP (Old series)	3.8 trillion KSh ($44.1 billion)	42.4 trillion naira ($270 billion)	53 trillion TSh ($33.3 billion)	60.5 trillion USh ($21.5 billion)	77.7 billion kwacha ($13.4 billion)
GDP (New series)	4.8 trillion KSh ($55.2 billion)	80.2 trillion naira ($510 billion)	70 trillion TSh ($43.8 billion)	68.4 trillion USh ($24.7 billion)	97.2 billion kwacha ($16.7 billion)
Percent change	25.3	89.2	27.8	13.1	25.2

Source: Sy (2015a)

a. For Zambia, comparisons between the old and new GDP series are available only for the benchmark year 2010.

Indeed, in reviewing the revised 2013 figures for these five countries, we see that, in addition to massive upward revaluations of GDP, the following changes in GDP composition by sector—largely increases in services, declines in industry, and relatively stable contributions from agriculture—took place (see figures 2-2, 2-3, and 2-4 for a comparison of changes among the five countries):

- In Kenya, the rebasing found slightly higher increases in the contribution of agriculture and industry to the economy than previously estimated and a minor decrease in the contribution of services. However, interestingly, within the services sector, many new subdivisions were created for fast-growing sectors such as information and communication technology, which was formerly classified under transport, storage, and communications. From 2010 to 2013, agriculture's share of GDP grew slightly, and industry and the services' sectors shares declined.
- In Nigeria, the revised GDP estimate included measures of forty-six industries (up from thirty-three in the previous calculation). Oil and gas's share of GDP decreased, from 32 to 14 percent, as did agriculture's, from 35 to 22 percent. Yet the share of telecommunications increased from 2 to 7 percent, contributing in part to the massive boost from 26 to 51 percent of the services sector's share of GDP. Manufacturing also rose from 0.9 to 9 percent. In terms of the changing composition of GDP over the period from 2010 to 2013, agriculture and mining generally declined in their contributions to GDP, while industry and services increased.
- In Tanzania, the revised GDP for the 2007 benchmark year saw small downward revaluations of agriculture (from 27.1 to 26.8 percent) and industry (from 21.1 to 20.2 percent) but an upward revision for the services sector (from 43.3 to 47.6 percent). In terms of the changing composition of GDP over the period from 2007 to 2013, the contribution of agriculture to GDP actually grew to 31.7 percent and services decreased to 40.4 percent. Industry declined to 15.6 percent in 2010 before rising again to 17.5 percent in 2013.

FIGURE 2-2 Agriculture, before and after Rebasing in 2013

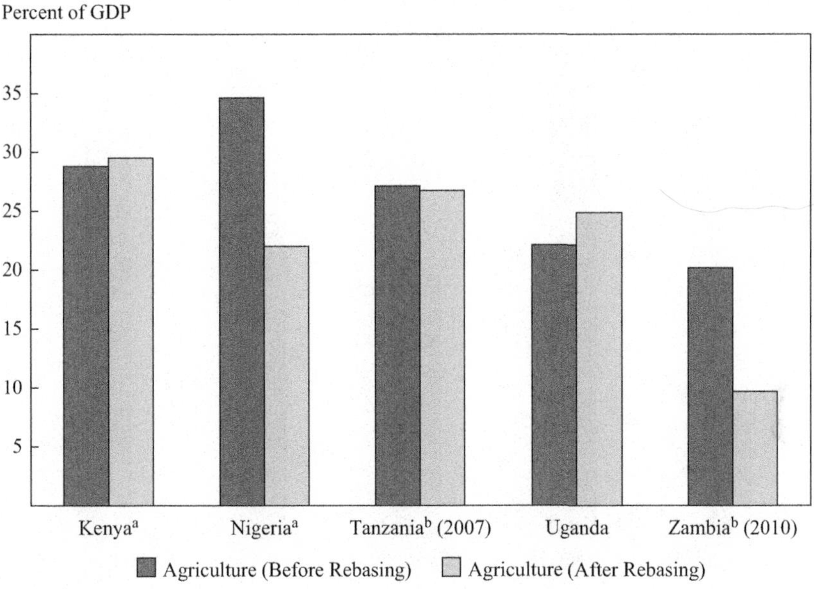

Source: Sy (2015a).

a. Values for Kenya and Nigeria are post-tax.

b. For Tanzania and Zambia, sectoral comparisons were available only in the benchmark years of 2007 and 2010, respectively.

- In Uganda, the share of industry in the revised GDP figure decreased from 26.6 percent to 20.8 percent, predominantly because of the previous overvaluation of the contribution of construction. Yet manufacturing (as a subsector of industry) rose from 8.0 percent to 10.0 percent in the recalculated figure, and agriculture and services also increased to 24.8 and 47.1 percent, respectively (from 22.2 and 45.4 percent) of the economy for 2013. Over the past several years the shares of these sectors in the economy have remained fairly stable.
- In Zambia, wholesale retail and trading made the largest contribution to the revised GDP for the 2010 benchmark year, at 18.4 percent, up from 14.4 percent. Construction and agriculture approximately halved from their prerevised figures to 10.9 percent and 9.9 percent, respectively. Mining, on the other hand, was revalued

FIGURE 2-3 Industry, before and after Rebasing in 2013

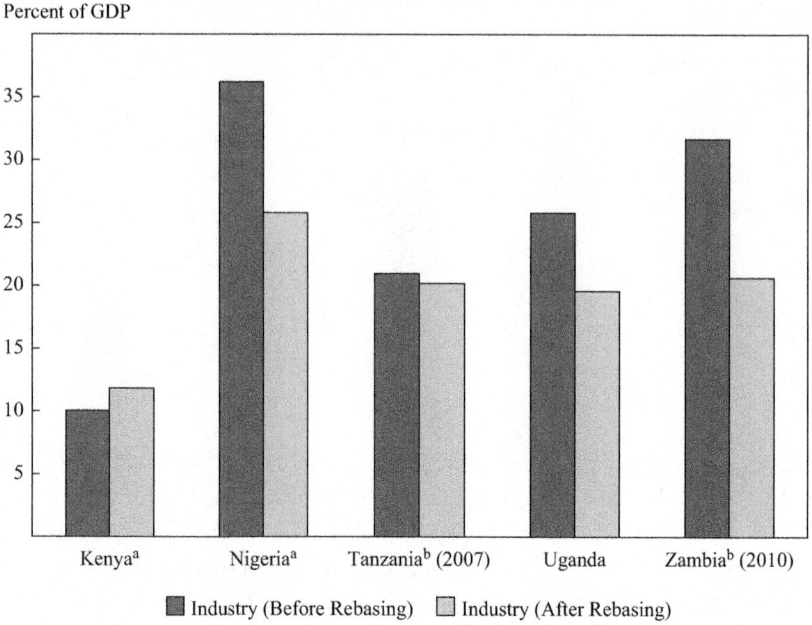

Source: Sy (2015a)

a. Values for Kenya and Nigeria are post-tax.

b. For Tanzania and Zambia, sectoral comparisons were only available in the benchmark years of 2007 and 2010, respectively.

from 3.7 percent to 12.9 percent of GDP. In terms of the changing composition of GDP over the period from 2010 to 2013, agriculture has remained stable in its share of GDP, while industry and the services sectors have increased their shares, and the share of mining has declined considerably.

A Case for Refocusing on Services Subsectors

These rebasing exercises have helped clarify the diversity within select African economies, providing policymakers with a better fundamental understanding of the structural changes their economies are undergoing. But revised statistics alone will not ignite economic growth across the continent—they must be integrated into the ongoing development

FIGURE 2-4 Services, before and after Rebasing in 2013

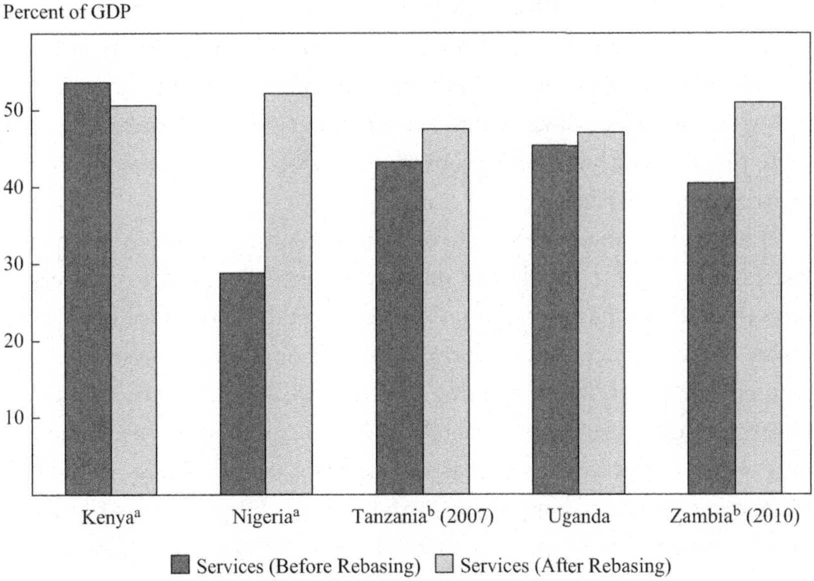

Source: Sy (2015a)

a. Values for Kenya and Nigeria are post-tax.

b. For Tanzania and Zambia, sectoral comparisons were available only in the benchmark years of 2007 and 2010, respectively.

policy debates occurring in these countries. In particular, the rise in the services sector's share of GDP together with gradual or no increases in the shares of industrialization and agriculture may have significant implications for sustaining the region's growth, as noted by Rodrik (2014, pp. 7–8):

> The traditional engines behind rapid growth and convergence, structural change and industrialization, are operating at less than full power. . . . If African countries do achieve growth rates substantially higher than what I have surmised, they will do so pursuing a growth model that is different from earlier miracles based on industrialization. Perhaps it will be agriculture-led growth. Perhaps it will be services. But it will look quite different than what we have seen before.

Keeping these changes in mind, policymakers must now focus on the sectors that are poised for transformation and consider how they can provide targeted support. A consensus seems to be forming for policies that draw more labor into and reinvigorate manufacturing (through, for example, agroprocessing activities), boost agricultural productivity by more plantings of high-value crops, and develop labor force skills to improve productivity in services.

A good start, in my view, is to delve more deeply into the African services sector. So far the debate on the services' potential to accelerate growth in Africa has centered on the opportunities presented by mobile phone technology, and the information and communication technology sector more generally, in creating jobs and raising productivity. But in Nigeria, as discussed above, the telecommunications sector accounts for only 7 percent of GDP, whereas the services sector's share of GDP is 51 percent. What is happening in the rest of the services subsectors, which account for 44 percent of GDP? Are the other key subsectors, including trade, creating sustainable and inclusive jobs for Nigerian workers? Are the sectors helping workers acquire new skills and use more technology? Or does service sector growth mostly constitute informal activities?

More exploration of the linkages between growth, employment, and productivity is needed beyond the information and communication technology subsector in often-understated subsectors, which could hold great, untapped potential to provide jobs and skills development to local workers, as it has done in other regions of the world.[2] In this sense, understanding the services sector requires a nuanced yet holistic approach that looks at the subsectoral employment and GDP data and determines which activities require additional investment to enhance productivity and lead to inclusive growth for the sector.

But formulating good policies will be easier than implementing them. As Pritchett and Summers (2014) put it, "Sustained economic growth typically relies on continued structural transformation in which new industries arise, but also old industries shrink—sometimes just relatively, but sometimes absolutely. While essential to sustained economic growth, neither governments nor existing firms like destruction—with

2 See figure 3 in Gutman (2015).

its geographic shifts, employment shifts, and firm exits that are a necessary part of weeding out uncompetitive industries."

As this chapter has demonstrated, African economies show a great deal of variation, and economic changes, such as rebasing their GDPs, are further evidence that much is changing on the economic front. These stories show the complex picture of the Africa we have; the next chapters delve into the vision for an Africa we want and how the continent is delivering on that vision.

3

Maintaining the Momentum

Much has been made of Africa's rising economic prosperity, whether it is sustainable and deeply rooted, and what it will do to reduce extreme poverty across the continent. In the following section I provide responses to the key questions being asked about Africa's growth and development.

FIVE QUESTIONS ON AFRICA'S RISING ECONOMIC GROWTH

Why Does Africa Show the Highest Growth Prospects of the World's Continents?

There is no doubt that favorable commodity prices have and will be a key driver of growth for sub-Saharan Africa. The so-called commodity supercycle, in which commodity prices have seen large increases since 2000, has benefited traditional oil exporters, such as Nigeria and Angola, and new ones, like Ghana. Demand for natural resources from emerging markets, especially China, has increased in the last decade and remains important. As noted in the *BP Energy Outlook 2035* (British Petroleum, 2014), Africa will remain an important producer of oil and natural gas, accounting for 10 percent of global oil and 9 percent of natural gas production in 2035. Even with oil prices lower in recent years, this remains a significant contribution.

In addition, the continuation of good medium-term policies and structural reforms bodes well for future growth in the region. Africa has democratized to some extent, and violence and armed conflicts have decreased, though a few hot spots remain. Half the world's future population growth will be driven by Africa (not because of higher fertility, which is declining, but because of longer life expectancy). This trend could lead to a demographic dividend of an adult population of 800 million by 2030 (compared to 460 million in 2010). Africa's rapid urbanization and burgeoning middle class could generate hundreds of millions of consumers.

To sustain its growth, however, Africa will need to continue reducing poverty and inequality and step up the transformation of its economy. As noted by Rodrik (2013), African countries, unlike East Asian countries, have not yet been able to turn their farmers into manufacturing workers, diversify their economies, and export a range of increasingly sophisticated goods. Moreover, many African countries are joining the resource-rich country club, and with that membership comes not only opportunities but also challenges. Good governance will be needed to enable future generations of Africans to benefit from this new wealth. Low global interest rates and high commodity prices have opened a window of opportunity for African countries to reform. This window will not always remain open, and reform is needed now.

What Role Does China Play in Africa's Economic Development?

China's economic performance shows that a transformational agenda can succeed and lift a large segment of the population out of poverty. Beyond being a benchmark, China has become the largest single trading partner for sub-Saharan Africa, with 17 percent of total trade. In comparison, India has a 6 percent share and Brazil a 3 percent share. The so-called Group of Five (Indonesia, Malaysia, Saudi Arabia, Thailand, and the United Arab Emirates) accounts for only 5 percent of sub-Saharan Africa's total trade.

China also accounts for 16 percent of total foreign direct investment to sub-Saharan Africa and has become a key investor and provider of aid. There is no doubt that China is interested in Africa's natural resources (such as copper in Zambia and oil in Nigeria and Sudan), but it is expanding its focus. Over 2,000 Chinese enterprises are investing and developing in more than fifty African countries, and South Africa is the leading recipient of Chinese foreign direct investment.

The key advantage of China in Africa is speed. Chinese firms are able to deliver quickly and work in close coordination with their financial and other national partners. Speed is a big comparative advantage in Africa. For instance, the continent has large infrastructure needs, and African policymakers are under pressure to deliver. An offer to build a coal-generated power plant in a couple of years tempts them when their population and businesses are disgruntled by sometimes daily power outages. They agree to the quick-and-dirty fix instead of adopting a less polluting technology.

Which African Countries Deserve Close Attention?

South Africa has always been a chief recipient of foreign investment, given the sophistication of its economy. In addition, natural resource–rich countries in Africa, such as Angola and Nigeria, will remain a key destination of foreign investment, especially given that the number of resource-rich countries will only increase with modern techniques in offshore oil exploration and extraction. In fact, Japanese prime minister Shinzo Abe visited Mozambique in 2017 to secure natural gas contracts. Countries in the East African Community (Kenya, Uganda, and Tanzania) have made oil and gas discoveries in recent years. Metal-exporting countries such as Burkina Faso, Ghana, and Tanzania are also attractive.

A country with few natural resources, Ethiopia has a large population of more than 80 million people, high GDP growth, and a government-led strategy to attract foreign investment in some sectors. Rwanda is a smaller economy, but it is growing rapidly and trying to leverage its membership in the East African Community. In West Africa, Côte d'Ivoire is fast recovering from armed conflict, Senegal boasts a long track record of political stability, and Ghana remains a darling of foreign investors.

What Are Key Areas of Opportunity to Capitalize on for Africa's Development?

Large infrastructure projects in Africa need foreign partners. Infrastructure spending in Africa is estimated to reach $93 billion per year, and tax revenues and other domestic resources will not be enough to fill the financing gap for infrastructure projects.

The needs of information and communication technology remain high in spite of the rapid growth in mobile phones and mobile banking. Major companies, including Google, Microsoft, Huawei, and GE, are betting on the continent and investing in research and development.

The rising African middle class is attracting investors in the retail sector. For instance, French supermarket chains Auchan and Carrefour and American big-box store Walmart have expanded their operations to Africa. Banking is also attractive given the low financial depth in Africa. Foreign investors are now focusing on urban centers with a high potential for consumer spending. In 2020, the household spending of Alexandria, Cairo, Cape Town, Johannesburg, and Lagos will total $25 billion. One untapped area for major investment is agriculture. Africa has about half the planet's arable land, and expected returns from this sector are potentially large, especially if its infrastructure gap is reduced.

Finally, investments in equity markets, domestic bond markets, and Eurobond markets are increasing, and private equity firms are increasingly investing in the region. In 2013, the Morgan Stanley Capital International African Frontier Market equity index was up 28.5 percent over the previous year, and $10.7 billion of sovereign bonds were issued by capital markets in Africa, which now has five times more countries with a sovereign rating than it did in 2000.

Is the Whole Continent Progressing?

The extent to which overall growth is shared by the fifty-four countries in Africa is quite impressive. This being said, some trouble spots remain. While some fragile countries like Liberia, Sierra Leone, and especially Rwanda have been able to move forward from unfortunate legacies of violence and in some cases even genocide, the situation in other countries is worsening, particularly in the Central African Republic and South Sudan (which is oil rich). The situation also remains unsafe in the east of the Democratic Republic of the Congo and in Mali despite recent progress, and press reports tell of terrorist acts by al-Shabab. Even the north of Nigeria experiences violence attributed to Boko Haram, and the Gulf of Guinea has piracy. An African-owned framework and response mechanism is needed to prevent and resolve violent conflict and crises on the continent. However, improving intelligence and local dialogue should be prioritized.

African efforts to increase economic integration are strengthening regional growth. Economic and trade integration across Africa will help foreign investors access larger markets and reduce transaction costs, including costs associated with regional infrastructure projects. African countries are trying to strengthen regional integration through regional economic communities and are negotiating free trade agreements and customs unions with the goal of ultimately having common currencies. The continent is far from one common African currency, but some steps forward have been made in this area. The East African Community—which includes Burundi, Kenya, Rwanda, Tanzania, and Uganda—is a market of 150 million people and is set to become a monetary union soon. The former French colonies in Africa all use the same currency, which is pegged to the euro, and have common financial institutions.

What is striking is that there is a consensus in African policy circles that we are witnessing Africa's moment. The challenge will be in implementing the policy road map quickly, as there is little time left for transformation. Filmer and Fox (2014) note that half the region's population is under twenty-five years of age. Each year between 2015 and 2035 will see 500,000 more fifteen-year-olds than the year before. The challenge will be to transform this youth bulge into an opportunity.

INVESTMENT IN AFRICA: WHO PROFITS FROM THE BOOM?

Foreign investment in Africa has undergone remarkable growth of late. However, this trend raises questions not only about the sustainability of the flow of capital to the continent but also its contribution to the improvement of the daily lives of the people of Africa. The debate is of course far from over, but here are answers to some of the most frequently asked questions.

Are Foreign Investors Flocking to Africa?

Indeed, there has been a decadelong increasing trend of foreign investment into sub-Saharan Africa with three notable highlights.

1. The flow of foreign private capital has multiplied by five times in the last ten years. Investment has increased from $14 billion in 2002 to $67 billion in 2012. This demonstrates a great interest in investment, especially if one takes into account the financial crisis of 2008. The flow of foreign private capital now exceeds the disbursements of official development assistance. Foreign aid increased from $18 billion to $43 billion over this same period. Taking into consideration growth rates, capital flow has increased by almost 20 percent per year against 12 percent annually for aid.
2. This growth of capital investment is partly driven by China and other members of the BRICS (Brazil, Russia, India, China, and South Africa) countries. These countries now account for more than one-quarter of capital investment to the continent, and this trend is increasing.
3. Investment focus has also changed. In recent years, some countries have had access to international capital markets for the first time. These countries include South Africa, Angola, Côte d'Ivoire, Gabon, Ghana, Namibia, Nigeria, Senegal, Seychelles, and Zambia. Additionally, foreign investment in local capital markets in the form of purchases of stocks, bonds, and treasury bills is growing rapidly.

Is an African Middle Class Emerging?

At the outset it should be noted that there are different ways to define *middle class* in Africa. Certain economists, such as my colleague Homi Kharas (2017), define it as households with daily incomes of between $11 and $110 per person (in 2011 purchasing power parity [PPP] terms). According to this definition, middle-class Africans represent 114 million people (4 percent of the world's middle-class population) with a total overall consumption of $915 billion in 2011 PPP terms (3 percent of the world's middle-class consumption). Kharas expects the middle class in sub-Saharan Africa to reach about 212 million people, with a total consumption of $1.661 trillion by 2030 (roughly the same size as the Middle East today).

On the other hand, according to the African Development Bank (2011), $2 to $20 is enough daily income to be considered as middle class. That equates to 350 million people (or 34 percent of the African population) as of 2010, up from 126 million (or 27 percent of the African population) in 1980. For other analysts, a range of $15 to $20 is a better definition because an income of $2 is far too close to the defined poverty line.

What is certain is that the growth of the African middle class could be the highest in the world (albeit from a low base), and this is what is attracting foreign investors. The World Bank estimates that the strong economic growth of African countries (of more than 5 percent per year) is driven by the consumption of the middle class. We can therefore expect investments targeting the mobile phone market, electronic products, and banking services. We are already seeing shopping malls developing very quickly in many African capitals. However, the 2017 failure of the Kenya supermarket chain Nakumatt is a reminder that rapid growth is not without risks.

Are Africans Benefiting from Increased Investment and Economic Growth?

Many Africans argue that increased investment and economic growth do not translate into benefits in their daily lives because of the persistence of unemployment, the high cost of living, and the poor quality of public services, as well as the high price of electricity and water. One reason is that foreign direct investments do not create enough jobs because, apart from the case of South Africa, they are primarily intended to finance projects in the natural resources sector (oil, gas, and mining). A high concentration of these investments flows toward South Africa and natural resource–rich countries, which together receive three-quarters of all such current investments. The mining and petroleum sectors primarily require skilled workers, and governments have not been able to provide training for sufficient numbers.

Throughout Africa there is very little growth in jobs, and I foresee a necessity for foreign creation of private sector jobs and foreign involvement in local small and medium enterprises. This requires foreign investments that are more closely associated with the transfer of knowledge and skills. Some progress in the area of information and communication technology has occurred, and Microsoft, Huawei, Google, and other large foreign companies have actively invested in training. There is even talk of a Silicon Savannah in Kenya.

The agricultural sector also has significant investment potential, which, if exploited, could lead to large-scale job creation. Africa has more than half the world's arable land, but because of lack of infrastructure, farmers can lose more than half their product on the way to market. The share of industry in Africa has also declined since the 1960s, and the development of the agricultural sector could happen in conjunction with that of the industrial sector. The success of horticulture in East Africa is a good example.

It is important to remember that foreign investments are only one component of external flows to the continent. Such flows also include remittances from Africans abroad (on average, $22 billion per year over the 2000–12 period and more than 10 percent of GDP for Nigeria and Senegal). We must also add public development aid. Many fragile countries emerging from conflicts continue to depend on official development assistance and remittances. There is a need to redefine the role of public aid so it can catalyze productive investment toward employment opportunities and infrastructure. South–South cooperation should also be strengthened.

Finally, external flows from abroad are lower than tax revenue collected by African governments. Ultimately, an improvement in fiscal management is indispensable for growth. In this context, illicit financial flows that escape national taxation must be reduced. Some foreign companies use these illicit financial schemes to offset their tax payment.

Will Foreign Investment Growth Be Sustainable?

The evolution of the growth of foreign investment in Africa depends on internal and external factors. Internal factors pulling foreign investment into the region include urbanization, the emergence of the new middle classes, and the natural resources boom. In external factors, an increase in U.S. interest rates (a measure of risk-free return) tends to slow down or even reverse portfolio flows. This has been the case in Ghana, Nigeria, and South Africa with the increased volatility in their short-term financial markets, including in the foreign exchange and equity markets. A sharp drop in the price of raw materials and commodities would have severe effects on long-term investment such as foreign direct investments.

But, for the moment, the numerous discoveries of gas in Mozambique, oil in East Africa, and gold in Burkina Faso attract investors and should support foreign direct investment. On a very positive note, Ethiopia managed to attract some foreign direct investments in the industrial sector and in the renewable energy sector. With the emphasis on infrastructure by many African countries and international initiatives, for example, the Power Africa initiative launched by U.S. president Barack Obama, this sector also sees a strong demand for foreign investment.

Regarding crises in Africa, conflict and insecurity discourage potential foreign investors, especially those who are interested in sectors other than natural resources or who are not entirely familiar with Africa, but this is not always the case. In Côte d'Ivoire, some investors achieved more profitable business in Abidjan during the crisis than in neighboring Ghana. In contrast, bad news for a particular African country can affect other countries on the continent. However, recent conflicts in Africa are confined to a few unfortunate areas. The Central African Republic has never been a very important destination for foreign investors. In Mali, the conflict is now contained, and the southern part of the country can rebound quite quickly. In South Sudan, the crisis there has affected oil production, and foreign companies have removed nonessential staff. But let us not forget that oil companies continued their operations in Angola even during the Cuban intervention in 1988.

HOW MUCH OF SUB-SAHARAN AFRICA'S GROWTH SLOWDOWN IS DRIVEN BY EXTERNAL FACTORS?

Sub-Saharan Africa's GDP growth forecasts are down. In early 2016, the International Monetary Fund (IMF) lowered its annual growth estimates to 3.0 percent from 4.3 percent. The last time the region achieved a similar growth rate was in 1999 (2.8 percent). Importantly, the expected slowdown largely reflects the impact of a more difficult external economic environment on African economies and, in particular, the effects of a sharp drop in commodity prices, the slowdown in China, and tighter financial conditions.

The lower growth forecasts follow long, robust growth in the region. Between 2004 and 2011, sub-Saharan Africa experienced 6.2 percent growth. Between 2012 and 2015, however, growth in the region slowed to 4.5 percent. Africa is not alone, though: this pattern of boom and subsequent slowdown was observed in every emerging region on the globe. This doesn't mean that these changes are insignificant, though. In 2016, GDP growth in sub-Saharan Africa slowed down sharply to 1.4 percent, the lowest in twenty years, but the IMF (2017b) expected it to reach 2.6 percent in 2017 as a third of the countries in the region continue to grow at 5 percent or more.

But How Much of the Region's Growth Is Driven by External Factors?

To determine the external influences on the region's growth, the Africa Growth Initiative partnered with the Brookings Global–CERES Economic and Social Policy in Latin America Initiative to study the role of external factors in explaining output fluctuations in sub-Saharan Africa (Sy and Talvi, 2016). The analysis focused on the seven largest economies (Angola, Ghana, Kenya, Nigeria, South Africa, Ethiopia, and Tanzania, the SSA-7), which account for three-quarters of sub-Saharan Africa's GDP.[1]

Some of the key findings of the study are the following:

1. Almost half of sub-Saharan Africa's output fluctuations since 1998 can be explained by a small set of external factors—namely, GDP growth in the Group of Seven countries,[2] GDP growth in China, oil and non-oil commodity prices, and borrowing costs for emerging economies in international capital markets.

1 For this more detailed analysis, see Africa Growth Initiative (2016).

2 The Group of Seven (G-7) is composed of Canada, France, Germany, Italy, Japan, the United Kingdom, and the United States.

FIGURE 3-1 Sub-Saharan Africa's Business Cycle: The Role of External Factors[a]

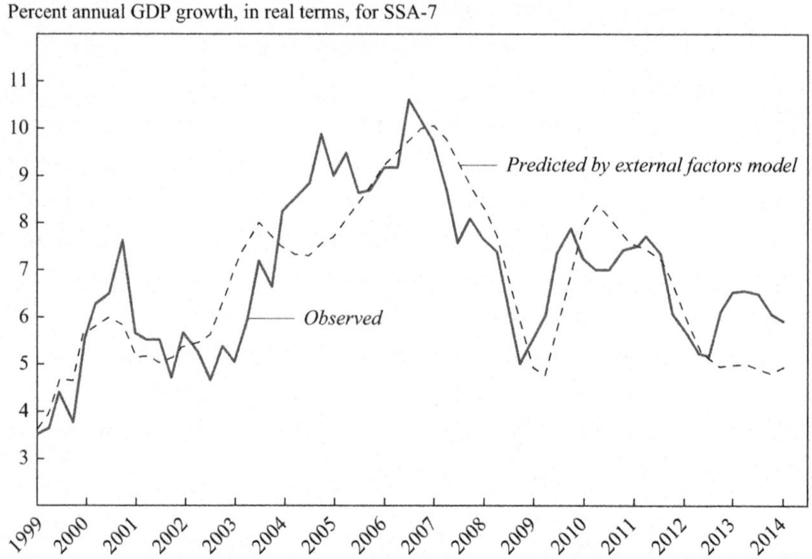

Sources: International Monetary Fund (2015b); Sy and Talvi (2016).

a. Predicted GDP growth corresponds to the prediction of a vector error correction model using only the observed external factors from 1998:1 to 2014:4. For technical details, see Izquierdo, Romero, and Talvi (2008).

Figure 3-1 illustrates that this small set of external variables helps explain about 44 percent of sub-Saharan Africa's output variance. As a result, both the boom experienced between 2004 and 2011 and the sharp deceleration observed since 2012 can, to a large extent, be attributed to significant changes in the external environment, from extremely favorable in the former period to more adverse in the latter.

2. Key downside risks for sub-Saharan Africa's growth include a sharp slowdown in China's growth, a further decline in commodity prices, and a tightening in international financial conditions for emerging economies. Whereas permanently lower commodity prices and tighter financial conditions for emerging economies would have only temporary effects on sub-Saharan Africa's output growth, a permanent Chinese slowdown would have a larger and persistent effect, as seen in figure 3-2.

FIGURE 3-2 Counterfactual Scenarios for Sub-Saharan African Growth[a]

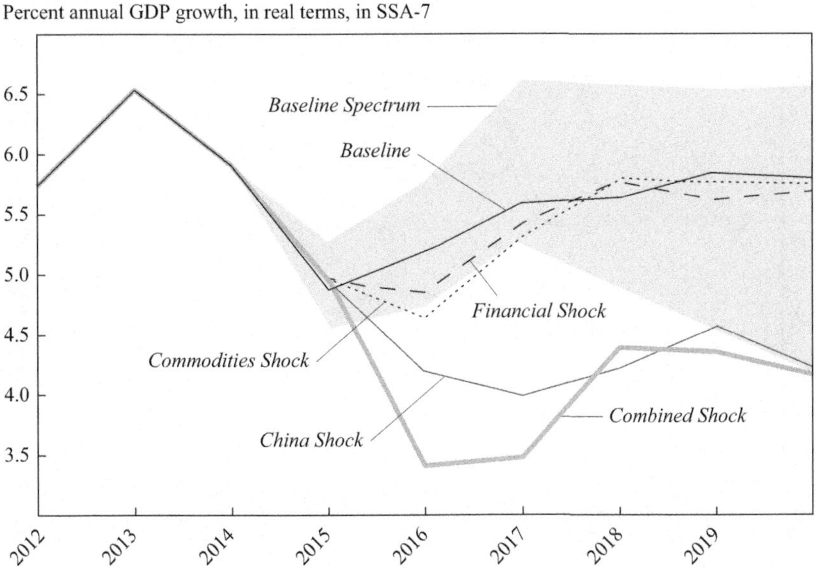

Sources: International Monetary Fund (2015b); Sy and Talvi (2016).

a. The baseline scenario corresponds to the prediction of a vector error correction model when external factors are assumed to evolve according to market expectations. The China shock is a reduction in growth from 6.5 percent to 4 percent; the financial shock is an increase of 300 basis points above baseline EMBI+ levels; the commodities shock is a price fall of 20 percent below baseline levels; the combined shock combines all of the above simultaneously.

3. Given the importance of external factors in explaining output fluctuations in sub-Saharan Africa, a key policy recommendation is that, to properly evaluate a country's fundamentals, policymakers should work with structural indicators of sustainability. For instance, the structural fiscal and current account balances are the fiscal and current account positions that result when the key external drivers of the business cycle of sub-Saharan Africa such as commodity prices are computed at their long-run values.

Fiscal sustainability refers to the ability to run fiscal deficits and pile up public debt without compromising a country's perceived solvency. Figure 3-3 shows that during the boom period (2004–11), the observed fiscal balance was consistently above the structural fiscal balance and

FIGURE 3-3 Structural Fiscal Balance

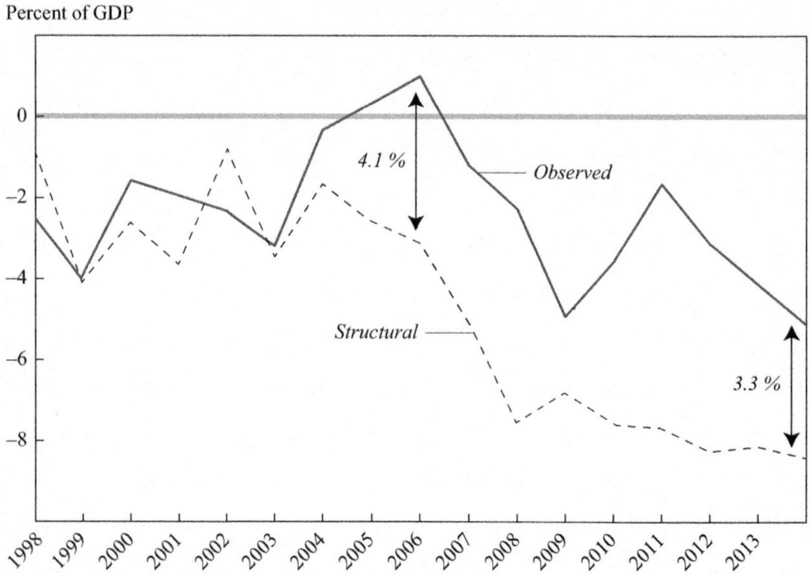

Sources: International Monetary Fund (2015b); Sy and Talvi (2016).

Note: The structural fiscal balance is calculated by performing a linear estimation on observed fiscal revenues between 1998 and 2003, before the boom began, and extrapolating from then on.

thus conveyed the impression that the fiscal position was stronger than it actually was. As commodity prices declined and output growth decelerated during the cooling-off period (since 2012), the observed fiscal balance began moving toward the structural fiscal balance, revealing that the underlying fiscal position was actually weaker than the observed one.

External sustainability refers to the ability to sustain spending over income with external capital inflows. Figure 3-4 shows that during the boom period (2004–11) the observed current account balance was consistently above the structural current account balance and thus conveyed the impression that the external position was stronger than it actually was. As commodity prices declined during the cooling-off period (since 2012), the observed current account balance began moving toward the structural current account balance, revealing that the underlying external position was actually weaker than the observed one.

FIGURE 3-4 Structural Current Account Balance

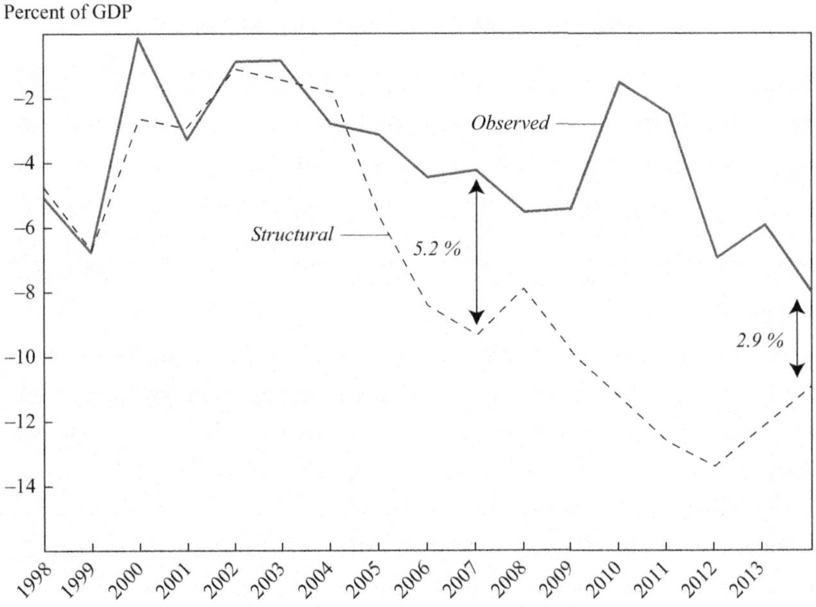

Sources: International Monetary Fund (2015b); Sy and Talvi (2016).

Note: The adjusted current account balance is calculated by using the average of export and import prices observed between 1992 and 2003, before the boom began.

These findings shed some light on the "Africa rising" narrative—the recent economic boom cycle in sub-Saharan Africa. In particular, they highlight the important role of external factors, which accounted for almost half of the region's output fluctuations. They also point to the need for policymakers to be cautious in boom periods and rely on structural economic indicators that are less sensitive to the boom-bust cycle of external factors such as commodity prices.

Indirectly, the findings above emphasize the important role of domestic policies in explaining Africa's growth. If external factors explain half of output fluctuations, then it is crucial to make sure we get the other half of domestic factors right. Now that we are in a bust cycle, the political appetite for policy reforms should be higher. Now is the time for implementation.

FOREIGN EXCHANGE RISK OF AFRICAN SOVEREIGN BONDS: NOT YET TIME TO SOUND THE ALARM

Africa needs significant financing to meet its ambitious sustainable development goals. While domestic financing sources such as tax revenues have increased, they are not sufficient. To fill the continent's financing gap, a number of governments are accessing international markets to complement domestic financing. However, as seen in the 1997–98 Asian financial crisis or more recently in the European crisis, external financing comes with risks.

In a useful and timely exercise, the Overseas Development Institute (ODI) assesses these risks and finds that the depreciation of local currencies with respect to the U.S. dollar is threatening sub-Saharan African governments' ability to repay the bonds to investors (Tyson, 2015). But is that really true? Before 2006, South Africa was the only sub-Saharan African country to issue a foreign-currency-denominated sovereign bond. From 2006 to 2014, at least fourteen other countries have issued more than $15 billion in international sovereign bonds. Unfortunately, the increased indebtedness of these countries increases their vulnerability to economic shocks. African currencies such as the Ghanaian cedi and the Nigerian naira have been depreciating recently, and servicing debt denominated in the U.S. dollar has become even more expensive (see figure 3-5). But how much riskier has African sovereign debt become as a consequence of currency depreciation?

Tyson (2015) uses a stress test exercise to find that "the foreign exchange rate risk of sovereign bonds issued by governments in sub-Saharan Africa in 2013 and 2014 is threatening losses of $10.8 billion—a value equivalent 1.1 percent of the region's GDP." African countries face such a risk because they have borrowed in U.S. dollars but typically earn a large share of their revenues in local currencies. If local currencies depreciate with respect to the U.S. dollar, borrowing countries experience a loss of value of their local currencies and have to raise more local currencies to pay back their U.S. dollar–denominated debt. This additional amount (expressed in U.S. dollars or as a percentage of GDP) is the foreign exchange impact in the ODI calculations. Table 3-1 shows the additional estimated amount that countries would have to raise in order to service their sovereign bonds following a depreciation of their local cur-

FIGURE 3-5 African Currencies and Sovereign Bond Interest Rate Spreads, 2014 and 2011

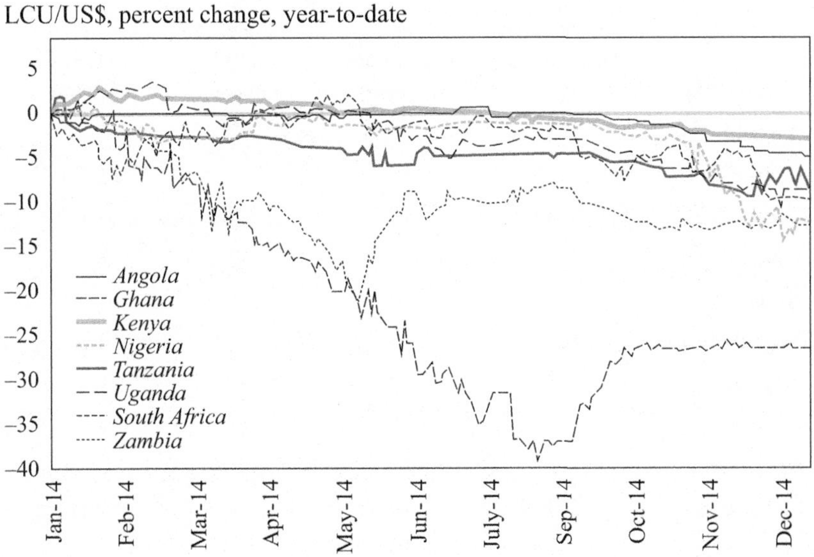

Sources: Bloomberg LP and World Bank (2015a).

LCU = Local Currency Units.

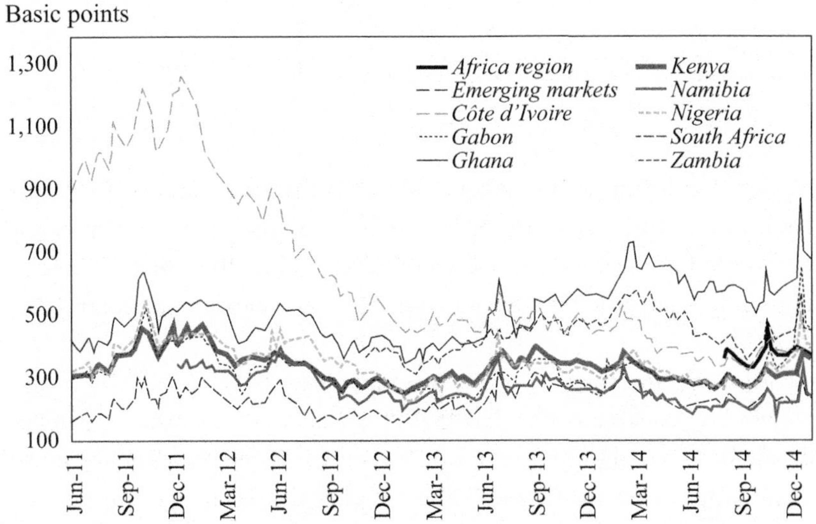

Sources: J. P. Morgan and World Bank (2015a).

TABLE 3-1 Stress Test Scenario of Foreign Exchange (FX) Risk, Using Worst Actual Currency Moves in the Region[a]

	Sum of Cash Flows (in US$ millions)	FX Depreciation (percent)	FX Impact (in US$ millions)	Percent of 2013 GDP
Angola	1,503	30	451	0.36
Côte d'Ivoire	12,398	30	3,719	11.60
Gabon	2,552	30	766	3.97
Ghana	3,325	30	998	2.09
Kenya	3,178	30	953	1.73
Mozambique	1,530	30	459	3.00
Namibia	792	30	238	1.94
Nigeria	2,322	30	697	0.13
Rwanda	670	30	201	2.64
Senegal	2,064	30	619	4.18
Seychelles	302	30	91	6.55
Tanzania	864	30	259	0.78
Zambia	3,034	30	910	3.39
Ethiopia	1,663	30	499	1.05
Total	**36,196**	**30**	**10,859**	**1.13**

Source: Tyson (2015).

a. Depreciation is 30 percent with respect to the U.S. dollar.

rencies. For instance, following a 30 percent depreciation of the Angolan kwanza with respect to the U.S. dollar, the authorities in that country would have to raise an additional $451 million to service their $1.5 billion debt, an amount equivalent to 0.36 percent of the Angolan GDP in 2013.

Allow me to disagree with these numbers.

My first concern is that the "$10.8 billion loss" assumes 30 percent devaluation based on "the worst actual currency moves in the region in 2014 (which were for Ghana)" and "applies the devaluation to all currencies." This assumption overestimates the impact of the foreign exchange shock. Take Côte d'Ivoire, Gabon, and Senegal—which together account for about 47 percent of the total estimated foreign exchange impact. These three countries share a currency (the CFA franc), which is pegged to the euro and has been devalued only once since 1960 (a 50 percent devaluation against the French franc in 1994). As a result, movements of the CFA franc with respect to the U.S. dollar exactly mirror movements of the euro with respect to the U.S. dollar, and although the euro has depreciated against the U.S. dollar, it has lost about 18 percent from early 2014 to early 2015 (a period including the Greek elections). Other currencies, apart from the Zambia kwacha and the Nigerian naira, have lost less than 10 percent. Markets have been somewhat discriminating between different African credits and the differences in the level of spreads among African sovereign bonds that incorporate their differentiated risks, including exchange rate risk. A more realistic scenario would have been to use the worst actual currency moves for each country rather than that of the Ghanaian cedi. In table 3-2, I have quickly reestimated the foreign exchange impact using such a scenario and find an average 15 percent devaluation, which leads to a foreign exchange impact of about $6.5 billion, or 0.68 percent of GDP. These figures are lower than the ODI estimates of $10.8 billion, or 1.1 percent of GDP.

My second concern is that Tyson does not account for the net present value of cash flows. The paper's assumption again overestimates the impact of the devaluation, as it ignores the time value of money ($100 now should be worth more than $100 in ten years because it can be invested in a low-risk asset and earn interest). Simply adding the cash flows of the bonds will lead to much higher value than discounting them, and the longer the maturity of the bond, the higher the difference with the present value of the cash flows. Côte d'Ivoire, which accounts for about one-third of the foreign exchange impact estimated in the paper, has issued two bonds with tenures of twenty-two years and ten years, respectively. To estimate the present value of cash flows, I assume that the interest rate spread of Côte d'Ivoire is about 400 basis points (4 percent) over a U.S. ten-year treasury yield of 2.25 percent and calculate a present value of $5.8 billion, which is less than half the figure of $12.4 billion used in Tyson (2015). Applying a devaluation of 18 percent instead of 30 percent to the Ivorian bonds yields a foreign exchange impact of about $1 billion (3.3 percent of GDP) rather than $3 billion (11.6 percent

TABLE 3-2 Stress Test Scenario of Foreign Exchange (FX) Risk, Using Worst Actual Currency Moves for Each Country and Comparison with Overseas Development Institute Findings

	Sum of Cash Flows (in US$ millions)	FX Depreciation (percent)	FX Impact (in US$ millions)	Percent of 2013 GDP
Angola	1,503	10	150	—
Côte d'Ivoire	12,398	18	2,210	—
Gabon	2,552	18	459	—
Ghana	3,325	40	1,330	—
Kenya	3,178	10	318	—
Mozambique	1,530	10	153	—
Namibia	792	10	79	—
Nigeria	2,322	20	464	—
Rwanda	670	10	67	—
Senegal	2,064	18	371	—
Seychelles	302	10	30	—
Tanzania	864	10	86	—
Zambia	3,034	20	607	—
Ethiopia	1,663	10	166	—
Total	**36,196**	**15**	**6,492**	**0.68**
ODI Findings	**36,196**	**30**	**10,859**	**1.13**
Difference		**15**	**4,366**	**0.45**

Source: Tyson (2015) and author's calculations.

of GDP). Even applying a devaluation of 30 percent leads to a foreign exchange impact of about $1.7 billion—about half what Tyson finds. So just by focusing on Côte d'Ivoire, the estimated foreign exchange impact falls from $10.9 billion (1.13 percent of GDP) to about $5.3 billion (0.55 percent of GDP).

My third concern is that the paper assumes that the effect of the devaluation is permanent. Implicitly, Tyson (2015) assumes that when a government has issued a ten-year U.S. dollar–denominated bond and the local currency depreciates with respect to the U.S. dollar, it will bear the resulting higher debt-servicing cost for ten years. Instead, it is more reasonable to assume that the government will not remain idle for ten years and will attempt to reduce the cost of debt repayment. For instance, the government could earn more U.S. dollars over a year or so if the value of exports rises following the depreciation of the local currency, which makes them cheaper to foreigners. Such an automatic stabilizer is rightly mentioned in Tyson (2015), but it is not taken into account in the stress test scenario. In practice, therefore, the government will focus its risk analysis on a shorter-term horizon than the maturity of its debt. For instance, the government will focus on a one-year horizon, in which cash flows are at risk from a depreciation of its currency.

Tyson (2015) is timely because it brings attention to the risks stemming from the increased indebtedness of African countries, and I find it quite useful in highlighting the importance of adequate sovereign debt management at this stage. However, it is not yet time to sound the alarm on these risks. Rather, it is time to check the fire alarm and make sure that African governments can properly and rapidly identify, measure, and manage the risks from their increased external indebtedness. Adams's paper "Africa Debt Rising" (2015) reaches a conclusion comparable to mine.

Rebalancing the Risks from U.S. Dollar External Debt to Local Currency Domestic Debt

In fact, there is some good news. African debt management offices have benefited from increased technical assistance from the World Bank, the IMF, and other bilateral partners such as the U.S. Treasury's Office of Technical Assistance, allowing them to strengthen their institutional capacity to manage public debt and providing them with analytical tools.

However, the work agenda is far from being finished. Indeed, beyond foreign exchange risk, there is a real risk that African countries become so dependent on external debt that they may not sufficiently develop their local debt markets. This type of structural risk is high because in many countries U.S. dollar–denominated external debt is cheaper than local-currency-denominated domestic debt. Ghana's experience is a case in point. In January 2013, its government could pay about 4.3 percent on a ten-year loan in dollars. However, when borrowing in local currency domestically, the interest rate was at least 23 percent on three-month Treasury bills. After inflation differentials are taken into account, the difference between U.S. dollar and local-currency borrowing costs reached 10.6 percent (or 5.4 percent when taking into account currency depreciation).

This wedge was due in part to changes in the policy environment—monetary policy was tightened in 2012, and the fiscal deficit increased to about 10–11 percent of GDP. But the wedge was also due to a low external cost that reflects foreign investors' search for yield. The difference also reflected underdeveloped domestic debt markets with an investor base dominated by banks—which raised domestic borrowing costs—and the likely effects of restricting foreign investors from buying short-term domestic government securities (with a maturity of less than three years).

By 2015, the economic situation had deteriorated significantly, leading the country to request an IMF program. However, Ghana's deteriorating fundamentals have not led to a loss of market access but have resulted in higher borrowing costs. In particular, in September 2014, Ghana was able to raise $1 billion for a twelve-year bond paying a coupon of 8.125 percent at the same time it was negotiating an IMF program.

The lesson from Ghana's experience is that African countries should pursue a two-pronged approach. The first priority should be to improve fiscal policy and strengthen debt management. The second priority should be to develop local capital markets. Armed with strong fiscal and debt management policies, African countries will be better placed to opportunistically exploit the boom-bust cycle of international interest rates, tapping international markets when borrowing costs fall and relying on local markets when such costs rise.

THE REAL CONCERN FOR AFRICA: A WEAKENED CHINESE ECONOMY, NOT A DEVALUED YUAN

The devaluation of the Chinese yuan has been an oft-discussed issue over the past several years (Sy, 2015b). Market analysts have been busy refining their assessments of what the devaluation means and examining the extent of the Chinese economic slowdown, timing of increases in U.S. long-term interest rates, pace of global economic growth, turbulence in commodities markets, and likelihood of competitive devaluation by other emerging markets. But what about the impact of the yuan devaluation on Africa?

After all, China is Africa's largest bilateral trading partner. Press reports and analysts have stressed that African exports to China may fall as they become more expensive following the yuan's devaluation. Currencies in African countries with strong exports to China, like South Africa (gold and wine), Angola (oil), and Zambia (copper), have already fallen following Beijing's move. In addition, the yuan devaluation may erode Africa's competitiveness, because domestic products will face stronger competition from cheaper Chinese imports, and local wages will cost more for Chinese firms seeking to open shop on the continent.

However, reports also point out that some African countries—such as Ethiopia, Kenya, and Mozambique—may benefit from the cheaper cost of Chinese goods that they import, such as Chinese-made heavy machinery, bulldozers, and electrical lines. African retailers and consumers will also have access to cheaper Chinese goods.

Despite these worries, I argue that the real concern should not be the yuan devaluation. Rather, African policymakers should focus on the impact of China's economic slowdown on their economies and the policy measures needed to manage it.

First, a 2 percent drop in a currency is not that large, especially when compared to movements of floating currencies. For instance, in August 2015 the U.S. dollar had appreciated by about 20 percent relative to the euro and the yen, and the South African rand had dropped by about 12 percent against the U.S. dollar.

Second, African countries trade with China mostly in U.S. dollars because the yuan is not internationalized. Because the U.S. dollar has been appreciating against African currencies, the impact of the Chinese devaluation is less important for African countries than for the United States. The yuan was devalued by about 2 percent against the U.S. dollar on August 11, 2015, and further fell by about 3 percent by August 13. However, the South African rand fell about 1.77 percent over the same period against the Chinese yuan (using cross-rates) because it also depreciated against the U.S. dollar by 1.24 percent.

Third, China's economic slowdown is the real issue. The turbulence in global markets following the devaluation has been mostly driven by market participants' concerns over a stronger-than-anticipated slowdown of the Chinese economy. China's official GDP growth rate dropped to 7 percent in 2015 from a double-digit average in 2010 and has been around 6 percent in the last year. There are questions as to whether it is on a downward trend. The answer is not clear, and some China specialists, like Brookings senior fellow David Dollar (2015), think that China is still growing in the 6–7 percent range and doing well.

The key issue is that a slowdown in China's economic growth is a serious risk to Africa's economic outlook. For instance, a recent *Africa's Pulse* (World Bank, 2015b, p. 11) observed that "the balance of risks to Africa's outlook remains tilted to the downside" and that "on the external front, a sharper-than-expected slowdown in China, a further decline in oil prices, and a sudden deterioration in global liquidity conditions are the main risks." Similarly, the latest IMF *World Economic Outlook* (IMF, 2015d, p. 66) section on sub-Saharan Africa, echoing earlier analysis in the *Regional Economic Outlook* (IMF, 2014a), notes that "further weakening of growth in Europe or in emerging markets, in particular in China, could reduce demand for exports, further depress commodity prices, and curtail foreign direct investment in mining and infrastructure."

More than the movements of the yuan, every African ministry of finance and central bank should be carefully watching the movements in the determinants of Chinese growth. I argue that they should even have specialized China Watch units monitoring the evolution of Chinese real estate and business investment, infrastructure investment and consumption, and urbanization and service industries trends.

For instance, a report by IMF economists Paulo Drummond and Estelle Liu (2014) focusing on the impact of changes in China's investment growth on sub-Saharan African exports finds that China affects the region's economies directly through its exports and indirectly through commodity price effects and international prices of manufacturing products. The authors find that a 1 percentage point decline in China's investment growth is associated with an average 0.6 percentage point decline in sub-Saharan Africa's export growth. The impact is larger for resource-rich countries, especially oil exporters, because they account for a large share of the region's exports to China.

What Should African Countries Do to Manage the Effect of a Chinese Economic Slowdown?

The bad news is that, unlike in the period following the global financial crisis, African countries will not be able to rely on trade and investment with China as a buffer now that they are struggling to manage the effect of domestic and external risks, such as large fiscal deficits, declines in oil and other commodities (especially metal), and domestic security-related risks (International Monetary Fund, 2015b).

The IMF and World Bank reports mentioned above indicate a menu of sensible policy options for sub-Saharan African countries, including

- allowing their currencies to depreciate;
- diversifying economies (both output and fiscal revenues) away from primary commodities;
- strengthening fiscal positions and restoring fiscal buffers while protecting the poor from income losses arising from these shifts;
- reducing or eliminating fuel subsidies or making room for higher energy taxes; and
- implementing deep structural reforms to increase productivity growth across all sectors, especially agriculture.

But these recommendations are a mix of short-term and long-term measures and, most importantly, involve tough policy trade-offs. For instance, diversifying an economy is typically a difficult and long process involving many potential winners and a few (but politically powerful) reluctant losers entrenched in rent-seeking activities. Allowing currencies to depreciate may help the economy adjust to shocks but, at least in the short term, may lead to higher inflation and higher exchange rate volatility and may discourage foreign investment. Some countries, like Nigeria, are struggling with these trade-offs and are using administrative measures in the foreign exchange markets rather than letting their currencies depreciate. Reducing subsidies or increasing the value added tax takes political will. To complicate things, many African countries were scheduled to have elections in 2016 and 2017.

A Chinese economic slowdown will definitely shrink the window of opportunity for policy action in Africa. But there is some light at the end of the tunnel. First, intraregional trade and investment has the potential to grow on the continent. Second, India is strengthening its trade with Africa, and India's growth is expected to be resilient (hovering around 5 percent). U.S.-Africa trade has the potential also to increase as initiatives such as the U.S. African Growth and Opportunity Act have not yet been fully utilized. Regardless of the extent of the Chinese slowdown, African policymakers should accelerate the pace of reform, hope for a resilient Chinese economy and European Union rebound, and perhaps start betting on India.

COUNTRY CASE STUDY: NIGERIA

I now look at policy and economic management in Nigeria. The country remains one of the two largest economies in Africa but has faced obstacles in the global market (for example, declining oil prices) and in governance and security that have made recent years difficult for the country.

Policies Regarding the Naira

Moving the naira to a flexible exchange rate must be accompanied by strong policies. Following the 2016 announcement by Godwin Emefiele, governor of the Central Bank of Nigeria (CBN), that the naira (N) would be allowed to float freely, the Nigerian currency fell by 22 percent, to N253.50 per dollar, within a week. The CBN's decision shouldn't have been a surprise, as the Nigerian economy had been suffering from the steep fall in oil prices since mid-2014. Economic growth had turned negative for the first time since 2004, and inflation reached levels last seen in 2010. Real GDP growth fell to 0.4 percent (year-on-year) the first quarter of 2016, down from 2.1 percent in the last quarter of 2015. Inflation increased to almost 16 percent in the month before this change (following higher electricity tariffs and fuel prices). It is likely that the financial sector was also experiencing more nonperforming loans. Foreign investment had declined markedly, and foreign exchange reserves stood at $26.5 billion at the end of May 2016 (3.6 months of imports), down from $39 billion about two years prior.

It was becoming evident that the previous currency arrangement, which held the naira at an official exchange rate of N197 per dollar and restricted access to foreign currency, was not helping achieve an orderly adjustment to the severe terms-of-trade shock the country experienced. Nigerian policymakers had de facto given up the option of letting the currency absorb some of the shocks. Choosing to peg the naira left fiscal policy the major if not the sole policy tool for managing the oil shock. But that was a risky decision, especially in the absence of an adequately funded oil fund (the country's Excess Crude Account was depleted). President Muhammadu Buhari's op-ed in the *Wall Street Journal* (2016) explained the priorities of his administration: fight corruption, rebalance away from oil dependence, and through that shift, create durable economic growth.

But for growth to return to positive territory and for Buhari to achieve his goals, he needs to first enact policies to combat a number of challenges. Attacks on the country's oil infrastructure must be stopped. Oil production has been estimated to be at its lowest level in more than two decades. Attacks by the Niger Delta Avengers on oil pipelines have hit the country's oil production hard. The expected increase in oil revenues following the increase in the price of oil ($47 per barrel at the time compared to a budget benchmark price of $38) has not materialized; oil production has fallen (from 2.2 million barrels per day to, at most, 1.4 million in May 2016). The country is no longer the number-one African oil producer, slipping behind Angola. The credibility of Nigeria as a reliable supplier should be safeguarded to reignite its growth. Planned initiatives to increase non-oil revenues must be given a high priority in order to help compensate for the fall in oil revenues. In the first half of 2016, the fall in economic activity was not likely to generate the expected tax revenues that were envisioned in the budget. Delays in passing the budget meant, however, that the decline in revenues may have been accompanied by lower expenditures, which may have helped reduce the impact of revenue decline on the deficit. Increasing the value added tax would complement the government tax administration initiatives to raise more revenues. Although the value added tax is regressive, some of the increased revenues can be passed to the poorest segments of the population. At the same time, measures in the budget such as achieving a lean and cost-effective government and fighting corruption remain as relevant as ever. Moving the naira to a flexible exchange rate must be accompanied by strong policies.

The biggest bang from the policy buck in a new exchange rate regime is expected to come from the effects of the increased flexibility of the naira on the economy. Government revenues from oil exports will increase, and economic activity and foreign investment, it is hoped, will resume. There are some risks, however. If the exchange rate overshoots and the inflation rate increases sharply, then monetary policy will need to be used. The central bank could hike interest rates to manage inflation and avoid outflows and encourage inflows—but if rates are too high for too long, those interest rates can hurt growth.

Credibility, Credibility, Credibility

Policy credibility will be needed to achieve an orderly adjustment as the CBN works to smooth the transition from a fixed exchange regime with a parallel market exchange rate to a floating exchange rate regime. To do this, the CBN needs to reduce uncertainty about the functioning of the currency market. However, some of the bank's latest announcements raise questions. For instance, forty-one items, including rice, cement, and tomatoes, are still classified as not valid for foreign exchange, which means that importers of these products will continue to face restrictions in accessing foreign currency. These administrative measures should not be continued because they will not eliminate the parallel exchange rate and will continue to create opportunities for arbitrageurs and corruption. Also, the CBN has changed the rules for the selection of primary dealers, and although some growing pains are to be expected when new markets are being set up, it will be important to converge rapidly to a well-functioning currency market. To do so, rules and regulations by the CBN on the functioning of the spot market as well as on the futures market will need to be clear and stable. Lack of credibility about the functioning of the new exchange rate regime can push investors to continue adopting a wait-and-see attitude and postpone their investment decisions. This will not achieve the expected growth dividends from increased currency flexibility.

4

Sharing the Benefits

Ensuring that Africa can deliver on its vision for economic growth is important, but it is also important that the benefits are shared. Employment is a huge issue for Africa, which boasts the largest percentage of vulnerable employment, or unpaid family workers and self-employed workers, in the world. Somalia is an example of where a lack of job opportunities and the deterioration of an existing sector of employment has aided the development of piracy. This chapter examines the state of jobless growth, looks at the example of piracy in the Gulf of Aden, and recommends ways for addressing jobless growth.

JOBLESS GROWTH IN SUB-SAHARAN AFRICA

Youth employment continues to be a critical issue for sub-Saharan Africa. The International Labour Organization's (ILO) *Global Employment Trends 2014* focuses on the "risk of a jobless recovery" and sheds a sobering light on the Africa rising story. The World Bank's *Youth Employment in Sub-Saharan Africa* is a reminder that African policymakers urgently need to address the challenges of providing jobs to the majority of the continent's population (Brooks and others, 2014).

Let's take a look at the numbers. We are all by now familiar with the story of the region's rapid economic growth. Over the 2003–13 decade, sub-Saharan Africa grew by 5 percent per year, and at this rate the continent may double the size of its economy before 2030. Sadly, this rapid rate of growth has not benefited the majority of the population. The ILO (2014) data show that sub-Saharan Africa has the highest rate of vulnerable employment in the world (77.4 percent in 2013).

Moreover, youth unemployment in sub-Saharan Africa remains stubbornly high. The ILO (2014) reports that the average regional youth unemployment rate decreased from almost 13.4 percent in 1991–2000 to only 12.3 percent during 2001–12. Although these unemployment numbers appear rather low (good data on labor markets in sub-Saharan Africa are not easy to get), the trend indicates that unemployment is not decreasing as fast as it should (see figure 4-1).

FIGURE 4-1 Economic Growth and Vulnerable Employment, by Region, 2001–12

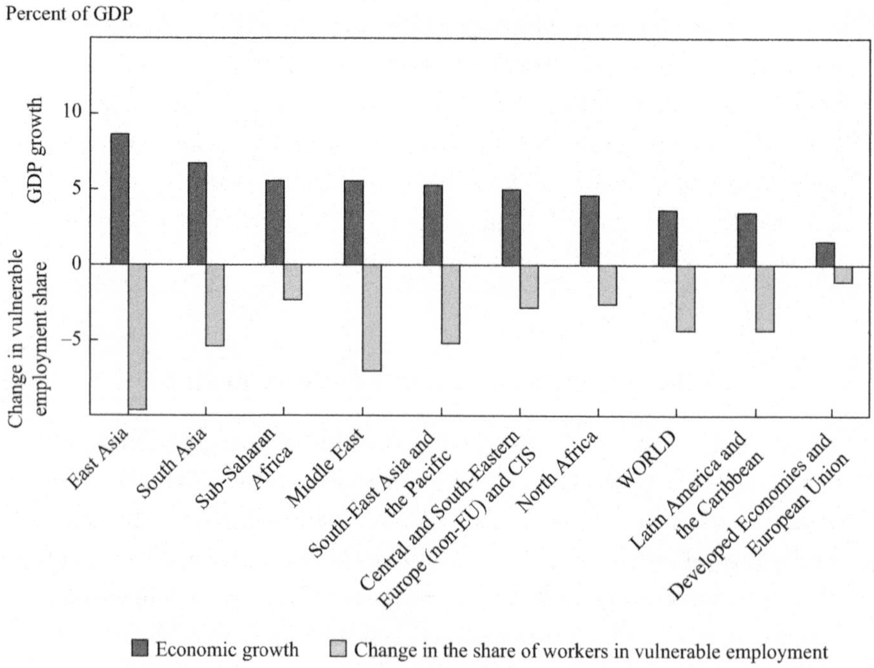

Source: International Labour Organization (2014).

Other sobering news from the ILO (2014) is that the manufacturing sector in sub-Saharan Africa, in contrast to other regions, has not been an engine of job creation. In countries such as Ghana that role is left to mining and construction. Manufacturing in the region has been declining as a share of GDP in the last two decades, ending in 2013. To put it simply, sub-Saharan Africa has deindustrialized, and the share of workers in industry in the region is extremely low, at only 10 percent. Similarly, in the rapidly growing oil and gas sector not enough new jobs are being created. To make things worse, agriculture's share of GDP has contracted in the region over the 1993–2013 period. Overall, the proportion of the working-age population in paid employment in the region is low, at only 13.7 percent (see figure 4-2; note that South Asian data are biased because of the importance of women in the services sector).

The ILO (2014) report notes that, in certain countries, almost one-quarter of young people ages fifteen to twenty-nine are now neither in

FIGURE 4-2 Paid Employment and Employment in Industry across Regions, 2012

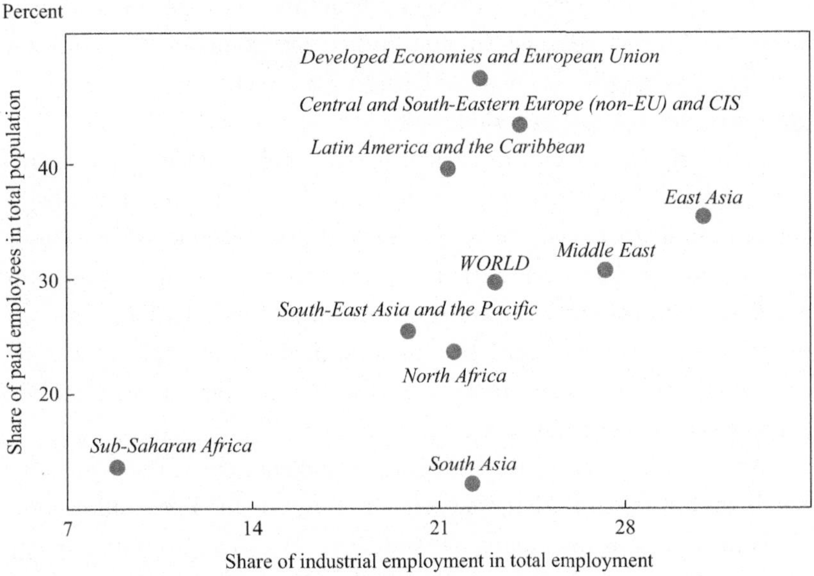

Source: International Labour Organization (2014).

employment nor in education or training. These figures do not include sub-Saharan Africa, but one can guesstimate they are higher in the region.

So sub-Saharan African economies have a serious problem of weak structural transformation. As noted by Rodrik (2014), sub-Saharan African countries, unlike East Asian countries, have not yet been able to turn their farmers into manufacturing workers, diversify their economies, and export a range of increasingly sophisticated goods. What is worrisome is that there is not much time left for transformation: between 2015 and 2035, each year will see 500,000 more fifteen-year-olds than the year before, in a region where half the population is under twenty-five. In contrast, the population in other regions is, or will soon be, aging. The challenge will be to transform this youth bulge into an opportunity, or the risk is an Arab Spring. Sub-Saharan African countries have not been doing a good job at it, and time is running out fast (see figure 4-3).

Even the narrative around a middle class rising in sub-Saharan Africa should not divert policymakers' attention from the urgency of transforming the region's economy to provide sustainable and inclusive growth. Indeed, a rising middle class creates an "expectation revolution" that has to be managed. As noted by Brookings vice president Kemal Derviş (2014), in Chile, Brazil, and Turkey, the young and parts of the aspiring new middle classes have been in the streets asking for respect, greater equality, less corruption, and a greater say in their lives.

Well-designed policies in agriculture can help reduce youth unemployment in at least three ways. First, high-value crops can offer jobs to youth in rural areas (a good example is horticulture production in Kenya). Second, linkages between agriculture and manufacturing can develop when agricultural products are transformed and even exported and in the process create jobs. Third, increased productivity of staple food crops can lower food prices and real wages, thereby making the manufacturing sector more competitive.

African policymakers are aware of the challenges of a jobless growth. But it should be clear that they are running out of time, and a good indicator of that is the rapidly expanding youth bulge. Economic transformation is needed, and it is needed urgently. As noted by my colleague John McArthur and his coauthor, Jessica Pugliese (2013), employment

FIGURE 4-3 Sub-Saharan Africa's Population Compared with Other Regions

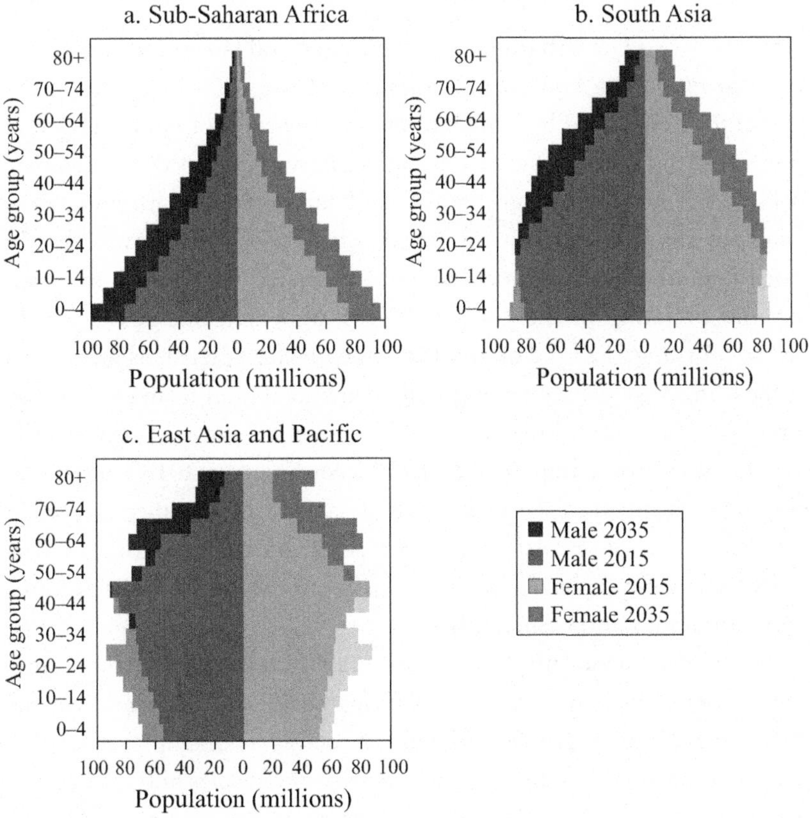

Source: Filmer and Fox (2014).

challenges can be broken into typologies: predominately rural, predominately urban, and mixed between rural and urban economies. As a result, highly tailored approaches to job creation based on economy type should be the focus of African policymakers trying to improve the employment situation for young people. In addition, as noted by Brooks and others (2014), solutions will need to be multidimensional and include increasing training opportunities for youth and addressing the quality of education, nutrition, and basic health care while also removing obstacles that hinder progress in agriculture, household enterprises, and manufacturing.

CAPTAIN PHILLIPS AND THE DRIVERS OF PIRACY IN EAST AFRICA AND SOMALIA

While at Africa Growth Initiative, a colleague and I examined the movie *Captain Phillips*, a Hollywood portrayal of the 2009 hijacking of the MV *Maersk Alabama* by Somali pirates off the coast of Somalia (Sy and Smith, 2013). While some media outlets have reported that the movie unfairly left out the background of the Somalis drawn into piracy, the film does allude to a widely discussed Somali piracy narrative—that is, that the pirates are fishermen who got their start combating overfishing and polluting in their waters (Alessi and Hanson, 2012; Walsh, 2013). Working as a kind of unofficial Somali coast guard, as mentioned in the film, these fishermen originally demanded fines from exploitative foreign commercial fishing vessels. This narrative, however, is generally overstated and oversimplified. In fact, according to a 2013 United Nations assessment, the fishermen-pirates focus less on commercial fishing vessels in the Gulf of Aden and the Somali Basin and more on commercial vessels from countries willing to pay out ransom (United Nations Office on Drugs and Crime, 2013).

In a UN survey of fifty-six pirates, only fourteen listed their former occupation as fisherman (United Nations Office on Drugs and Crime, 2013). A bulk of respondents listed themselves as unemployed or employed in informal business activities, such as khat sales and transportation. In the movie, Muse, the captain of the pirates who board the *Maersk Alabama*, also bemoans his lack of opportunities, and the pirates come across as young and desperate to get a large ransom payment.

Idealistic as the Somali pirates may have been initially, it becomes clear in the movie that by 2009 the original piracy motivations no longer applied. At the beginning of the film, the pirates are roused from their village by men with guns who work for a kingpin. A sleepy-eyed Muse, played by Somalia-born actor Barkhad Abdi, is forced at gunpoint to assemble his pirate crew. In another instance, when asked by the titular Captain Phillips, played by Tom Hanks, the pirates respond rather sarcastically that of course they are all just fishermen. Thus, the movie presents a subtle and nuanced view of the current scenario for piracy in East Africa.

Indeed, ransom payments are the main venture of real-life Somali pirates, unlike the small-scale robberies of the initial Somali piracy narrative. Ransoms have increased in value from under a million dollars on average in 2005 to an average payment of $5 million in 2011 (although the average dropped in 2012 to $4 million). As mentioned repeatedly in the film, the hijackers are rarely the sole profiteers from a hostage-taking scenario. A band of pirates is usually headed by a kingpin, who organizes the mother ship, and negotiators, who have higher education and can command up to 5 percent of the payout. Pirate crews need to nearly equal the crew members on the commercial vessels being hijacked, so the ransom generally is divided among a lot of people.

According to the United Nations, financiers of planned hijackings can buy shares of attempts, and the typical cost of an attempt is about $50,000. Thus, the payout needs to cover pirate crew, the kingpin's costs, and the original outlay, as well as a high return to investors (investors typically claim at minimum 30 percent of the payout). The UN argues that piracy in Somalia in the past garnered public support because of the perception that it redistributed wealth. However, this support has recently waned, hinting that communities do not really see the benefits of piracy. As Somalia reconstructs and attracts more legitimate business investors, there may be less support for an activity that increases risk and negative perceptions of the business environment (Joselow, 2013).

WHAT CAN BE DONE ABOUT PIRACY IN SOMALIA AND EAST AFRICA?

The number of successful pirate hijackings has dropped since November 2011, when over forty successful attacks were recorded for that month alone. In comparison, in all of 2012 there were only fifteen successful attacks off the East African coast, according to UN figures. The drop has been attributed to increased private armed security on commercial vessels and antipiracy task forces from foreign governments, which have been supported by enforced prosecution of hijackers. Maritime law before 2011 did not allow armed security on commercial vessels, but the International Maritime Organization has since added it to its guidance on best management practices for areas at high risk for piracy.[1] Although

1 See www.imo.org/Documents/IMO_Piracy_Guidance.pdf.

the situation has seen improvement, some pirate groups have turned to inland hostage taking, and hijacking attempts still continue.

There are three main potential methods to prevent piracy:

- Provide the people involved with alternative employment.
- Increase the costs of hijacking for pirate networks.
- Remove the kingpin and increase security to raise the costs of attempted hijackings for the pirates—that is, loss of life and imprisonment.

In terms of finding alternative employment, it may be tough to replace hijacking with a lucrative option. As far as fishing goes, it is difficult to determine if it is still a viable option for the Somalis. According to a UN Food and Agriculture Organization country profile from 2005, the area's fish stocks may be overexploited, though there may be some opportunities for increased fishing of large, high-value fish, such as tuna and mackerel.[2] The UN Security Council (2011) reported that fishery programs in Somalia are generally neglected by NGOs and assistance programs. Thus, this is a largely untested prevention mechanism.

A Brookings colleague, Vanda Felbab-Brown, an expert on conflict, has pointed out that piracy will continue unless the financiers and kingpin networks on land are dismantled (Felbab-Brown, 2011). She has studied piracy in the Strait of Malacca, which stretches between Malaysia and the Indonesian island of Sumatra (and carries about 40 percent of global trade). The Malacca Strait area reduced piracy by nearly 75 percent from the beginning of 2000 to the end of that decade. Felbab-Brown attributes this reduction to a concerted effort by Singapore, Indonesia, and Malaysia to increase security in their waters. Unfortunately, the lessons learned from the experience in the Strait of Malacca might not be helpful for the East African context.

Somalia, on the other hand, has a very weak government compared to the countries that border the Malacca Strait. The interdiction effort by the commercial vessels and their foreign governments currently under way in the waters of East Africa seems to be working. However, this may

2 See www.fao.org/fi/oldsite/FCP/en/som/profile.htm.

actually increase the threat of greater violence for hostages and patrol units because of the use of armed guards on ships and the intensified counter-response from pirates. Thus, East Africa is faced with the long-term and difficult obstacles of strengthening governance in Somalia as well as finding alternative livelihoods for pirates.

Perhaps the onus will be on the foreign governments and transport industry for the foreseeable future. Fortunately, Belgian authorities have had some success in tearing apart the Somali kingpin network, as demonstrated by the capture of Mohamed Abdi Hassan, a kingpin similar to the boss of the pirate captain Muse in *Captain Phillips*. The notorious kingpin was lured to Belgium with a fake offer to serve as adviser to an upcoming documentary on Somali piracy and was arrested by authorities when he showed up to the meeting. With such drama and continued obstacles in preventing piracy in Somalia and East Africa, we may see another Hollywood movie about piracy in the near future.

5

Financing Africa's Development

While at Brookings I wrote extensively on financing for development. The topic is vast, and there are many new approaches and new takes on old approaches to discuss and evaluate for African policymakers. This chapter examines the importance of financing for an Africa after replacement of the Millennium Development Goals, how finance flows to Africa, and the continent's infrastructure deficit. It also looks at financing solutions, which include Islamic sukuk finance, and at trends in frontier bond markets.

POST-2015 MILLENNIUM DEVELOPMENT GOALS: MORE AND BETTER FINANCING WILL NOT BE ENOUGH

In 2013, I participated in a panel organized by the UN General Assembly Open Working Group, which was tasked with preparing a proposal for creation of the Sustainable Development Goals (SDGs) (Sy, 2013b). The SDGs build on the Millennium Development Goals and include economic, social, and environmental dimensions. The panel included Amar Batthacharya, director of the Group of Twenty-Four Secretariat; Mukhisa Kituyi, secretary general of the UN Conference on Trade and Development; and Jeffrey Sachs, director of the Earth Institute at Columbia University.

In this event, it was clear that the current consensus for more and better financing for development would not be enough to meet the SDGs. In addition, it was clear that the quality and quantity of financing would need to evolve—governments need to come up with policies to associate financial flows with the other inputs of sustainable growth, such as the transfer of skills and technology. In the current vision for financing for development, which originates from the 2002 Monterrey Consensus and the 2008 Doha Declaration, both from an International Conference on Financing for Development, financing is a critical input for attaining the SDGs, and governments should encourage more and better financing.

The more financing argument: most of the money to finance sustainable development will continue to come from domestic resources. The UN High-Level Panel on the Post-2015 Development Agenda (tasked to advise on the global development framework beyond 2015, the target date for the Millenium Development Goals) rightly stressed that countries should therefore continue efforts to invest in stronger tax systems, broaden their domestic tax base, and build local financial markets. Raising domestic revenues to expand public services and investments remains vital for sustainable growth, and creates ownership and accountability for public spending. However, domestic revenues alone—especially in low-income and fragile countries—will not be enough given the scale of the resources needed to attain the SDGs. External financing, which includes official development assistance, private capital flows (foreign direct investment, portfolio investment, and loans), and remittances, will complement domestic sources.

The better financing argument: external flows can bring risks such as the volatility associated with hot money (short-term and volatile capital flows). The vulnerability of countries to the volatility of private capital flows can be reduced by attracting more long-term financing (that is, typically more stable than short-term financing) from institutional investors including sovereign wealth funds, private corporations, development banks, and other investors.

Encouraging more and better financing for development is good policy, but it will not be enough. Beyond the quality and quantity of financing, it will be crucial for governments to get a bigger bang for their buck and ensure that the money they raise helps achieve the SDGs in the most effective way.

The evidence on capital flows to sub-Saharan Africa illustrates this point, as the region has benefited from more and better financing since the 2002 Monterrey Consensus. During the period from 2002 to 2012, private capital flows to sub-Saharan Africa have grown by 19.4 percent per year and have overtaken official debt assistance. Stable long-term flows in the form of foreign direct investment remain the engine of external financing to sub-Saharan Africa, with 75 percent of total private capital flows.

However, although sub-Saharan Africa has attracted more foreign direct investment, about three-quarters of it went to resource-rich countries and extractive industries over the 2002–12 period. The prospects for increased investment in the natural resources sector look strong given the discovery of new resources on the continent. Yet in most sub-Saharan African countries, the linkages among extractive industries, local firms and employment markets, and domestic financial systems are tenuous.

One way for governments to better leverage foreign direct investment flows for long-term economic growth in sub-Saharan Africa is to associate them with knowledge and skills transfer from multinational companies to the domestic private sector. In the medium to long term, policymakers can also anticipate the type of foreign direct investment their countries will attract and build a strategy in advance to develop the future technology and skills that will be needed for the expected investments. In the short term, policymakers can provide incentives for investors to include local businesses in the value chain and invest in education and training. This is increasingly happening, for instance, in the information and communication technology sector. Initiatives to develop local content legislation in resource-rich countries should take a flexible and strategic long-term view to meet the SDGs.

Other avenues for governments to better use financing to attain SDGs include the use of innovative technologies to increase financial literacy, financial inclusion, and the use of green energy in power projects.

In sum, for financing that will help attain the SDGs, governments will need to ask for more than just money from financial flows. Supporting the SDGs will entail ensuring that financing supports development and engaging the private sector through initiatives like the UN Global Compact that provide forums to discuss ways to make financing an effective input for achieving the SDGs. To extract nonmonetary benefits from financial resources will require involvement of both domestic and foreign governments.

HOW FINANCING FLOWS TO AFRICA

Understanding how different sources of development financing flow to different parts of Africa can help identify priority areas of intervention.

In a recent study with Fenohasina Maret Rakotondrazaka (Sy and Rakotondrazaka, 2015), I explored the different types of external financial flows and their prevalence in sub-Saharan Africa and discussed what those trends suggest about and for the region. This report was third in a number of studies the Brookings Africa Growth Initiative conducted on financing for development in the run-up to the Financing for Development Meeting in Addis Ababa in July 2015. Previous reports looked at the financing of African infrastructure and the trends and developments in the burgeoning African bond markets—the so-called frontier markets (Gutman, Sy, and Chattopadhyay, 2015; Sy, 2015c).

The good news is that external financial flows to sub-Saharan Africa have increased significantly over the last twenty years or so. In fact, the volume of external flows increased from $20 billion in 1990 to about $120 billion in 2012. As seen in figure 5-1, the composition of external flows has also changed a lot: Most of the increase in external flows to sub-Saharan Africa can be attributed to the increase in private capital flows, which are now higher than official development assistance. The share of official development assistance fell from 62 percent of total external flows in 1990 to 22 percent in 2012, and seventeen countries received more foreign direct investment than official development assistance in 2012.

But have these changes in the scale and composition of external flows to sub-Saharan Africa equally benefited countries in the region? Did the rising tide lift all boats? Is aid really dying? Are all countries attracting private capital flows and benefiting from remittances to the same degree? Finally, how does external financing compare with domestic financing?

FIGURE 5-1 Sub-Saharan Africa: Composition of External Flows, 1990–2012

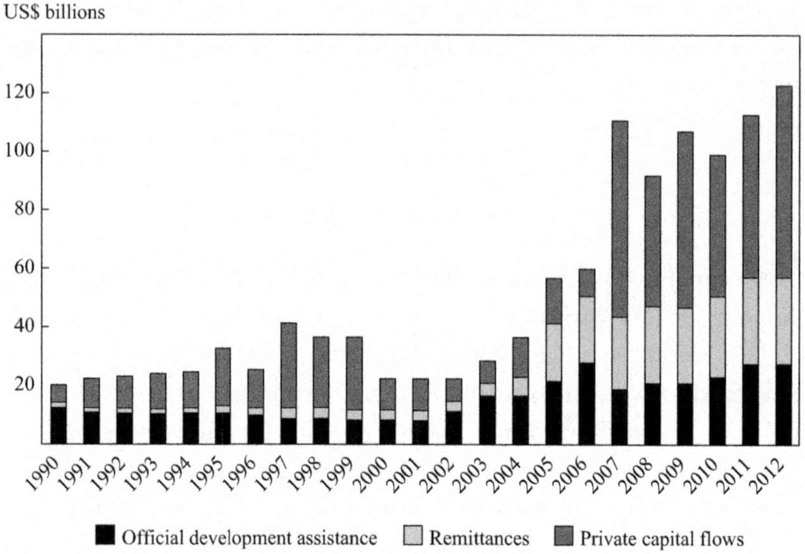

Data sources: IMF and World Bank databases, and authors' calculations.

Source: Sy and Rakotondrazaka (2015).

To answer these questions, in our study (Sy and Rakotondrazaka, 2015) we group sub-Saharan African countries into several different categories to compare the types of flows that they receive. We also compare countries in terms of the government revenues they raise. We group countries by income levels, growth performance, access to international capital markets, geography, colonial heritage, and regional economic community to explore how the external flows differ around the continent. For example, as seen in figure 5-2, we find that the type of external financial flow to non-resource-rich, high-growth states and fragile and low-income countries differs significantly from that of countries that are both middle income and oil exporting.

Our main finding is that changes in the scale and composition of external capital flows have not benefited all sub-Saharan African countries equally. We also find that the claim of the demise of aid is premature, the growth of private capital flows has benefited only a few countries, remittances have become significantly more important for some countries,

FIGURE 5-2 Sub-Saharan Africa: External Flows by Income Level (Deviations from SSA 1990–2012 average, in percent of GDP)

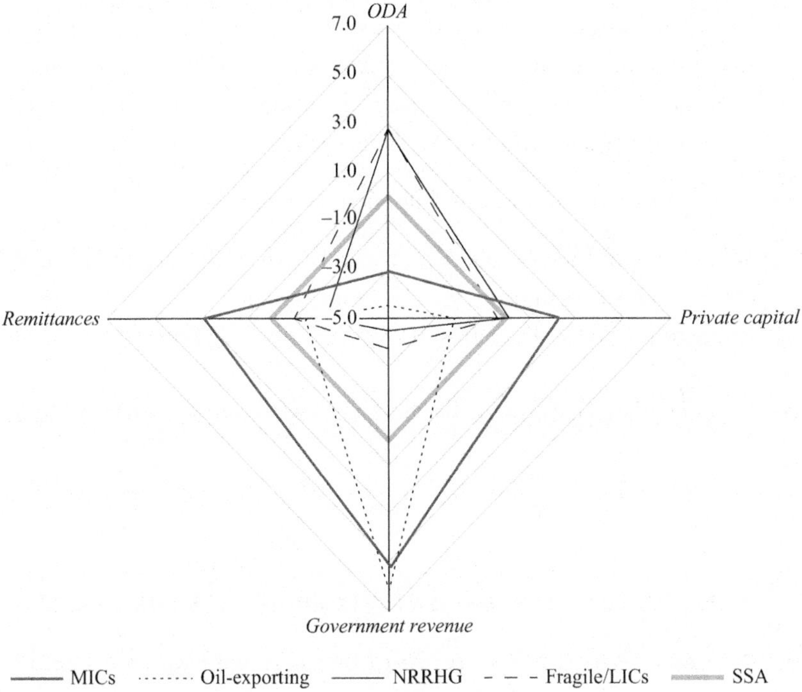

Source: Sy and Rakotondrazaka. 2015.

LIC = low-income countries; MIC = middle-income countries; NRRHG = non-resource-rich high-growth; ODA = official development assistance; SSA = sub-Saharan Africa.

and the rise of external flows means that sub-Saharan African countries will have to manage the volatility associated with such flows. In particular, we find the following:

- Fragile countries and low-income countries, not surprisingly, are regional laggards in terms of access to both external and domestic financing.
- Even resource-rich countries, which are able to attract large volumes of private capital flows, fare relatively poorly when external financing flows are scaled to the size of their economies. In addition, these countries, although they raise more domestic government revenues

than other countries, do so mostly because they benefit from fiscal revenues linked to volatile commodity prices.

- Francophone countries both in the West African Economic and Monetary Union and the Central African Economic and Monetary Community are not able to attract the same level of private capital flows as other sub-Saharan African countries.
- Remittances are high for middle-income countries.
- When external financing is contrasted with domestic financing, it seems that sub-Saharan African countries do not have a natural hedge to the risks of reversal of external financial flows.

For more detail on these and other findings, see Sy and Rakotondrazaka, 2015.

FINANCING FOR DEVELOPMENT: SIX PRIORITIES FOR AFRICA

In 2015, Addis Ababa hosted the third International Conference on Financing for Development. The African development financing context has certainly changed a great deal since the conference's previous gatherings in Monterrey, Mexico, in 2002 and in Doha, Qatar, in 2008: for example, private capital flows, mainly foreign direct investment and remittances, have now overtaken official development assistance. Similarly, China and the other BRICS countries have strongly increased their presence on the continent. Given the challenges Africa faces, African stakeholders have much to contribute to the dialogue, but because Africa's context has changed, its priorities must be reconsidered.

My recommendations on surmounting Africa's financing gaps to achieve its development goals are as follows:

Priority No. 1: Do not consider financing in isolation; rather, link it clearly with its purpose. This priority may seem quite obvious, but it is very tempting to focus on raising more financing without questioning its intended use. For instance, a consensus is forming around the need to invest in upgrading and developing Africa's infrastructure. Yet the focus of the ongoing conversation is on energy infrastructure, whereas urban infrastructure has largely been omitted from the discussion. I believe, instead, that urban infrastructure should be considered a priority given that African cities are growing quickly and have vast needs, including new roads, public transit, and water and sanitation systems. Mechanisms such as municipal bonds issued by cities could be a unique means of filling these financing voids—the U.S. Agency for International Development and the Bill and Melinda Gates Foundation,[1] for example, are currently working with the city of Dakar to issue its first municipal bond, which will be the first nongovernment guaranteed municipal bond for sub-Saharan Africa (outside of South Africa).

Priority No. 2: Focus on domestic financing by increasing government revenues and developing domestic financial and capital markets further. A multifaceted approach, including public and private, domestic and international financing will be necessary to meet the continent's vast financing needs. Over the last fifteen years, external financing from the private sector, especially foreign direct investment, has risen relative to public financing through official development assistance. Meanwhile, domestic public financing has increased, as countries have received some debt relief, improved revenue collection mechanisms, and benefited from commodity price booms (although tax revenue generation still remains relatively low).

However, an important question to ask when examining the roles of these different sources of financing is: What can African governments really control? Governments can influence public financing and to some extent domestic markets, so they should start by focusing on these two areas. Taking a regional view when developing capital markets can make a lot of sense because it allows for economies of scale and has worked well for the West African Economic and Monetary Union. When it comes to capital markets, for instance, why not have continental or at least regional targets and commitments to put in place regional legal and regulatory frameworks, develop the money markets (the cornerstone of capital markets), and integrate payment systems that reduce transaction costs? These strategies would provide the basis for strengthening domestic markets and public financing.

1 The Bill and Melinda Gates Foundation contributes to the funding of the Africa Growth Initiative.

Priority No. 3: Reduce the cost of remittances and increase their developmental impact. Remittances are increasing too, averaging $21.8 billion over the last decade—with some countries, including Nigeria and Senegal, receiving approximately 10 percent of their GDP in remittances. Yet the costs of sending remittances to Africa are the highest in the world, and transfers within Africa cost even more. Since remittances mostly fuel consumption within the social sectors (health and education) and thus have developmental impacts, let's reduce the cost of sending remittances and transform the ways they can be invested to spur entrepreneurship and development. For instance, if a bank sees that an individual regularly receives remittances, it could invite the recipient to join the bank's clientele, and on the basis of the history of remittances received, make a loan to further the recipient's entrepreneurial pursuits.

Priority No. 4: African policymakers should anticipate (or at least identify) the unintended consequences of global financial regulation on Africa and work with global partners to mitigate them. While remittance flows to Africa have increased over time, recent trends in global financial regulation, such as stiffer rules for antimoney laundering (AML) and combating the financing of terrorism (CFT), have had unintended consequences for the continent and have stifled remittances. For instance, AML-CFT regulations have hurt Africa, as seen when many U.S. banks discontinued remittance services to Somalia after AML-CFT regulations were implemented there. Even Basel III (international measures developed by the Basel Committee on Banking Supervision after the 2007–08 global financial crisis), with its disincentives for banks to engage in long-term financing because of more stringent liquidity ratios, can have negative consequences for Africa's attempts to reduce its financing gap in long-term infrastructure projects. Cost of compliance can push global banks to reduce or even cease their activities in small African markets: Why take the risk in small markets when the costs are so high? The $9 billion fine imposed on BNP Paribas for its business in Sudan and Iran is still fresh in the mind of global bankers.

Priority No. 5: Work with foreign governments and the private sector to reduce illicit financial flows. Illicit financial flows are relatively high by some estimates, with African countries losing nearly $60 billion a year, predominantly because of tax evasion by commercial firms and the undervaluing of services and traded goods but also through corruption and organized crime. This loss in capital has translated to lost opportunities for advancing economic and human development in Africa. Efforts by African countries and global institutions such as the United Nations are under way to engage foreign governments and corporations to track and reduce illicit financial flows, and they should be strengthened.

Priority No. 6: Partner with bilateral, multilateral, and private sector (even philanthropic) actors to get the nonfinancial benefits of financial flows. Improving the quantity and quality of financing to Africa is necessary but not sufficient to secure sustainable development for the region. For instance, in dollar terms, foreign direct investment still predominantly goes to resource-rich countries such as Nigeria, Angola, and South Africa (although there has been some progress in recent years in diversification to other countries with large consumer markets or financial sectors). Importantly, the risks from African countries issuing foreign-currency-denominated bonds must be managed, as I discuss in "Trends and Developments in African Frontier Bond Markets" (Sy, 2015c). But African countries must focus on getting a bigger bang for their buck through partnerships that will promote the transfer of knowledge and skills and integrate African businesses into global value chains. At the same time, they should avoid detrimental regulation such as excessive local content regulation. For instance, it may be mutually beneficial for both African governments and foreign firms to foster local participation in some parts of the value chain (such as the downstream oil sector) and be less demanding initially in other parts (such as the upstream oil sector).

Finally, it is worth highlighting that Africa is not a country. Fragile and low-income countries still receive a lot of aid. New "green" (climate change) and "blue" (ocean preservation) areas require aid. African governments must remember to be granular in their approaches and at times focus on one particular type of financial flow.

Coordination of the different types of stakeholders can lead to important gains for all. Again, take infrastructure. My and others' work (for instance, see Gutman, Sy, and Chattopadhyay, 2015) shows that many stakeholders (including the United States and China) are committed to investing in the African power sector, but that means that coordination and cooperation are needed among the various actors. Sweden, for instance, is investing in the U.S. Power Africa initiative. But how about engaging other partners in the energy sector? The African Development Bank could play a central role coordinating this.

The good news is that Africa is increasingly speaking with one voice, as seen in the case of the Common African Position on the Post-2015 Development Agenda. The priorities above are consistent with Pillar Six of the Common African Position, which is about financing and partnerships. Clearly, African policymakers have emphasized the need to (1) improve domestic resource mobilization, (2) maximize innovative financing (remittances and long-term, nontraditional financing mechanisms), and (3) implement existing commitments and promote the quality and predictability of external financing.

These are all relevant issues, but we should strive to have Pillar Six strengthen the five other pillars. Financing should underpin the SDGs.

AFRICA'S INADEQUATE INFRASTRUCTURE

Inadequate infrastructure—including unreliable energy, an ineffective urban-rural road network, and inefficient ports—is one of the largest impediments to economic growth in Africa. It limits the returns from human capital investment—such as education and health. Hospitals and schools cannot function properly without electricity (Sy, 2016).

A 2009 World Bank study estimated that sub-Saharan Africa's infrastructure needs are about $93 billion a year (Foster and Briceño-Garmendia, 2009). In 2014, the International Monetary Fund (IMF) (2014c) estimated that budget spending on infrastructure by sub-Saharan African countries reached about $51.4 billion, meaning a residual financing gap of about $41.6 billion.

External commitments, both private and public, appear to fill a substantial share of this gap (see figure 5-3). They rose to about $30 billion a year in 2012 from $5 billion in 2003 (Gutman, Sy, and Chattopadhyay, 2015). Official development financing has increased—especially from the World Bank and the African Development Bank. Private participation in infrastructure has surged and now accounts for more than half of external financing. China has become a major bilateral source of financing.

FIGURE 5-3 Foreign Commitments to Infrastructure

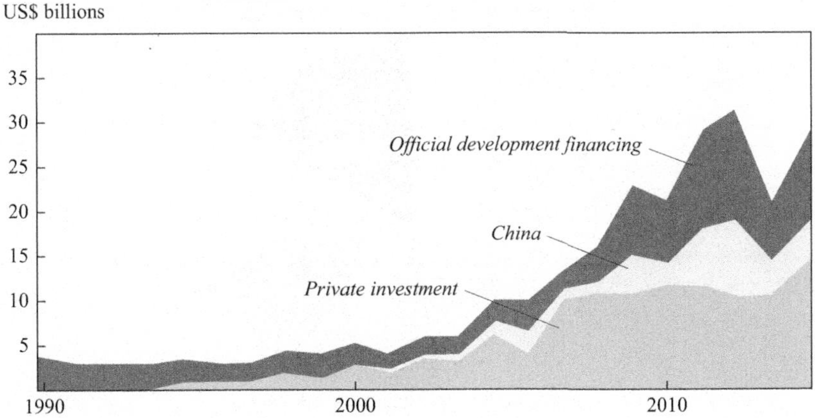

Source: Gutman, Sy, and Chattopadhyay (2015).

But the remaining gap of about $11.6 billion is probably too low an estimate and one that global assistance in any event will not fill under current circumstances. First, the 2009 World Bank calculation underestimates current needs, such as urban infrastructure. Second, the $30 billion in external commitments is not comparable to budget spending. These commitments materialize over time and do not arrive evenly. One large deal, such as a major energy investment in South Africa in 2012, can distort that year's data. Third, overall numbers don't tell the whole story. Of the $59.4 billion in budget spending on infrastructure by African governments, South Africa accounted for about $29 billion in 2012, with the number-two country, Kenya, allocating about $3 billion. Countries also vary widely in their commitment to infrastructure spending. Angola, Cape Verde, and Lesotho invest more than 8 percent of GDP, whereas oil-rich Nigeria and fragile South Sudan allocate less than 1 percent.

In addition, most external financing is concentrated in a few large countries and a few sectors. Five countries attracted more than half the total external commitments to infrastructure development in 2009–12 (see figure 5-4).

Except for Nigeria and South Africa, sub-Saharan African countries have been unable to attract significant private investment outside the telecommunications sector. In 2013, sub-Saharan Africa received about $17

FIGURE 5-4 Dominant Destinations of External Financing

Percent of total external commitments, 2009–12

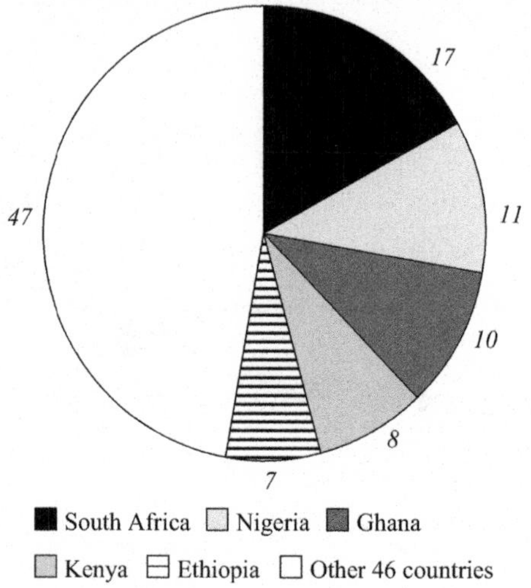

Source: Gutman, Sy, and Chattopadhyay (2015).

billion in private funds, of which all but $2 billion went to South Africa and Nigeria in sectors other than telecommunications. Overall, private investment (which includes public-private partnerships) went mostly to information and communication technology and electricity from 2005 to 2012.

A policy agenda for building and maintaining infrastructure in sub-Saharan Africa under these circumstances should have at least three priorities.

First, domestic budget spending—the largest source of African infrastructure financing—should be increased. African countries generate more than $520 billion annually from domestic taxes and can mobilize more domestic revenue through improved tax administration and measures to broaden the tax base. The average tax-to-GDP ratio increased from 18 percent in 2000–02 to 21 percent in 2011–13—equivalent to half the development aid Africa received in 2013 (Africa Progress Panel, 2015). The increase in domestic financing is no doubt the result of debt relief, some increased tax revenue collection, gains from the commodity price boom, and improved macroeconomic and institutional policies. But it will be hard for many countries to find more domestic revenue. Tax mobilization remains low despite significant effort and recent reforms in non-resource-rich countries (Bhushan, Samy, and Medu, 2013). The ratio of general government tax revenue to GDP in 2013 ranged from 2.8 percent in the Democratic Republic of the Congo to 25 percent in South Africa (one of the highest among developing economies).

Helping African countries raise more funds domestically for many purposes, including infrastructure, should be a priority for African policymakers and the international community. In 2015, global donors committed to helping African countries improve tax collection. In 2011, the latest year for which figures are available, less than 1 percent of official development assistance went to domestic revenue mobilization.

Second, sources of domestic revenue should be broadened. From 2006 to 2014, thirteen countries issued a total of $15 billion in international sovereign bonds, often intending to use the proceeds to finance infrastructure. But a more prudent and sustainable way to finance infrastructure would be to increase the participation of domestic institutional investors, such as pension funds (see table 5-1).

African pension funds have about $380 billion in assets under management, 85 percent of which are in South Africa (see table 5-1). In countries such as Cape Verde, Kenya, South Africa, Swaziland, Tanzania, and Uganda, funds are investing in infrastructure (Inderst and Stewart, 2014). Pension fund trustees and managers should consider whether risk-adjusted investments can be made within the context of their fiduciary duty to beneficiaries. Countries must also improve the governance, regulation, and development of domestic financial and capital market instruments for infrastructure investment—and seek to attract foreign institutional investors too.

Third, funds must be spent efficiently. Most of the debate on infrastructure needs in sub-Saharan Africa focuses on financing issues. But there is evidence that efficiency, not financing, is often the barrier to investment. For example, the IMF estimates that about 40 percent of the potential value of public investment in low-income countries is lost to inefficiencies in the investment process due to time delays, cost overruns, and inadequate maintenance. Those inefficiencies are often the result of undertrained officials, inadequate processes for assessing needs and preparing for and evaluating bids, and corruption. Reducing inefficiencies could substantially increase the economic dividends from public investment (International Monetary Fund, 2015a).

TABLE 5-1 Mine the Gap: Pension Fund Assets in Africa Could Be Tapped as a Source for Investment in Infrastructure

Country	Pension Fund Assets under Management (billions of U.S. dollars)
South Africa	322.0
Nigeria	25.0
Namibia	10.0
Kenya	7.3
Botswana	6.0
Tanzania	3.1
Ghana	2.6
Zambia	1.8
Uganda	1.5
Rwanda	0.5
Total	**379.8**

Sources: Ashiagor and others (2014); Sy (2017).

Note: Asset amounts represent the latest figures available as of 2013.

The Foster and Briceño-Garmendia (2009) study estimated that if inefficiencies were addressed through such measures as rehabilitating existing infrastructure, targeting subsidies better, and improving budget execution—in other words, more efficient use of existing infrastructure—the \$93 billion financing need could be reduced by \$17 billion. That means that the focus of attention on infrastructure should be broadened beyond financing issues to include efforts to improve efficiency. This is a complex task that requires African governments and the international community to focus on individual sectors and how they operate in particular countries and requires robust monitoring capability.

TOP FIVE TRENDS IN AFRICAN INFRASTRUCTURE FINANCING

Since 2009, infrastructure financing to Africa has seen unprecedented growth. Chinese financing, official development financing, and private participation in infrastructure investments have been key sources in this rapid growth—as have national African governments and their domestic resources. However, this financing is still not enough to reach the estimated $93 billion gap in the continent's infrastructure needs. In addition, while infrastructure financing has seen massive growth, until now an understanding of what that growth looks like was lacking. Specifically, what countries and sectors still aren't getting the attention they need? Is the current global governance on this financing sufficient? Where are efficiency and sustainability gaps? Is there a balance between regional, national, and subnational infrastructure? In a 2015 paper, "Financing African Infrastructure: Can the World Deliver?," Gutman, Sy, and Chattopadhyay explored these questions and identified five major trends in infrastructure financing in Africa:

Trend 1: External financing saw a major surge during the period from 2002 to 2012, but its composition looks much different now. As seen in figure 5-3, while infrastructure commitments have been growing from all major sources, private investment has particularly been taking off. Indeed, private investment accounts for 50 percent of infrastructure financing. Chinese financing has also seen significant growth since 2002 and now accounts for about 20 percent of external financing. Importantly, official development financing, private investment, and Chinese financing often (but not always) emphasize different sectors and target different countries (Gutman, Sy, and Chattopadhyay, 2015), creating the need for a central actor to coordinate these disparate efforts.

Trend 2: The importance of private investment and nontraditional sources has grown. Not only have the proportions of Chinese and private sector investments grown, but their significance for particular sectors on the continent has become increasingly important. Among other interesting trends, we find that private investment is the major contributor to the telecom sector. In fact, 64.1 percent of private investment goes to telecommunications. Electricity receives 18.6 percent of private investment, seaports 9.6 percent, and the last 7.6 percent is split among six other sectors. Clearly, private investment has grown and contributed significantly to African infrastructure, though it has been narrow in scope: as seen in figure 5-5, excluding information and communication technology, the number of countries receiving private investment drops from forty to twenty-one. This trend suggests the need for better-targeted measures to promote private investment for other sectors in a broader range of countries.

FIGURE 5-5 Private Investment Commitments in Sub-Saharan Africa, by Count of Countries, 2005–12

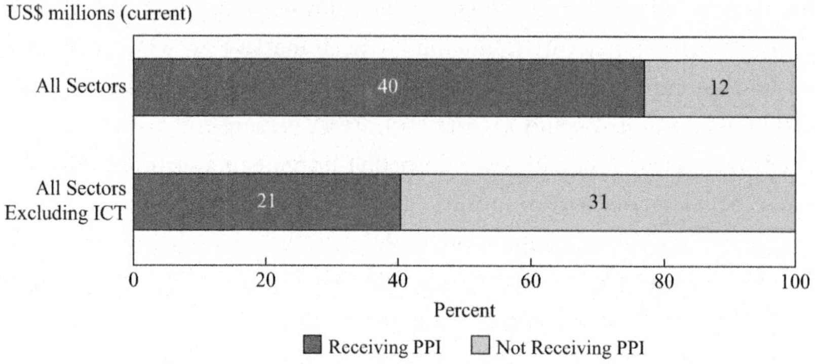

Sources: Gutman, Sy, and Chattopadhyay (2015); authors' calculations using World Bank PPIAF database (ppi.worldbank.org).

ICT = information and communication technology; PPI = private participation in investment.

As seen in figure 5-6, Chinese financing and private investment often cover sectors and subsectors that national governments and official development financing do not. We find that Chinese infrastructure financing emphasizes transport (particularly railways and roads) and hydropower. Importantly, Chinese funding has significantly complemented official development financing, private investment, and domestic financing in terms of both countries served and sectors supported—once again calling for good coordination and alignment of efforts throughout the continent.

Trend 3: Traditional multilateral banks remain relevant in certain sectors and subsectors. While private investment and Chinese financing have been growing, official development financing contributes a major share of infrastructure financing. As seen in figure 5-7, official development financing still plays a particularly important role in transport, water supply and sanitation (which receives only 10 percent of external infrastructure financing on the continent), and energy. In fact, Chinese financing and private investment financing to water supply and sanitation is almost nonexistent. Another advantage of official development financing is that, because of the criteria for multilateral concessional

FIGURE 5-6 Major Financing Source by Sector

Sector	Government	ODF	China	PPI
Energy	✓	✓	✓	✓
Telecom				✓
Transport	✓	✓	✓	✓
Water	✓	✓		

Transport Sector	Government	ODF	China	PPI
Seaports	✓			✓
Airports	✓	✓	✓	
Railroads	✓	✓	✓	
Roads	✓		✓	✓

Sources: Gutman, Sy, and Chattopadhyay (2015); authors' calculations using World Bank PPIAF database (ppi.worldbank.org).

ODF = official development financing; PPI = private participation in investment.

loans, allocation across countries is broadly distributed (which is not the case for private investment or Chinese financing). In fact, for low-income fragile states, official development financing is the largest source of external commitments (excluding telecom).

Trend 4: Overall external commitments as a share of GDP indicate a surprisingly reasonable distribution by country. As could be expected, large economies such as South Africa and Nigeria receive the largest absolute amounts of external financing. When controlling for the size of the economy, however, four of the top six recipients of external financing as a percentage of GDP are all low-income fragile states—Liberia, Togo, Malawi, and Sierra Leone—with Liberia standing out by having external financing that totals more than 25 percent of its GDP.

Recipients of the lowest external financing (as a percentage of GDP) represent a variety of country types. For example, large economies such as South Africa and Nigeria rank near the bottom, and so do resource-rich economies such as Angola because of domestic resources or the size of the economy. Many fragile states like Eritrea, South Sudan, the Republic of the Congo, and Chad rank at the bottom. Looking ahead, analysis of the strengths and weaknesses of middle-range countries (Senegal, Lesotho, the Democratic Republic of the Congo, Cameroon, and Côte

FIGURE 5-7 Official Development Financing Infrastructure Investment in Sub-Saharan Africa, by Sector, 2000–12

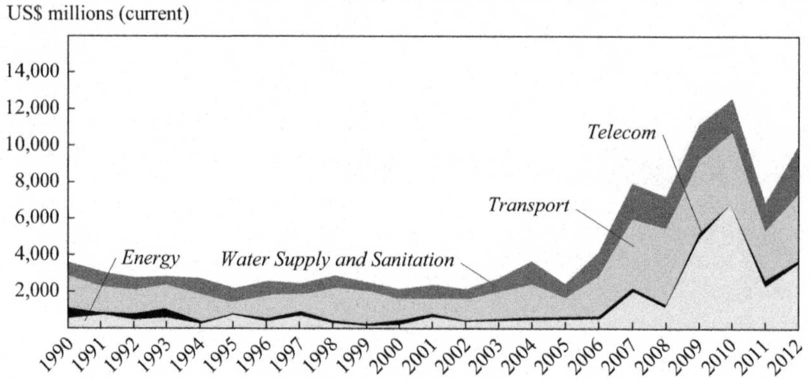

Sources: Gutman, Sy, and Chattopadhyay (2015); authors' calculations using World Bank PPIAF database (ppi.worldbank.org).

d'Ivoire) might offer more opportunities for enhancing access to financing.

Trend 5: Domestic financing remains the largest source of African infrastructure financing. Unfortunately, some governments face many obstacles, including a lack of domestic revenues, a narrow base of revenues, and little capacity to collect those revenues. In addition, these governments have not yet been able to exploit what revenues they do have in an efficient way. Finally, a lack of strategy around infrastructure projects—including uneven financing among national and local, urban and rural, projects—makes it difficult for them to get ahead of the game. When it comes to domestic financing for infrastructure (Fay and others, 2011), experts argue that 5–6 percent of GDP should be sufficient. As seen in figure 5-8, while some countries do surpass this threshold (for example, Angola, Botswana, the Central African Republic), there is no rhyme or reason to who does and who doesn't. Fragile states and resource-rich states fall all over the spectrum. Governments in sub-Saharan Africa also fund the transport and energy sectors—at 41 and 37 percent, respectively, of their infrastructure financing. Water and telecom are on the other end, at 20 and 3 percent, respectively. However, these averages mask extreme differences across countries (see Gutman, Sy, and Chattopadhyay, 2015 for more details).

FIGURE 5-8 National Budget Allocation to Infrastructure in 2013

Percent of GDP

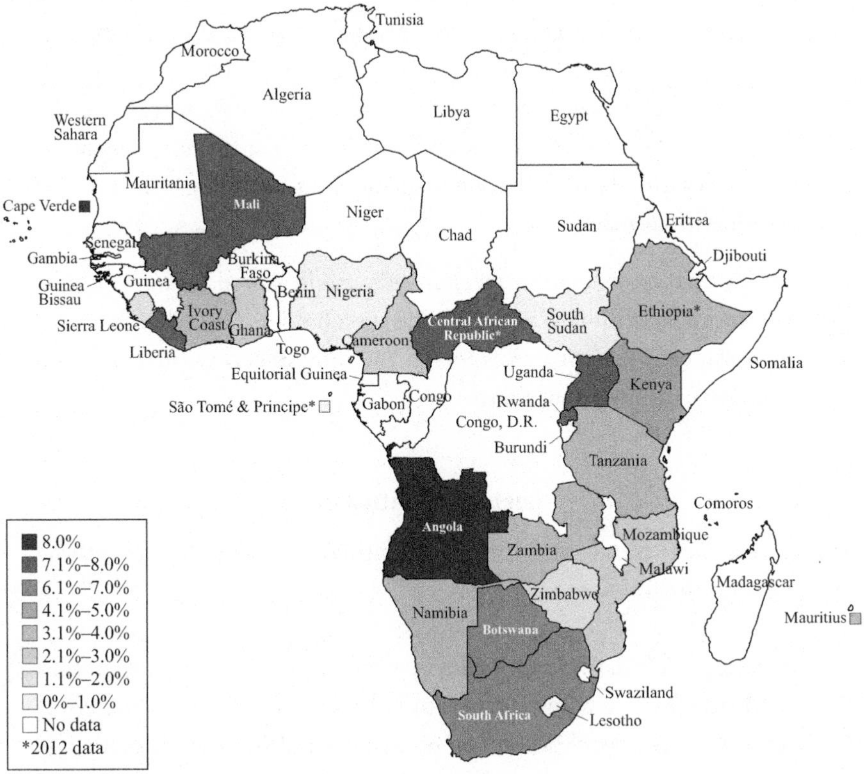

Source: Infrastructure Consortium for Africa (2014).

Major Concerns

In addition to these trends, Gutman, Sy, and Chattopadhyay also find areas of major concern when it comes to African infrastructure financing:

- Subnational and urban infrastructure—both in need for accessing infrastructure and financing it—is largely ignored, which, given rapid population growth and intense urbanization across the continent, raises some red flags.
- Until recently, the emphasis on facilitating projects has led to ignored governance, coordination, and efficiency gains in infrastructure, cre-

ating unnecessary and avoidable obstacles and leaving great potential untapped.

- At the moment (as seen in figure 5-6), the complementarity in financing across sources, countries, and sectors is purely serendipitous, creating the concern that, in the future, African infrastructure financing in certain sectors and countries will suffer major deficits. A coordination body is needed to ensure that financing will continue to address all needs.
- Traditional coordination mechanisms are ill suited in an economic environment with new and multiple stakeholders. Stakeholders need to consider new approaches for raising infrastructure financing and capitalizing on current financing.

Recommendations

In light of these trends and concerns, Gutman, Sy, and Chattopadhyay recommend the following:

- building on existing institutional structures and functions rather than inventing new institutions to enhance collaboration and coordination across traditional and nontraditional sources of financing;
- promoting regional guidance of investment practices for economic, social, and environmental sustainability;
- extending opportunities for private investment beyond the telecom sector to a broader range of countries;
- improving public financing support, including subnational and urban financing and investment; and
- focusing on broader sectoral governance reform opportunities.

Although African infrastructure financing has been taking off, policymakers, private sector actors, multilateral banks, and other stakeholders need to be aware of the complexities surrounding current financing and begin to coordinate as financing continues to shift. See Gutman, Sy, and Chattopadhyay, 2015 for a more detailed breakdown of financing by sources, sectors, subsectors, and countries, as well as a more nuanced look at our concerns and recommendations.

FINANCING AFRICA'S INFRASTRUCTURE DEFICIT: FROM DEVELOPMENT BANKING TO LONG-TERM INVESTING

Africa is the continent of the future. To realize its potential, Africa needs to reduce its massive infrastructure deficit to achieve both structural transformation and market integration. Africa is, however, constrained by its limited domestic revenue base and thus needs to tap into foreign finances. While progress has been made on the origination of large regional infrastructure projects (the first stage of project life), the needed scaling up of financing infrastructure has not yet materialized. While research on the incentive issues in a context of public-private partnership has been prolific, little attention has been paid to the appropriate structure of financing of infrastructure investment in developing countries and in Africa in particular. This chapter fills that gap.

From the perspective of investors, including long-term investors such as sovereign wealth funds (SWFs),[2] investing part of their assets in infrastructure would provide them with the obvious benefit of portfolio diversification while helping achieve their risk-adjusted return objectives. Long-term investors such as SWFs constitute a pool of savings that can help alleviate the financing constraints of Africa's infrastructure. SWFs as a class of institutional investors have gained prominence mainly as a result of the rapid rise of their assets under management. As of 2016, SWFs have accumulated nearly $6 trillion in assets, and if the reserves accumulated by central banks are added, total accumulated savings in this sector approach $15 trillion. The enormous size of this global sovereign wealth becomes apparent by comparing it, for example, to U.S. nominal GDP ($16.6 trillion in 2012), or to the IMF's new borrowing arrangements ($576 billion in 2013), or even to the total market capitalization of U.S.-listed companies ($18.7 trillion in 2012). In addition to their relatively large size, SWFs have long investment horizons and are

2 Sovereign wealth funds are state-owned investment funds. See www.swfinstitute.org/sovereign-wealth-fund/.

relatively much better placed to invest in long-term global infrastructure assets than most investors. In the infrastructure asset class, where there is a huge demand for funding, SWFs are likely to face less competition. One major reason that SWFs are in a better position to invest in such long-term assets is that, unlike other traditional long-term investors such as pension funds, most SWFs do not have substantial explicit liabilities. They are also not subject to the "prudent person" investment regulations, which prevent other institutional investors such as pension funds from building a large exposure to long-term infrastructure projects.

While the case for SWFs and other long-term investors to invest in infrastructure-based assets is strong, the modalities of such a shift in their asset allocation, especially toward Africa-based infrastructure assets, constitute a real challenge. Indeed, the asset allocation toward infrastructure by SWFs has been very modest thus far. SWFs have invested $26 billion of their assets under management in infrastructure assets (TheCityUK, 2013). SWFs differ widely in terms of their objectives and their asset allocation. Notable exceptions to SWFs not investing significantly in infrastructure are Singapore's Temasek and the United Arab Emirates' Mubadala.

The Canadian Pension Plan is one of a few major global pension funds that also invest noticeably in infrastructure assets, and it invests about 5.7 percent of its total assets. Existing evidence for African countries suggests that pension assets are relatively small and dominated by often poorly performing pay-as-you-go schemes for public sector employees. However, countries in southern Africa such as Botswana, Namibia, and South Africa and a few others such as Kenya and Nigeria have larger pension assets. But even when pension reforms toward fully funded systems have been implemented (as in Nigeria) and assets are available for investment, governance and regulatory obstacles as well as a dearth of adequate financial instruments limit African pension funds' allocation to infrastructure.

More generally, SWFs and other long-term investors contemplating investing in infrastructure assets have three main challenges. First, investment in infrastructure entails different types of risk compared to other asset classes. For example, the construction risks inherent in large-scale infrastructure can deter long-term investors whose propensity to take risks is relatively low in light of their main objective, which is to preserve wealth.

Second, SWFs and other long-term investors lack in-house expertise specific to infrastructure. At times, it is even crucial to possess the adequate expertise on infrastructure at the sectoral level (for instance, transportation, energy, information and communication technology, or water). A report from the Organization for Economic Cooperation and Development (2014) stresses that more expertise at the level of board members will be required, perhaps including specialists who have appropriate asset and risk management skills. Third, the lack of standardization of underlying infrastructure projects is an important impediment to the scaling up of investment into infrastructure-based assets. Large physical infrastructure projects are indeed complex and can differ widely from one country and from one sector to the next.

For these reasons, banks and, in particular, development banks and multilateral development banks (MDBs) that have expertise in infrastructure and flexibility in terms of investment horizon and contract renegotiation may play a key role in paving the way for a viable engagement of institutional investors. In addition, MDBs' claims on the governments that receive their loans are senior to other claims. MDBs indeed possess unique characteristics in providing financing that is related to the design and implementation of structural reforms and institution-building programs adopted by governments. The (credible) commitment of governments to the policy reforms and changes in government practices embodied in MDB conditionality and their monitoring and enforcement measures are fundamental to MDB operations and differentiate MDBs from private lenders. Importantly, the advent of infrastructure investment platforms has further extended the practice of cofinancing whereby MDBs and private lenders join forces to support infrastructure investments (Arezki and others, 2017).

Indeed, Armedáriz de Aghion (1999) shows that the provision by MDBs of well-targeted guarantees (or subsidies) alongside the use of cofinancing (limiting the opportunities for politically motivated credit allocation) can lead to superior outcomes. Among the international efforts to leverage institutional investment for infrastructure and other long-term investment, the principles in "G20/OECD High-Level Principles of

Long-Term Investment Financing by Institutional Investors" aim at facilitating and promoting long-term investment by institutional investors, including pension funds (Organization for Economic Cooperation and Development, 2013). In particular, the principles seek to help policymakers design a policy and regulatory framework that encourages institutional investors to invest in long-term assets in a manner consistent with their investment horizon and risk-return objectives.

The main difficulty that Africa faces in terms of structuring its infrastructure financing is the balancing of differences in terms of investors' preferences. Considering the greenfield (that is, projects that are still under development and hence more risky at the outset) nature of the infrastructure needs that Africa faces, development banks need to play a bigger role in not just the origination but also the financing of the earlier stages of large infrastructure projects. They then need to manage a careful but prompt balancing act to promote the involvement of institutional investors in order to avoid crowding out those arm's-length investors. The focus here is on development financial institutions rather than regular commercial banks to support the early—and riskiest—phase of projects. In practice, a large share of the growth in infrastructure financing worldwide is currently shouldered by banks. Banks will surely remain an important source of financing, in particular in the early stages of new projects. However, banks have mostly short-term liabilities and are not well placed to hold long-term assets on their balance sheets for an extended period. More stringent banking regulation, including compliance with Basel III solvency and liquidity requirements, following the global financial crisis has further discouraged long-term lending by banks. As a result, development banks, which are not subject to the same regulatory constraints, need to step up and help with the early stages of the development of projects to pave the way for institutional investors such as SWFs, which constitute a viable source of financing for Africa's infrastructure.

Another rationale for the greater involvement of development banks in the early stage of projects is that in the absence of that engagement, institutional investor preferences would likely lead to a crowding out of greenfield infrastructure assets. Considering that Africa's infrastructure needs are mostly in greenfield investment, it is essential for development banks to step in at the earlier stage of the development of infrastructure projects. Indeed, most institutional investors are comfortable holding only debt instruments (bonds), preferably guaranteed, in relatively safe infrastructure assets, with a payback horizon as short as possible. This generally means that private infrastructure investors crowd into the relatively safe brownfield infrastructure-asset class (that is, projects that are already built and operating), in which yields are no longer that attractive. Far fewer investors venture into greenfield infrastructure projects, which expose them to significant construction risk and involve much longer payback periods. Moreover, in the greenfield space, most private investors want to hold only senior, secured, and if possible, guaranteed debt.

New initiatives, like the Program for Infrastructure Development in Africa, have the ambition to scale up infrastructure investment in Africa but mainly reveal progress on the origination front as opposed to the financing one. Considering differences in investors' preferences, Africa's success in filling its largely greenfield (and hence risky) infrastructure gap hinges on a delicate balancing act between development banking and long-term institutional investing. First, greater involvement of development banks, which have both the flexibility and expertise in these projects, should help finance the riskier phase of large infrastructure projects. Second, development banks should disengage and offload their debts to pave the way for a viable engagement of long-term investors such as SWFs. To promote an Africa-wide infrastructure bond market in which SWFs could play a critical role, the enhancement of Africa's legal and regulatory framework should start now.

FINANCING AFRICA'S INFRASTRUCTURE GAP: LOOKING AT LIBERIA

What uses more electricity: Liberia or the stadium of the Dallas Cowboys on game day? This question was the theme of a *Wall Street Journal* blog and prompted by President Ellen Johnson Sirleaf's declaration that the stadium uses more electricity than the total installed capacity of her country, Liberia (Lefebvre, 2013).

In that small West African country, only 1 percent of people living in cities have access to electricity. That lack hurts hospital patients who cannot be treated properly, children who cannot get access to refrigerated vaccines, students who cannot study at night, girls who have to hunt for firewood instead of going to school, women who cannot venture outside their homes after dusk, businesspeople who pay more than half their operating costs on power alone, and as a result, consumers who pay higher prices to buy goods or services (Sy, 2013a).

Given that Liberia only emerged from a terrible conflict in 2003, one would think that the rest of sub-Saharan Africa fares better when it comes to access to power. Unfortunately, this is not the case: 550 million Africans are in the same situation as Liberians. Africa started fifty years ago with infrastructure comparable to that in Southeast Asia, but now it is lagging behind other developing countries. Blame the lack of maintenance and poor investment decisions, especially in the postindependence period—the so-called bridges to nowhere and white elephants. Furthermore, Africa's infrastructure services, whether for power, water, road freights, mobile telephones, or Internet services, are twice as expensive as elsewhere. Sadly, Africa's infrastructure problems are most acute in fragile states such as Liberia.

Improving infrastructure should contribute to economic growth and help achieve the Sustainable Development Goals. About 60 percent of the world's uncultivated, arable land is in Africa, but because of poor roads and a lack of storage, African farmers can lose up to half their crop just trying to get it to market. Some studies (e.g., Calderón, 2009) indicate that from 1990 to 2005, investments in infrastructure—especially in telecommunication services—contributed almost 1 percent to sub-Saharan African per capita economic growth.

According to Foster and Briceño-Garmendia (2009), the continent's infrastructure spending needs stand at about \$93 billion per year, and about 40 percent of total spending needs are associated with power. Using their meager fiscal resources, African governments spend about \$45 billion—about one-third of which is contributed by donors and the private sector—per year in infrastructure. Two-thirds of the public sector money is used to operate and maintain existing infrastructure and one-third is to finance new projects. This leaves a financing gap of almost \$42 billion and raises the question of how to finance the remainder.

In setting up policies to finance Africa's remaining infrastructure gap, two areas should be on top of the agenda for African policymakers:

1. *Engage, coordinate, and leverage different sources of funding.* The long-term maturity of infrastructure projects and their large scale require different types of financiers, including private sector, bilateral, and multilateral partners. Policymakers therefore need to engage and coordinate with many partners. One challenge will be to find ways to leverage aid flows so as to attract the private investment necessary to implement a sub-Saharan Africa infrastructure agenda.

Recent developments are encouraging: During the period from 2008 to 2013, the African Development Bank (AfDB) has delivered more than $5.4 billion in critical infrastructure investments on the continent through private sector and public-private partnership financing. The Africa50 Infrastructure Fund that the AfDB recently launched with the Made in Africa Foundation will not only finance projects but also help develop bankable projects. It currently takes an average of seven years to go from project identification to financial closure.[3]

The World Bank Group, which includes its private arm, the International Financing Corporation, and the Multilateral Investment Guarantee Agency, which provides political risk insurance, has a new strategy that aims to use financial innovation and partnerships with the private sector to fund selected sectors, including infrastructure. China pledged $3 billion for joint investments with the International Financing Corporation to support private sector development in emerging markets, including in African infrastructure. The China-Africa Development Fund—a subsidiary of the China Development Bank—has already financed projects in more than thirty African countries. The projects are expected to bring further Chinese investment in Africa.

2. *Financial innovation.* African policymakers will also need to create appropriate innovative financing solutions. Private sector investment has in the past focused on areas such as mobile telephones, power plants, and shipping container terminals. In other areas, such as power, water, and railways, the private sector has preferred the use of concessions and other types of contracts. Innovative financing can play a role in attracting private sector funds to these areas. Financing of infrastructure projects is

3 Financial closure, or financial close, occurs when all the project and financing agreements have been signed and all the required conditions contained in them have been met. It enables funds (e.g., loans, equity, grants) to start flowing so that project implementation can actually start. See www.eib.org/epec/g2g/iii-procurement/32/323/index.htm.

challenging because of the large size, long tenures, and complexity of projects. In sub-Saharan Africa, local banks, which dominate the financial sector, are not able to provide sufficient long-term financing.

Untapped sources of funding are also relevant. The use of diaspora bonds (like those issued by Ethiopia) and the offering of infrastructure bonds (like those in Kenya) are being explored by other African countries. For instance, Kenya marketed infrastructure bonds to retail investors, including from the diaspora. Islamic financial instruments such as sukuk have been used to finance infrastructure projects. In project financing, solutions to mitigate credit risk could involve multilateral partners. Berne Union data show that medium- and long-term credit guarantees in sub-Saharan Africa reached $9.1 billion in 2012 but were highly concentrated in Angola, Congo, Ethiopia, Ghana, Nigeria, South Africa, and Zambia (Masse, 2013).

Do not forget investments in financial infrastructure: most efforts are currently dedicated to investments in social infrastructure (education, and health) and physical infrastructure (transportation, power, and information and communication technologies). However, given the potential role of deeper financial markets and more developed capital markets in helping find the necessary resources for such investments, policymakers should also consider improving the infrastructure of the financial system, starting with the payment system.

Regional solutions make sense for building the infrastructure necessary to exploit the new oil and gas fields in East Africa. There is, at the moment, a coordinated approach to address the very large gap in financing of projects. The New Partnership for Africa's Development Infrastructure Project Preparation Facility (IPPF) is a fund set up to assist in developing high-quality infrastructure proposals. Managed by the AfDB, the 2016–20 IPPF financial pipeline aimed between $160 million and $250 million to prepare sixty to eighty projects.[4]

I offer a note of caution, however. Large infrastructure projects are expensive, complex, and require adequate and transparent governance structures to avoid a misuse of public funds. To avoid the bridges to nowhere of the past, policymakers should separate political promises from

4 See www.afdb.org/en/topics-and-sectors/initiatives-partnerships/nepad-infrastructure-project-preparation-facility-nepad-ippf/.

technical decisions, which should be based on appropriate evaluation methods to assess costs and benefits. To avoid the white elephants of the past, they should improve infrastructure planning and assessment, assess risks from execution, avoid cost overruns, and carefully assess expected maintenance costs. This will need an institutional strengthening of the ministries and public sector entities in charge of implementing infrastructure projects.

By the way, the results of the Liberia versus Cowboys Stadium question are, according to Bob Brackett (energy analyst and football fan), that "during moments of peak demand on game day, Cowboys Stadium may consume up to 10 megawatts of electricity and Liberia has the capacity to pump less than a third as much power into its national grid" (Lefebvre, 2013).

ISLAMIC SUKUK FINANCING CAN HELP MEET AFRICA'S INFRASTRUCTURE GAP

Sukuk have financed infrastructure projects in Malaysia, Indonesia, and the Middle East and could attract investors from other countries. Islamic financing requires a clear link with real economic activity, and transactions have to relate to a tangible, identifiable asset, which comes in handy in the case of infrastructure financing.

Nascent market activity shows that some African countries have already set the course toward a greater use of Islamic financing to fund their infrastructure projects. Nigeria's Securities and Exchange Commission approved new rules facilitating the issuance of sukuk in 2013. At the end of that year, the southwestern Nigerian state of Osun issued a local currency sukuk. The seven-year instrument raised about $62 million from domestic pension funds and international investors and paid 14.75 percent in nominal terms (which is equivalent to about 6.75 percent in real terms given the prevailing 8 percent inflation rate). It received an A rating from a local credit rating agency and was expected to be listed on the Nigerian Stock Exchange.

After the recent trend of Eurobond issuance by African countries, Osun's offering is sowing the seeds for more African sukuk. Before Osun's issuance, only Gambia and Sudan had issued local-currency short-term domestic notes (Sudan sold local currency sukuk worth $160 million in 2012).

Senegal issued a $180 million sukuk program in 2014 to finance infrastructure and energy projects. The Islamic Corporation for the Development of the Private Sector said that the Senegalese sukuk would be the first of a series of programs that would be offered to West African countries. The Central Bank of the West African States agreed in principle to allow banks in its eight member countries to use the sukuk in repurchase operations. Other countries such as South Africa, Nigeria, Senegal, and Mauritania also have plans to issue Islamic securities.

There are two lessons from the Osun offering. The first is that African countries should continue to be innovative to fund their development needs. In this regard, developing a strategy to tap the large pool of money seeking Islamic financial products is good policy. About 600 Islamic financial institutions operate in seventy-five countries, and global Islamic financial assets stand at about $1.3 trillion with a growth rate exceeding 20 percent. African sukuk issuers will be able to diversify their investor base and, as is the case for conventional sovereign bonds, help establish benchmarks for other domestic borrowers. For investors, African sukuk are worth considering as they offer different geographic and credit exposures.

But a second lesson from the Osun issuance is that sukuk can help develop domestic capital markets, which is typically a difficult and long process. Osun issued a local currency instrument that was rated by a domestic agency and placed to domestic investors. For years, Malaysia has used Islamic securities to grow its domestic bond market, which is now the third largest in Asia, after Japan and South Korea. Malaysia's total sukuk issuance in 2012 was $97 billion with a total outstanding stock of $144 billion as of the end of 2012. In countries with a large Muslim population, there is a demand for Islamic securities, and it makes sense for policymakers and the private sector to consider financial securities that can meet this demand. About half of Nigeria's 160 million people are Muslim, and the Pew Research Center (2011) estimates that the Muslim population in sub-Saharan Africa, about a quarter of a billion (243 million in 2010), will increase to about 386 million by 2030. The challenge, however, is to set up the conditions for Islamic financial products to be attractive to all investors. There may be lessons from the evolution of socially responsible investment industry too. When I visited Kuala Lumpur a few years ago, I was struck by how one bank, which catered to Malaysians of Chinese origin, was very active in Islamic products because its non-Muslim customers demanded fixed-rate products instead of the conventional floating-rate mortgages.

Zeti Akhtar Aziz, the former governor of the Central Bank of Malaysia, noted that "Islamic finance is well-positioned to assume a much larger role as a competitive form of financial intermediation for supporting economic activity, and as a channel for enhancing greater global connectivity" (Aziz, 2013). Malaysia is still working to improve its Islamic financial markets. Its focus is now on internationalization, but its road map to building a stable Islamic financial sector that can finance inclusive growth is useful to Africa as well. It starts with developing the legal framework for Islamic financing and establishing sound regulatory and supervisory frameworks.

FINANCING AFRICA: MOVING BEYOND FOREIGN AID TO ISSUING EUROBONDS

Most sub-Saharan African countries have long had to rely on foreign assistance or loans from international financial institutions to supply part of their foreign currency needs. But now, for the first time, many of them are able to borrow in international financial markets, selling Eurobonds, which are usually denominated in dollars or euros.

South Africa has issued Eurobonds for a number of years. But more recently, Angola, Côte d'Ivoire, Gabon, Ghana, Namibia, Nigeria, Rwanda, Senegal, Seychelles, and Zambia have been able to raise funds in international debt markets. Kenya, Tanzania, and Uganda are expected to issue Eurobonds in the near future. In total, more than 20 percent of the forty-eight countries in sub-Saharan Africa have sold Eurobonds.

This sudden surge in borrowing in a region that contains some of the world's poorest economies is due to a variety of factors, including rapid growth and better economic policies, low global interest rates, and continued economic stress in many major advanced economies, especially in Europe. On several occasions, African countries have been able to sell bonds at lower interest rates than in troubled European economies, such as Greece and Portugal.

Whether the rash of borrowing by sub-Saharan African governments (as well as a handful of corporate entities in the region) is sustainable over the medium to long term, however, is open to question. The low-interest-rate environment is likely to change at some point, which will raise borrowing costs for these countries and reduce investor interest. In addition, strong and sustained economic growth may not continue, which would make it harder for these countries to service their loans. Moreover, political instability in some African countries could make the situation more difficult for borrowers and lenders alike.

To assess whether the favorable climate for bond issuance is likely to persist, it is useful to focus on factors that drive the cost of borrowing and determine the direction of capital flows. "Push" factors affect the general climate for bond sales to international investors; "pull" factors are country specific and depend to a degree on a country's policies.

When global interest rates increase and concerns about the global financial crisis abate, governments in sub-Saharan Africa will have to compete for funding with other issuers.

Push factors indicate that the capital inflows driving the purchase of Eurobonds issued by sub-Saharan African countries are sustainable only in the short term. One reason for this is that interest rates in the United States, currently historically low, are likely to increase in the medium term. The other is a change in the risk appetite of foreign investors, which has been increasing as they search for yields higher than they can get in the United States and other safe havens. This greater appetite for risk favors Eurobonds from sub-Saharan Africa. However, when global interest rates increase, governments in sub-Saharan Africa will have to compete for funding with other issuers.

Pull factors also indicate that capital inflows are sustainable in the short run. Whether African countries will pull in capital over the long run depends on the ability of the policymakers in these countries to strengthen their policies. Low-income countries in sub-Saharan Africa have been helped by stronger policy frameworks, improved governance, favorable commodity price trends, and sharply reduced external debt burdens (at least for now). The strength of projected growth in the region is also helped in part by supply-side factors, including an expanding natural resource sector. The near-term outlook for the region remains broadly positive: GDP growth reached 5.3 percent in 2013. But downside risks have intensified, mostly stemming from the uncertain global economic environment.

The spate of international borrowing by sub-Saharan African countries, at rates sometimes below what some crisis-affected European countries are paying, is probably unsustainable in the long run, unless these countries are able to generate high and sustainable economic growth rates and further reduce macroeconomic volatility.

Policy actions are therefore important. First, short-term policy actions must continue to focus on achieving macroeconomic stability, maintaining debt sustainability, ensuring adequate use of proceeds from financing and investing in projects with high economic multipliers, avoiding the buildup of balance sheet vulnerabilities from currency and maturity mismatches, and managing the risk of significant slowdown or reversal. Second, long-term policy actions should focus on developing domestic capital markets and institutions and adequately sequencing the liberalization of capital accounts.

Taking examples from a variety of countries, African policymakers could aim for successful second-best policies and then transition to the best ones. However, countries must also consider the net benefits of unconventional policies because more conventional policies will take time to develop and implement. For example, developing a well-functioning domestic bond market to attract domestic and foreign savings, especially in the long term, is not easy. To that end, in addition to developing their investor base, the conventional advice is that African countries must improve macroeconomic policies, debt management, and regulatory, legal, and market infrastructure. Money markets are the cornerstone of capital markets and a natural place to start reforms. Commercial banks are typically the largest investors in Africa, and a well-functioning interbank market is key. Ensuring the liquidity of domestic markets should also be a priority.

Implementing these conventional policies takes time, however, and policymakers should explore a number of innovative measures. First, regional solutions are promising. By strengthening common institutions, the governments in the West African Economic and Monetary Union are increasingly able to mobilize domestic savings from banks and other investors in the eight union countries and issue Treasury bills and bonds separately from each other.

Second, the diaspora should be better engaged. Ethiopia has tapped savings from nonresident nationals by issuing diaspora bonds, and Nigeria is planning to do the same. Kenya marketed an infrastructure bond issue to retail diaspora investors, and nonresident Kenyans can now send money back home using mobile phone payment systems.

Third, natural resource wealth creates challenges that must be addressed, including how to ensure the efficiency of public spending arising from this wealth. Nigeria and Angola have set up SWFs that have the potential to fund infrastructure or other long-term projects.

Most important, African policymakers must continue innovating if they want to raise the vast resources needed to finance the continent's development needs. Innovation will be risky, but aid is simply not large enough, and Eurobond flows are just not stable enough.

6

Big Risks and Big Opportunities

Many risks confront the African continent as it works to achieve its vision. Changes in the external geopolitical and economic environment and accompanying shocks are, of course, a major risk for African countries. Resource-rich and soon-to-be-resource-rich countries also face very specific challenges when it comes to navigating such shocks. Climate change poses challenges to African countries, and global epidemics such as the recent Ebola crisis obviously posed a huge risk to the health, livelihoods, and economic progress of the region.

However, some of the risks confronting African countries also present opportunities. Climate change and the way that Africa is both affected by and approaches climate-friendly policy in the future is a critical topic of discussion. Similarly, Africa's rapidly increasing urbanization offers an opportunity for creative policymaking. In addition, an examination of past crises, such as Ebola, aids the development of new and better ways to confront similar future events.

While this chapter could address countless issues, I limit myself to a few examples that focus on major challenges and the opportunities they present for strengthening and ensuring better analysis and development outcomes.

SUB-SAHARAN AFRICA AND THE EXTERNAL ENVIRONMENT

In recent years, sub-Saharan Africa has experienced slower growth rates for the first time since the 1998 global financial crisis. The International Monetary Fund's *African Regional Economic Outlook* (International Monetary Fund, 2017b) stated that the 2016 growth rate was the lowest the continent has seen in the last twenty years, at 1.4 percent. The region's real GDP growth fell from 5.0 percent in 2014 to 3.75 percent in 2015, and then to 1.4 percent in 2016. The 2017 forecast showed a slight recovery, with expectations around 2.6 percent, but at a rate still much lower than the decade preceding the decline. What is even more worrisome is that the IMF growth forecast for 2018 is just a baseline projection. There is, therefore, an implicit interval of confidence around the growth projection, and downside risks to the baseline are looming large. Not all is lost, though: changes like these create opportunities for appropriate and timely policy measures that can make a difference and help sub-Saharan African economies regain their growth momentum both in the short and long term.

Such a path does, however, mean that the growth momentum in the region may be running out of steam. This trend is worrisome: when looked at on a per capita basis, Africa's growth rate is still too low to make a permanent dent in Human Development Index indicators. GDP per capita growth averaged 3.4 percent in 2004–14, and if the region regained this level of per capita GDP average growth rate, GDP per capita could be doubled by 2036. If it cannot, improving human development indicators will take much longer.

As the continent takes its first steps in meeting the UN Sustainable Development Goals, it is crucial that it achieve faster and better-quality economic growth, meaning growth that has a high growth elasticity of poverty reduction (the percentage reduction in poverty rates associated with a percentage change in mean per capita income) and relies on more engines of growth, such as agriculture and manufacturing, rather than on exports of oil and other commodities.

In 2008, the continent, like the rest of the world, faced a global financial shock but was in part insulated from it thanks to its less pronounced financial linkages with the rest of the world. Now, however, the continent faces a triple threat: (1) prices of Africa's main exports, oil and metal, have fallen significantly, driven by robust supplies and low demand, and are expected to remain low now that the commodity supercycle has come to an end; (2) the economy of Africa's main bilateral trading partner, China, is slowing; and (3) external borrowing costs are increasing as the U.S. Federal Reserve further raises interest rates, and the options for borrowing are becoming more limited. One could even add a fourth threat—climate change, which has particularly affected East and Southern Africa recently.

Throughout 2015, the effects of the triple threat were felt across the continent. Almost all currencies have depreciated against the U.S. dollar, inflation is higher, stock markets are down, and bond yield spreads are up. But all of this provides an opportunity for sub-Saharan African countries to assess their existing vulnerabilities and enact policy measures taken to manage them.

The different ways of looking at the region's vulnerabilities to current external shocks all point to a regional economic slowdown:

- Oil and metal exporters in the region will experience slower growth. World Bank (2015b, p. 6) data show that fuel, metal, and mineral exports represented about two-thirds of sub-Saharan Africa's exports in 2010–14. Oil exporters, which include Angola, Cameroon, Chad, the Republic of the Congo, Equatorial Guinea, Gabon, Nigeria, and South Sudan, alone represent about half the region's GDP and will be a drag on the region's growth. In contrast, oil-importing countries such as Ethiopia, Kenya, Rwanda, and Tanzania will help mitigate the impact of lower oil prices on the region.

- Growth in the largest economies in the region, Nigeria and South Africa, is slowing. The two countries together account for more than half the region's GDP and have suffered from falling commodity prices as well as structural problems, including electricity shortages. Nigeria's real GDP growth is expected to be 0.8 percent in 2017 (Vanguard Media, 2017). South Africa is expected to grow at 1.0 percent.

- Economies that are the largest exporters to China are mostly commodity exporters and, as a result, are vulnerable to both a Chinese economic slowdown and lower commodity prices (the two trends are

> related). Exports to China from South Africa (the second-largest economy in the region) exceeded 29 percent of its total exports in 2010–14 and are above 40 percent for the Gambia, the Democratic Republic of the Congo, the Republic of the Congo, Angola, Mauritania, and Sierra Leone. One of the best examples of a vulnerable country is Zambia, which is major exporter of copper, most of which is sold to China (46 percent of Zambia's exports in 2010–14), the world's largest consumer of the metal (45 percent of global demand in 2014).

Unfortunately, unlike in the aftermath of the 2008 global financial crisis, policy buffers are thin, and most countries are suffering from twin deficits—both current account and fiscal. Deteriorating terms of trade have widened current account deficits, and public investment in infrastructure has contributed to widening fiscal deficits. To make things more complicated, these deficits need to be financed at a time when the cost of external borrowing is increasing and access to capital markets is becoming more difficult.

Sub-Saharan African countries need a two-pronged approach to accelerate their growth. Basically, countries need to implement macroeconomic policies to cope with the short-term effects of the external shocks, and they need to stay the course in implementing medium- to long-term structural policies. A typical policy strategy for countries facing external shocks is to sacrifice long-term gains to avoid short-term pain—for example, by cutting public investments to avoid fiscal adjustment instead of cutting current expenditures. This is often because politicians—who at the end of the day lead the way—have a short-term horizon dictated by the electoral calendar.

This changing environment makes now an opportune time for policymakers to act. Significantly reduced revenues make fiscal reforms in commodity exporting countries necessary. With oil prices down, countries must now consider removing oil subsidies and increasing non-oil fiscal revenues—such as by raising the value added tax. Countries will need to alleviate the impact of these policies on the poor, such as through social protection programs. Other revenue boosting measures that should be considered include reducing tax expenditures, improving tax administration, and reviewing tax policy on luxury goods. Now is also the time to review and prioritize expenditures and maximize the efficiency of every dollar spent from the budget. In addition, given the reduction in policy buffers, countries with flexible exchange rate regimes may consider letting their exchange rates depreciate to absorb some of the economic shocks. As global liquidity conditions are tightening, cash and debt management should become a priority.

At the same time, beyond the narrow macroeconomic response to external shocks, policymakers must consider broader policy responses: the key challenge is to strengthen the resilience of African economies to shocks. This task involves successfully implementing the economic transformation agenda of the continent, starting with investment in infrastructure and kick-starting the engines of the economy beyond commodity exports.

Increased domestic revenue mobilization also depends on a growing economy, and the changing environment should be a catalyst to expand the non-oil economy. The rebasing of Nigeria's GDP in 2013 showed how large the non-oil economy had become and how little it contributes to fiscal revenues. Strengthening the non-oil economy will require increasing investment and implementing structural reforms to improve competitiveness, reduce the infrastructure gap, enhance the quantity and quality of education and training, and improve skills. It will also mean addressing tough issues, such as how to best design land tenure systems in a continent where land is often customarily owned in rural areas. These measures need financing. In the case of infrastructure, local-currency financing through the development of domestic capital markets and local institutional investors should be the first option. For countries with unsustainable pension systems, this means implementing pension reform. For countries with existing pension assets, this means increasing the liquidity of domestic markets. But financing is not the only way to increase investment; significant productivity gains can be achieved through more efficient spending and better organization of line ministries responsible for implementing government programs and public utilities. Finally, engaging the private sector and multilateral partners can help reduce the infrastructure financing gap.

Building the non-oil economy will also involve economic and financial integration, including through both regional and global value chains. It will involve broadening access to financial services and improving the payment system, including mobile payments. It will involve adapting economies to climate change and avoiding the high-carbon growth path that other countries like China have gone through. It will also involve avoiding homegrown shocks that could arise if Africa's high demographic growth and rapid urbanization are not leveraged.

Because of these past shocks and future global changes and uncertainties, sub-Saharan Africa's external environment is definitely becoming less supportive of African growth. In the short term, timely and appropriate macroeconomic policies can help the region absorb the shocks of declining commodity prices, the slowing Chinese economy, and higher U.S. interest rates. Rather than seeing these and other trends and developments as impediments, policymakers should view them as opportunities to strengthen the resilience of their economies. For example, average growth numbers mask differences between economies, and some African countries such as Côte d'Ivoire, the Democratic Republic of the Congo, Ethiopia, Mozambique, Rwanda, and Tanzania will be among the fastest-growing economies in the world. Interestingly, in light of the supportive announcements at the conclusion of the Forum on China-Africa Cooperation at the end of 2015, China is making a $60 billion bet that, with support, sub-Saharan Africa can ride the current shocks and return to its previously high growth.

SUB-SAHARAN AFRICA'S OIL EXPORTERS: ADDRESSING GROWING FINANCING NEEDS

While prospects remain encouraging for many sub-Saharan African countries, how things have changed for the oil-exporting ones! Before 2014, oil exporters boasted a current account surplus and even managed to generate a small government budget surplus. But then in 2014, oil prices fell so abruptly that by early 2016 they had reached a ten-year low. As revenues from oil exports shrank, government revenues that largely depended on them fell, and so government financing requirements increased. Sub-Saharan African oil exporters were faced with the twin deficits of their current account and government budget.

The challenge is that external financing requirements are increasing at exactly the same time as financial conditions are tightening. U.S. interest rates are increasing, which not only raises refinancing costs and the cost of new borrowing but also dampens the search for yield and reduces the appetite for risk that had pushed investors to venture into frontier markets, including in Africa. Capital flows to oil-exporting countries may decline further or, even worse, reverse. Tighter financial conditions leave credible and decisive domestic adjustment as the main policy option to address growing financing needs. Unfortunately, oil exporters have so far been rather tentative in their adjustment efforts. In the face of depleted buffers and tighter financial conditions, they have been slow and at times even reluctant to implement much-needed macroeconomic adjustments.

Now, then, is the time to use the oil shocks to not only implement the right macroeconomic policy mix but also to put oil-dependent economies on a better footing so that they can make significant progress toward the Sustainable Development Goals. There is really no other choice, as oil prices are expected to remain low for a long time (even though they have been rising of late). Short-term adjustment will lessen only immediate pain, and sectoral policies, including in agriculture, will be needed to diversify oil-rich economies and strengthen their structural transformation. Financing is only one part of the equation, and raising more revenues from the non-oil economy is an option that should be exercised. But now that oil rents have shrunk, it is time to accelerate the pace of reforms that do not require much funding, such as improving the efficiency of spending. Policymakers will need the right combination of political will, effective communication, and private sector and other stakeholders' involvement. The social contract in place during the boom years should be revisited.

The boom-and-bust cycle of oil prices is leading to macroeconomic imbalances that will need to be financed. Fluctuations in the price of oil give a sense of how brutal the shock has been for oil exporters. The price of oil fell from $112 per barrel in mid-2014 to less than $39 in early January 2016. Falling oil prices have led to lower export revenues and deteriorated current account balances, and have put pressure on currencies. The current account deficit for oil exporters moved from positive to negative from 2013 to 2014. Oil-exporting countries managed to generate a current account surplus of 3.8 percent of GDP in 2013, which fell to a deficit of 0.6 percent in 2014 and worsened to a deficit of 4.7 percent of GDP in 2015. Fiscal balances have worsened over time. The large oil shock led to increased financing, and now a crucial question is to what extent external financing will be available in 2017. Unfortunately, although oil prices have somewhat recovered, prospects do not look good, and external financing was difficult to obtain in 2017.

One buffer against falling oil prices is the level of international reserves, but such a buffer is limited. Oil-exporting countries in the region have been depleting their international reserves and, as noted by World Bank (2016a), cumulative decline in international reserves was more than 30 percent between the end of June 2014 and March 2016. The IMF (2016) also remarks that these countries have financed about two-thirds of their current account deficit by drawing on international reserves to the tune of 1.5 percent of GDP each year since 2014.

Foreign borrowing can also help finance the widening current account of oil exporters. But accessing the international debt market is becoming increasingly difficult and costly. In 2016, only South Africa and Ghana tapped international bond markets, the latter raising $750 million at a yield of 9.25 percent after having delayed the issuance because of the higher price demanded by investors. It is useful to note that unlike oil-exporting countries like Nigeria and Angola, Ghana was already under an IMF program and had already started its domestic macroeconomic adjustment.

The pace of credit rating downgrades has accelerated over the past year (World Bank, 2016a). In the first half of 2016 alone, a number of oil-exporting countries, such as Angola, Gabon, and the Republic of the Congo, saw credit rating downgrades. Higher interest rates and lower ratings are complicating these countries' efforts to access international markets. Oil-exporting countries, and those exporting other commodities, paid a relatively higher cost to issue debt. Nigeria's $3 billion international bond issuance in November 2017, its first since 2013, provides a litmus test for other African oil-exporting countries seeking to finance themselves externally. However, foreign investors' appetite for risk is notoriously fickle, and there is no guarantee that other oil-exporting countries will be able to issue or to do so at a reasonable cost. Nigeria issued its 10-year notes at a cost of 6.5 percent and its 30-year bonds at 7.625 percent.

The typical medicine against a negative oil shock for oil exporters is a combination of fiscal contraction, currency depreciation, and monetary tightening (to limit inflationary pressures). In addition, state-owned enterprises and the financial sector are closely watched to avoid any bad surprises such as the materialization of quasi-fiscal liabilities and higher nonperforming loans from exposures to oil and gas and currency mismatches. To make the medicine easier to ingest, existing policy buffers can be used to smooth the adjustment. When policy buffers are too low, multilateral institutions such as the IMF, the African Development Bank, and the World Bank and bilateral donors, including China, are asked to pitch in (when the political economy environment allows it).

But unlike more diversified economies, oil-dependent economies are like oil tankers—they are difficult to turn around quickly. Still, implementing the right set of policies quickly and in a credible way is crucial. Unfortunately, African oil exporters have typically not been able to manage this difficult situation as credibly and decisively as they need to.

Slow exchange rate adjustment is evident not only in the dwindling international reserves of African oil-exporting countries but also in the scarcity of foreign exchange (getting U.S. dollars has become increasingly difficult in Nigeria, for instance) and in the large gap between parallel markets and official exchange rates such as in Angola and Nigeria. Budget outturns show that many countries were not able to rein in current expenditures or to execute capital expenditures (as in Nigeria, which sought to use it as countercyclical policy). In many countries, government debt has risen and a larger share of falling revenues is now allocated to service debt. The IMF (2016) notes, for instance, that public debt has increased sharply among oil exporters by twenty percentage points of GDP since 2013 (although from a low level in Nigeria). Government arrears have also increased, and some governments have even resorted to central bank financing. Reasons for not achieving the right and timely policy mix have been numerous and include treating the oil shock as a temporary shock rather than a permanent one, long delays in coordination between ministries and in policy execution, and difficulty in managing the political economy of reform.

A silver lining, however, is that the current shock and its negative consequences on the economies and lives of the citizens of African oil-exporting countries can be an opportunity to fix the machine. Indeed, the sharp fall in oil prices has highlighted the fragility of the current growth model. Structural transformation is not deeply rooted, and there has been little progress in diversifying economies and reducing overdependence on oil-export revenues. The time to accelerate the implementation of the domestic revenue mobilization agenda, which was much heralded in the 2015 Addis Ababa Action Agenda, and to improve the taxation of the non-oil economy, consider the merit of increasing the value added tax, and revisit poorly targeted tax exemptions and subsidies, is now. It is also the time to ensure that capital expenditures (which are needed to finance the large infrastructure gap) have a value for money and outcomes that are really growth enhancing. It is the time to revisit how current expenditures in the oil economy were part of an ineffective social contract in which oil windfalls would result in a higher wage bill and increased government spending for goods and services.

Now is the time to reconsider the roles of the private sector and the financial sector as engines of broad-based growth beyond their typical dependence on government contracts and oil and gas revenues. In the oil economy, the government is too often the be-all and end-all and crowds out or even stunts the private sector. Now is the time to level the playing field and revisit the role of the state and its areas of interventions, including reducing the cost of doing business and providing adequate infrastructure to boost private sector–led growth and competitiveness. Such measures are also part of the needed new social contract.

Now is the time to step up the improvement of institutions to complement the macro stabilization effort and set the foundation for sustainable and inclusive growth. Too often, poor governance has arrested the effectiveness of public expenditures to improve outcomes and enhance growth. Good governance is also critical for the domestic revenue mobilization agenda. Recent work shows that good governance is more relevant for raising tax revenues than for attracting foreign direct investment. This is important because tax revenues are typically the largest source of financing for development.

Now is also the time to take a serious look at the social compact in oil-exporting countries. Social protection expenditures can be very low in oil-exporting countries and should be revisited. After all, how much did the poor really benefit from the boom cycle in oil prices? Now that adjustment times have come, how much of the adjustment costs should the poor bear? Now is the time to build the capacity to implement targeted interventions and proceed to implement targeted social protection measures to help smooth the effects of the necessary macroeconomic adjustment. For instance, increasing the value added tax, a regressive tax, should be accompanied by well-targeted compensation of the poorest segments of the population.

Policymakers in oil-exporting countries need a three-pronged approach that will credibly and decisively focus on macroeconomic adjustment, set the basis for medium-term broad-based growth, and revisit the social contract. These objectives are vital at this juncture, and short-term issues must be addressed to avoid jeopardizing medium-term growth.

BREXIT: WHAT IMPLICATIONS FOR AFRICA?

On June 23, 2016, British citizens voted on a referendum determining the future of the United Kingdom and its place in the European Union (EU). British voters decided to leave the European Union. Supporters argued that the EU has seen tremendous changes over the years, thus diminishing the sovereign role of the United Kingdom and its influence. Advocates of staying in the EU argued that being part of a large regional community provided the United Kingdom with greater influence and security on a global scale.

Leaving the EU is estimated to have costly economic consequences (Erlanger, 2016). The departure of the United Kingdom from the EU, or Brexit, is expected to negatively affect the global economy. In late May 2016, Kenya's Central Bank governor, Patrick Njoroge, warned about the risks to the global economy, especially increased market volatility, following Brexit. Several commentators have focused on the potential effect of Brexit on fellow European countries and advanced economies, but what potential consequences might Brexit have on African economies?

The End of British Outwardness

Perhaps the biggest impact of Brexit on Africa would be the end of British outwardness—the country's concern with and responsiveness to global development issues—which, from an African development perspective, reached its peak in 2005 with the U.K. presidency of the Group of Eight (G-8) countries. Indeed, at the G-8 Summit in Gleneagles, Scotland, that year, leaders agreed to double aid to Africa and eliminate outstanding debts of the poorest countries. Indeed, one of the major successes of the G-8 U.K. presidency was the agreement to provide debt relief to the poorest African countries. The G-8 countries also agreed to increase aid to developing countries by $50 billion a year by 2010 with at least half of this commitment going to Africa. Other commitments included increased support for African peacekeeping forces and additional investment in education and the fight against HIV/AIDS, malaria, tuberculosis, and other diseases.

The Gleneagles Summit benefited from prior extensive consultation in Africa and elsewhere, including from African leaders like the late president of Ethiopia, Meles Zenawi, and the then–South African minister of finance, Trevor Manuel. Jump ahead eleven years, and the United Kingdom was the number-one funder of the World Bank Group's International Development Association for 2017 (the concessional borrowing window at the World Bank), with about a 13.20 percent share.

Brexit could lead to a retrenchment from outwardness with possible negative implications on U.K. development initiatives. At a time when the process for International Development Association for 2018 replenishment is under way, Brexit may not be good news for aid recipients. Let's have a closer look at its effect on bilateral development assistance.

Bilateral Development Assistance

An exit from the EU is likely to have dire consequences for development assistance. In a 2016 article, Kevin Watkins, a Brookings nonresident senior fellow and then–executive director of the Overseas Development Institute—an international development think tank based in London—highlights the consequences of a Brexit on development assistance. The United Kingdom is one of the biggest contributors to the European Development Fund, the EU's development assistance arm, which provides funds to developing countries and regions. The United Kingdom currently contributes £409 million ($585 million), or 14.8 percent of contributions, to the fund. The fund is one of the world's largest providers of multilateral concessional aid, with disbursements exceeding those channeled through the International Development Association. While Brexit would deprive the European Development Fund of British resources for development assistance, Watkins argues that the direct disbursement of aid—set to replace the U.K. contribution to the fund—from the United Kingdom to recipient countries will have a more narrow geographic reach than aid funneled through the fund.

Not everybody agrees. In an interview with Radio France International, James Duddridge, British member of Parliament who was an advocate of leaving, states that development assistance would be more effective under a situation in which the United Kingdom is not part of the EU (Finnan, 2016). He states that when U.K. development aid is channeled through the European Development Fund, it is less efficient than when it is directly allocated to African countries through British organizations such as the Department for International Development. In addition, he stresses that in a post-Brexit era, the United Kingdom would increase security assistance to African nations. He gives the example of the EU reducing funds available to the African Union Mission in Somalia by 20 percent—a decision the United Kingdom opposed.

But the U.K.-Africa relationship is not restricted to just development assistance (which increasingly goes to fragile and low-income countries). How about the impact of Brexit on bilateral trade?

Stronger Bilateral Relations but Weaker Bilateral Trade?

Analysts have stated that Brexit would weaken trade ties between the United Kingdom and African nations. The renegotiation of trade agreements can be a lengthy process, which could cause a decrease in trade volumes between the United Kingdom and Africa. Indeed, a Brexit would prompt the United Kingdom to renegotiate over 100 trade agreements (Hüttl and Merler, 2016).

Bilateral trade agreements signed between the EU, on one hand, and other countries and regional communities, on the other, will also have to be renegotiated. One example of such a deal is the recent EU–Southern African Development Community Economic Partnership Agreement. The agreement, signed on June 10, 2016, includes clauses on allowing free access to the EU market for select Southern African Development Community countries (Botswana, Lesotho, Mozambique, Namibia, and Swaziland). The agreement also introduces more flexible rules of origin, with the aim of promoting the development of regional value chains. Within the European Union, the United Kingdom is one of Africa's largest trade partners. The share of U.K. trade in bilateral trade between the EU and Africa has recently declined. Brexit and the annulment of trade agreements could accentuate this decline. For instance, scholars from North-West University argue that Brexit would cause a 0.1 percent decline in South Africa's GDP because of the strong trade ties between the two nations (Vollgraaff, 2016).

Another key issue that could be affected by Brexit is one of agricultural subsidies. For years, the United Kingdom has criticized the current subsidies European countries have in place, which have hindered African farmers' trade capacities. In his argument in favor of leaving, James Duddridge voiced his concerns over the EU's Common Agricultural Policy, whose subsidy systems harm African farmers' competitiveness. With more than 60 percent of Africa's economically active population working in agriculture, the subsidies take an important toll on the livelihoods of a majority of Africans. The United Kingdom has been a key opponent of the subsidies (Madu, 2016). With the United Kingdom leaving the EU, there may no longer be a strong voice within the EU advocating for the livelihoods of African farmers.

In sum, Brexit will likely affect African countries in many ways, starting with its impact on the global economy, reduced British outwardness when it comes to global development issues, and decreased bilateral development assistance and trade. The affects are all difficult to quantify but broadly point to a negative impact on African countries. Brexit is inopportune both for the United Kingdom and for African countries, which are facing serious external shocks, such as the fall in commodity prices, an economic slowdown in China, and higher external borrowing costs. However, African countries can at least prepare for the potential effects of the coming exit in the short period that remains.

CLIMATE CHANGE: EXAMINING THE PARIS AGREEMENT

Africa contributes the least to global warming in both absolute and per capita terms. The entire continent of Africa accounts for 3.8 percent of global greenhouse gas emissions. This compares to the largest emitters—

China, the United States, and the EU—which account, respectively, for 23 percent, 19 percent, and 13 percent, or Russia and India, which each account for 6 percent of global emissions. In a telling example, the Africa Progress Panel (2015) notes that it would take the average Ethiopian 240 years to register the same carbon footprint as the average American. Africa's low contribution to global warming is not surprising, as about two-thirds of its greenhouse emission is from land use, particularly from forest degradation and deforestation tied to the production of charcoal.

Yet despite its low emissions, Africa is one of the regions most vulnerable to climate change. It remains highly dependent on low-productivity agriculture for food, income, and employment. Agriculture accounts for 30–40 percent of GDP in Africa, and about 80 percent of Africans remain dependent on low-yield, rain-fed agriculture. Global warming, even if limited to below 2 degrees Celsius, increases the risk of drought in southern and central Africa and the risk of flooding in east Africa, which would lead to higher food prices and lower yields—by 2050, warming of less than 2 degrees Celsius could reduce total crop production by as much as 10 percent. Reduced agricultural production will have dire consequences on human development, as poverty in Africa predominantly affects rural agriculturalists, or pastoralists, in countries with some of the highest poverty rates in the world. For higher levels of warming, yields may decrease by 15–20 percent across all crops and regions. Progress in many areas will be reversed: health will suffer through increased mortality and morbidity because of events like extreme heat and flooding. A reversal of progress in health attainment will have a negative impact on childhood educational performance. Recent research has even found strong causal evidence linking climatic events to human conflict across all major regions of the world.

Africa needs to not only implement climate adaptation strategies to reduce its vulnerability to climate change but also adopt mitigating measures in order to achieve sustainable growth. Whereas climate mitigation focuses on uprooting the causes of climate change, adaptation focuses on adjusting to the effects of climate change in order to reduce vulnerability and risk. In contrast to developed economies, which focus on climate mitigation, both climate mitigation and adaptation are pressing issues in Africa. Climate mitigation will help the continent avoid a high-carbon lock-in that other countries such as China have experienced in their economic trajectory. Rapid economic growth and demographic and urbanization trends will increase Africa's emissions of greenhouse gases unless mitigating actions, such as the adoption of renewable energy in power generation technologies, are taken. For instance, under the International Energy Agency baseline scenario to 2040, power generation in sub-Saharan Africa would quadruple, and the region's share of global carbon dioxide emissions would increase from 2 percent to 3 percent. The likelihood of this scenario can be reduced when renewable technologies, including hydropower, solar, wind, and geothermal energy, are included the continent's energy mix. Furthermore, adopting such technologies can help broaden access to energy through both on- and off-grid solutions. In Africa, many national governments are initiating governance systems for adaptation such as disaster risk management, adjustments in technologies, and infrastructure and ecosystem-based approaches. Basic public health measures and livelihood diversification are also reducing vulnerability. The Africa Progress Panel notes examples from Ethiopia, Niger, and Rwanda, where small-scale landowners and communities are adapting to climate risk and leading the way for sustainable land use at a large scale.

A key challenge for African countries is that even with an increase in domestic revenue mobilization, their own resources will remain insufficient to tackle both climate mitigation and adaptation. As a result, international cooperation is needed to help fill Africa's climate funding gap. A study by the United Nations Environment Programme (2013) estimates that in a scenario of a 2-degree-Celsius increase, meeting adaptation costs in Africa by the 2020s will require a steep increase in annual funding for adaptation in Africa by 10–20 percent. It concludes that present trends in funding will not meet these needs, and there is at present no clear and agreed-on pathway or identified sources of funding through which such a rapid scaling-up can be achieved. The international community could help fill the climate financing gap that Africa currently faces, but this would require that the current governance of the global commons be addressed. Indeed, Africa will bear the brunt of global warming, which will be mainly caused by developed economies and some emerging ones; but Africa often has limited bargaining power in international negotiations. Given that the 2015 United Nations Climate Change Conference in Paris (COP21) resulted in a binding agreement for all countries, notwithstanding the possible change in the U.S. position, it is of the utmost importance for the continent to take a leadership role in the governance of the global commons.

Africa is speaking with one voice, and the continent is committed to achieving an inclusive, ambitious, and equitable agreement that would lead to lower carbon emissions. The Paris meeting aimed to keep global warming to less than 2 degrees Celsius above preindustrial levels (as agreed to in Cancun in 2010 Climate Summit). It also seeks to keep global warming to below 1.5 degrees Celcius by 2100. The basis for the position that African countries took to Paris in December 2015 is the African Common Position developed by the African Group of Negotiators and endorsed by the African Ministerial Conference on the Environment. African negotiators sought to ensure that global climate governance will include the concerns of all 195 countries, and in particular those of poor countries and small islands. They set a high bar in terms of targets for reducing carbon emissions and seek firm commitments from developed economies to a mechanism that will adequately finance climate adaptation and not just climate mitigation.

Among the issues agreed on in Paris, climate finance and in particular the need for financing both climate adaptation and mitigation were probably the most important concerns for African negotiators. At the third International Conference on Financing for Development Meeting in Addis Ababa, in July 2015, the international community recognized the need to increase financing for low-carbon and climate-resilient development. In particular, developed countries committed to a goal of jointly mobilizing $100 billion a year by 2020 from a wide variety of sources, including public and private sources, to finance mitigation actions and transparency on implementation (a goal previously set by the global community at the 2009 United Nations Climate Change conference in Copenhagen but not reached). In addition, the international community welcomed the initial resource mobilization process of the Green Climate Fund—the largest dedicated climate fund—which aims for a fifty-fifty balance between mitigation and adaptation over time and a floor of 50 percent of the adaptation allocation for particularly vulnerable countries (such as least-developed countries, small-island developing states, and African countries). In Addis Ababa, the international community also noted the importance of continued support to address remaining gaps in the capacity to gain access to and manage climate finance.

The October 2015 United Nations Meeting on Climate Change in Bonn, the last meeting before Paris, offered a preview of the African position on climate finance, in which African countries pushed for the main contributors of greenhouse gas emissions to commit to—and act on—their commitments in the level of financing, the use of financing for adaptation, and the sources of financing. In Bonn, African negotiators put climate finance at the center of the negotiations and strengthened their bargaining power by joining the Group of Seventy-Seven and China group of countries, which together included 130 nations, accounting for 80 percent of the world's population. African negotiators are seeking more finance, including a binding commitment from developed economies of greater than $100 billion by 2020. They are also warning that new public finance should be used to fill the climate financing gap and that existing official development assistance should not be diverted to climate finance. In addition, the current fragmentation of the climate finance architecture, with many separate multilateral agencies, does not serve the continent well and may not be conducive to leveraging private investment.

In addition to climate finance for adaptation, discussions about loss and damage associated with climate change in developing countries proved a stumbling block in Paris. Extreme events (such as hurricanes and heat waves) and slow-onset events (such as desertification, sea level rise, and ocean acidification) can bring relatively high loss and damage in developing countries, given their vulnerability to the adverse effects of climate change. According to the World Bank, losses to insurers due to weather events have reached about $200 billion a year, from about $50 billion a year in the 1980s. In spite of the establishment of the Warsaw International Mechanism at the 2013 United Nations Climate Change Conference (COP19), which represents a first step in addressing loss and damage associated with climate change in developing countries, loss and damage will remain a contentious issue given concerns from developed economies about an "unending string of liability" and the binding nature of the Paris agreement (Schueneman, 2015).

The successful agreement in Paris strengthened global governance to some degree, but African countries should still take the lead in developing and implementing sustainable strategies that can lead to a triple-win scenario. As noted by the Africa Progress Panel (2015), Africa can lead the world on climate-resilient, low-carbon development and achieve the triple-win of boosting agricultural productivity, reducing poverty, and strengthening national efforts to combat climate change. The "Intended Nationally Determined Contributions"—countries' publicly pledged actions for reducing carbon emission and adapting to climate change—or the Paris meeting offer an opportunity for African governments to develop ambitious but realistic strategies leading to the triple-win scenario. Regional cooperation and the support of regional development banks such as the African Development Bank, and multilateral institutions such as the World Bank and the Green Climate Fund, which was established within the United Nations Framework Convention on Climate Change to assist developing countries in climate change adaptation and mitigation, can help kick-start the process while the continent works to attract more international support, including through innovative financial solutions such as carbon finance.

MOBILIZING AFRICA'S RAPID URBANIZATION FOR SUSTAINABLE CLIMATE CHANGE

More than half the world's population lives in cities that could be responsible for over 75 percent of all greenhouse gas emissions (depending on definition, the urban share of global greenhouse gas emissions is estimated to be between 30 and 40 percent and up to 75 or 80 percent) (United Nations Environment Programme, 2012). Thus, given their enormous contribution to climate change, cities should be at the heart of the discussions on climate change. I refer not only to New Delhi or Beijing, but also to African cities where pollution levels are rising at an unprecedented scale but go largely unmonitored (Evans, 2015). As Africa urbanizes at a rapid pace—it is the second-fastest urbanizing region in the world, and by 2020 is projected to surpass Asia as the fastest—there is an increasing need to prioritize urban management and adaptation policies for sustainable climate change action.

African Cities on the Move

Though Africa has the lowest proportion of its population living in cities compared to other regions, this is quickly changing: Africa was nearly as urbanized as China in 2010 and had as many cities with over 1 million people as Europe (Leke and others, 2010). Forecasts from the 2014 *World Urbanization Prospects* suggest that, by 2050, Africa's urban population is projected to triple, making the continent the host of the world's second-largest urban population, behind Asia (United Nations, 2014b). At the moment, three African cities—Lagos, Cairo, and Kinshasa—meet the definition of megacity (10 million people or more). This rapid growth of African cities will push at least another six cities—Johannesburg, Luanda, Nairobi, Addis Ababa, Casablanca, and Khartoum—into the megacity class within the next couple of decades.

Increasing urban populations have been driving up energy demands and pollution levels, as anyone who has been stuck in traffic in Lagos already knows. Thus, this trend not only raises global warming concerns but also, if these rising demands and greenhouse gas emissions are left unmonitored, potentially poses further challenges for urban planning needs. This outcome results from urbanization on the continent being driven by more than the standard models of structural transformation that have been explored in economic literature. Many have argued that urbanization in Africa is also driven by factors such as climate change: In some areas the lengthened dry seasons and environmental shocks are forcing Africa's rural workforce to seek employment in the city. As they move into cities, a large proportion of rural migrants get stuck in low-productivity employment in the nontradable sector—increasing demand for better urban planning for basic services, infrastructure, housing, waste management, human livelihoods, and health.

The Urban Divide

A large urban population by itself is not a cause for major concern—in fact urbanization and growth should go hand in hand—but the looming challenge lies in the lack of urban planning, which can present environmental problems. This is the ultimate dilemma at the heart of the climate change negotiations: how to balance economic development and climate responsibility even though the two aims are not separate.

The poor are particularly vulnerable to climate change and natural disasters, which is bad news for sub-Saharan Africa. Cities in sub-Saharan Africa are grappling with issues of rapid urban inequality, poverty, and insecurity. According to a World Bank report, sub-Saharan Africa is the only region where a growing urban population has not had a corresponding overall poverty reduction (Ravallion, Chen, and Sangraula, 2008). In addition, while child mortality is, on average, lower in urban areas, child mortality of the poor is often higher in urban areas (World Health Organization, 2010). These rising problems are related to inefficiency and exclusion: lack of basic services, dysfunctional land and housing markets, underdeveloped manufacturing, insufficient transport infrastructure, and slums. In fact, over 70 percent of Africa's urban population is estimated to be living in slum conditions (CitiesAlliance, 2010). Rising global warming and an increase in the number of extreme weather events such as floods, droughts, and storms tend to adversely affect the poor more than other groups, leading them further into the vicious cycle of poverty and inequality.

Better Cities, Better Growth

The challenge of addressing climate change mitigation and adaptation is also the opportunity to successfully implement sustainable urban management policies. Huge and long-lasting investments are pouring into infrastructure for cities in Africa—making cities, energy grid systems, and land use policies open to opportunities and risk. There is an urgent need to emphasize the increasing dangers of delay to avoid locking in capital and infrastructure investments to high-carbon technologies.

The Sustainable Development Goals adopted in 2015 include making cities and human settlements inclusive, safe, resilient, and sustainable, and have a specific focus on decreasing the impact of disasters and reducing the adverse per capita environmental impact of cities. Urban planners are increasingly concerned about the issue as well—assistance for climate projects was among the top concerns for city officials according to a World Bank Institute's Municipal Finance Self-Assessment exercise (World Bank, 2014a). Cities' response on climate change has been gaining momentum, although rather slowly. In the lead-up to the 2015 United Nations Climate Change Conference (COP21), ten cities worldwide, including Cape Town, announced that they had met all planning and reporting requirements of the Compact of Mayors (the world's largest coalition of city leaders addressing climate change by pledging to reduce their greenhouse gas emissions). In 2018, about 7,400 cities and local governments, out of which 73 are African, share the vision to deeply reduce carbon dioxide emissions, improve transparency of targets, and move to global reporting standards as part of the Global Covenant of Mayors for Climate and Energy (www.globalcovenantofmayors.org/).

The comparatively late onset of urban growth in Africa allows embracing new urban paradigms that are more conducive to building green cities that support positive economic, social, and environmental links at an early planning stage. Investment in labor productivity, greener solutions, vulnerability reduction, public health hazard mitigation, social integration, and technological innovation will ensure that sustainable urbanization and economic development of African cities does indeed go hand in hand. In his message on World Cities Day, United Nations Secretary General Ban Ki-moon emphasized the importance of designing cities for living together to create opportunities, enable connection and interaction, and facilitate sustainable use of shared resources.

Financing is, however, a key constraint for African cities. Other than a few cities like Johannesburg, African cities depend on transfers from their central governments for financing, in part because of the predominance of informal economic activities and the narrowness of the formal tax base. Strengthening municipal financing tools, including through local banking and capital markets, and developing new ones will be important to meet the growing demands on African cities.

TAKING STOCK OF FINANCIAL AND DIGITAL INCLUSION IN SUB-SAHARAN AFRICA

Expanding formal financial services—including traditional services (offered by banks) and digital services (provided via mobile money systems)—to previously excluded individuals can improve their capacity to save, make payments swiftly and securely, and cope with economic shocks. Importantly, having access to financial services is also considered a critical component of women's full economic participation and empowerment. Many countries, therefore, are working to increase accessibility to and usage of formal financial services as important strategies to improving individuals' financial stability and, at a macro level, supporting inclusive development and growth.

In sub-Saharan Africa, where the provision and uptake of traditional financial services is limited by a wide range of factors (including poverty, lack of savings, and poor infrastructure), governments are creating an enabling environment for various entities (including bank and nonbank formal providers) to offer digital financial services. In turn, the region is a global leader in adoption of digital financial services: According to the GSM Association (2017), there are 420 million unique mobile subscribers in sub-Saharan Africa for a penetration rate of 43 percent. New mobile subscriptions in the region are growing rapidly with an expected average growth of 6.1 percent over the five years to 2020, about 50 percent higher than the global average. In the first of a series of publications exploring and sharing information that can improve financial inclusion around the world, the Brookings Financial and Digital Inclusion Project (FDIP) takes stock of progress toward financial inclusion in twenty-one countries from various economic, political, and geographic contexts and scores them along four key dimensions of financial inclusion: country commitment, mobile capacity, regulatory environment, and adoption of traditional and digital financial services (Brookings Institution, 2015). Four of the five top-scoring countries are in sub-Saharan Africa. On the other hand, some of the lowest-ranked countries were also African, demonstrating regional diversity in financial inclusion.

Here are some of the main takeaways from four of the nine African case studies featured in the report: Ethiopia (ranked twenty-first overall), Kenya (ranked first), Nigeria (ranked ninth), and South Africa (ranked second). Kenya and Ethiopia are the highest- and lowest-ranked African countries in the report, respectively. Nigeria and South Africa, the continent's two largest economies, have achieved disparate outcomes in terms of financial inclusion.

Ethiopia: A Developing Mobile Services Ecosystem

Ethiopia's overall low financial and digital inclusion score was due in large part to its poor mobile capacity and the low adoption rates of formal (particularly digital) financial services. The World Bank's Global Financial Inclusion Index (Findex)[1]—one of the major datasets highlighted in the report—reveals that only 22 percent of adults in Ethiopia had a formal financial account and about 0.03 percent of adults had a mobile money account in 2014. In addition, limited development of the information and communication technology sector and mobile communications infrastructure have inhibited mobile and digital access, reducing the array of financial products and services available to underserved populations.

However, Ethiopian digital financial inclusion has the potential and political support to grow. The government adopted a mobile and agent banking framework in 2013, and is taking other steps to provide digital financial services. This framework allows banks and microfinance institutions to provide services through mobile phones and agents. The government also set up the Financial Inclusion Council and secretariat to enhance participation from mobile-network operators in developing policies for achieving greater digital financial inclusion.

Kenya: Mobile Money Innovations Drive Uptake

That Kenya scored highest in the overall rankings was due to its highly accessible mobile networks, a regulatory framework conducive to the development of digital financial services, and products that cater to consumer needs and so promote adoption. Kenya also has the highest rate of women with financial accounts.

Between 2011 and 2014, Kenya increased its levels of formal financial and mobile money account penetration by thirty-three percentage points, owing mostly to robust take-up within the country's vibrant mobile money ecosystem. Nearly 90 percent of Kenyan households reported using mobile money services as of August 2014, and the M-Pesa system (operated by Safaricom) is widely considered the leading driver of adoption of mobile money usage.

1 See http://datatopics.worldbank.org/financialinclusion/.

Innovative services that have helped spur financial inclusion among marginalized groups have been developed within Kenya's mobile-network-operator-led approach. For example, in 2012, the Commercial Bank of Africa and Safaricom partnered to provide the M-Shwari service, which offers interest-bearing mobile money accounts and microfinance.

Still, one aspect of the mobile money system the Kenyan government could improve on is consumer protection of clients of credit-only institutions, such as microfinance institutions and savings and credit cooperatives, as these institutions are not adequately regulated and supervised.

Nigeria: A Stalled Bank-Led Approach

Nigeria achieved only a moderate score in the FDIP rankings because, despite a number of country commitments to increasing financial inclusion in recent years, low levels of adoption persist. In fact, while the proportion of adults ages fifteen and older who have a mobile money or traditional bank account increased from 30 percent in 2011 to 44 percent in 2014, only 0.1 percent of adults had a registered mobile money account in 2014 and had used it at least once in the ninety days prior, according to an Intermedia survey (2014).

The Central Bank of Nigeria has taken a bank-led approach to mobile money in which banks promote their traditional services via the mobile network. This is an alternative to Kenya's approach, in which mobile-network operators provide the network of agents and manage customer relations. Some experts have noted that in cases where a bank-led approach is adopted—for example, in India—the financial incentives are not strong enough for banks to expand their services to the unbanked, whereas mobile-network operators have greater assets, expertise, and incentives to launch and expand mobile money services.

South Africa: Strong Mobile Capacity and Room for Growth

South Africa was ranked highest of all countries in the FDIP report (Brookings Institution, 2015) in mobile capacity for its robust mobile infrastructure and large proportion of the population subscribing to mobile devices (70 percent) and area covered by 3G mobile networks

(96 percent). It tied for the highest score for formal account penetration, including among rural, low-income, and female groups.

In 2004–14, financial inclusion (as measured by the proportion of the population using financial products and services, formal and informal) has increased dramatically from 61 percent in 2004 to 86 percent in 2014. This uptick can be partially attributed to the increase in banking and ownership of ATM or debit cards. Disparities in penetration exist, however, in gender and race, with women and white populations being more likely to use bank accounts than men and black populations.

As cited in the Brookings (2015) report, the 2014 Global Findex found that 14 percent of adults (ages fifteen and older) possessed a mobile money account in 2014. The top 60 percent of income earners were more than twice as likely to have accounts as the bottom 40 percent of the income scale. So despite strong mobile capacity, there is still room for growth in terms of mobile money penetration, especially among low-income adults.

So what's next for expanding financial and digital inclusion?

The FDIP case studies offer insights into the policies and frameworks conducive to the uptake of formal financial services. In African countries considered to be mobile money success stories, such as Kenya, mobile-network operators play a substantial role in spearheading the drive toward financial inclusion and have collaborated closely with central banks, ministries of finance and communications, banks, and nonbank financial providers. Ensuring the participation of all stakeholders—not just governments and banks—in setting the national financial inclusion priorities and agenda, then, is critical. Furthermore, actively participating in multinational financial inclusion networks can enhance knowledge sharing among members and lead to further country commitments. Finally, surveys of financial inclusion can help governments and financial service providers target their strategies and services to the local needs and context.

CONJURING THE RESOURCE CURSE: FOUR GLOBAL TRENDS TO WATCH FOR IN AFRICAN COUNTRIES

The natural resource sector is an engine of Africa's growth. Resource prices have more than doubled since 2000 and, over the past decade, about three-quarters of foreign direct investment to sub-Saharan Africa ended up in resource-rich countries such as Angola and Nigeria, largely in extractive industries.

As exploration and production increase thanks to technological innovation and new players, sub-Saharan Africa will become even more reliant on its natural resource wealth. Resource-rich countries will increase their production, and countries from East Africa with newly discovered oil deposits, such as Kenya, Uganda, and Tanzania, will join the club. In addition to oil, production of gold (such as in Burkina Faso and Tanzania) and coal and gas (in Mozambique) are set to increase. Non-oil producers are also encouraging exploration, such as Ethiopia in the Ogaden Basin and Rwanda in Lake Kivu.

The economic literature has a large body of research on the effect of the boom and bust cycle on the price of oil and other natural resources, how resource-rich countries can manage the associated risks, and how to harness the power of natural resource wealth for the benefit of current and future generations (Arezki, Gylfason, and Sy, 2011). The challenges are enormous: How will sub-Saharan African countries diversify their reliance on commodity exports? How can their corporate sector benefit from a transfer of knowledge and technology and join the value chain of extractive industries? How sustainable will the social contract for managing the resource rents be? These questions and others will have to be addressed, but it is also crucial to identify global trends that will affect resource-rich sub-Saharan African countries in order to design more adequate policies. The following four trends come to mind:

Slowing Growth in China

A slowdown of growth in China and more generally in emerging markets is an important driver of commodity price declines. An IMF (2013) simulation studies the impact on other countries of Chinese growth slowing from an average of 10 percent during the previous decade to an average of 7.5 percent over the next decade. The result for Nigeria is that its GDP level in 2025 would be about 1.5 percent lower because of the lower Chinese demand for oil. This is much less than the 7 percent lower GDP for Mongolia, which depends on export of coal, iron ore, and copper to China, but still not trivial.

Financialization of Commodities

What happens in the stock and bond markets can also occur in commodities, from cotton and soybeans to oil and copper. The links between financial assets such as stock prices and commodities seem to have been important in explaining the commodity supercycle, the large increase in different commodity prices since 2000. The Institute of International Finance (2011, p. 4) estimates that, between 2005 and 2011, the value of commodity-related assets under management increased almost ninefold, to $450 billion. Commodities have become a new asset class as huge investments have flowed into commodity-index-related instruments after the dot.com equity market collapse. One rationale is that commodities offer a diversification benefit to portfolios of stocks and bonds. Some researchers like Tang and Xiong (2010) argue that, as index investors focus on their strategic asset allocation across different asset classes such as stocks, bonds, and commodities, they tend to move in and out of all commodities in a chosen commodity index at the same time. Their trading can thus cause prices of different commodities in the index to move together.

The U.S. Energy Boom

The United States is in the midst of an energy boom and will import less oil and gas from sub-Saharan Africa. Nigeria's crude oil exports to the United States have been falling, according to the U.S. Energy Information Administration,[2] from a peak of 425 million barrels in 2005 to a low of 162 million barrels in 2012. The 2013 figures represent a continuation of that downward trend, with 103 million barrels. U.S. imports bottomed out before rebounding slightly to 86 million in 2016. The culprit is the energy boom in the United States, where natural gas output increased 25 percent and crude oil and other liquids increased 30 percent during the period from 2005 to 2013, reducing net oil imports by nearly 40 percent. The Energy Information Administration shows U.S. production of shale oil increasing until 2020 before falling off during the next two decades. The baseline also shows U.S. shale gas production increas-

2 See www.eia.gov/dnav/pet/pet_move_impcus_a2_nus_ep00_im0_mbbl_m.htm.

ing steadily until 2040, and the United States is expected to be a net exporter of natural gas in the 2020s.

Africa's Use of Renewable Energy

Sub-Saharan Africa has relied heavily on nonrenewable energy to fuel its rapid growth, but it should also consider investing in renewable energy. Sub-Saharan Africa's demand for energy is set to increase if it wants to sustain its current rapid growth rate. Sub-Saharan Africa imports a lot of refined oil to meet its energy demand, and some countries, such as Uganda, are considering building new refineries. But beyond whether it is preferable to continue importing refined oil or build refineries, it is important to discuss whether sub-Saharan African countries should turn to renewable energy technology. This choice would not address just global warming and climate change. It would also be about diversifying energy sources, improving energy efficiency, and importing new technologies.

Ethiopia, no doubt because it is less endowed in nonrenewable energy, has made the choice to invest in renewable energy technologies such as the Ashegoda wind farm, the Grand Renaissance Dam on the Nile, and geothermal projects. Kenya has a wind power project on Lake Turkana and is involved in plans for geothermal energy production. Further northeast, Morocco is investing heavily in solar power plants. In terms of global warming and climate change, the Growth Commission, chaired by Nobel Prize Laureate Michael Spence, argues that it makes economic sense for developed countries to bear some of the costs of developing-country investments in cutting carbon emissions to safe levels. Interestingly, renewable energy is also part of former president Barack Obama's Power Africa initiative.[3]

In short, resource-rich and soon-to-be-resource-rich sub-Saharan African countries should (1) anticipate China's economic performance carefully, as slowing growth in China will lead to slower growth in resource-rich sub-Saharan African countries; (2) study how global stock and bond prices move with commodity prices, as the financialization of commodities indicates that financial assets can be linked to commodity

3 For more information on Power Africa, see www.usaid.gov/powerafrica.

prices; (3) prepare to redirect oil exports to the United States to other regions as the U.S. energy boom strengthens; and (4) invest in renewable energy sources to meet part of their growing own demand for energy.

FOUR QUESTIONS ON THE STATE OF REGIONAL ECONOMIC COMMUNITIES

Regional economic integration has been an increasing priority among many African nations in recent years.[4] Take, for instance, the Continental Free Trade Area, which convened its first negotiating forum in Addis Ababa on February 22–27, 2015. The forum aimed to incorporate all fifty-three African countries, representing over 1 billion people and $3 trillion in GDP, and is set to launch in 2018. The agreement's major goal is to boost trade among African countries.

To achieve economic integration, policymakers are counting on regional economic communities such as the West African Economic and Monetary Union (WAEMU), both a currency union and a free-trade zone, to be the main building blocks. The WAEMU is one of four existing currency unions in the world, the other three being the eurozone, the Eastern Caribbean Currency Union, and the Central African Economic and Monetary Community. Created in January 1994, the WAEMU is composed of former French colonies (Benin, Burkina Faso, Côte d'Ivoire, Mali, Niger, Senegal, and Togo) and a former Portuguese colony (Guinea-Bissau) and is a stepping stone to further integration in West Africa. The eight WAEMU countries are also members of the Economic Community of West African States, a group that also includes the six West African Monetary Zone member countries (the Gambia, Ghana, Guinea, Nigeria, Sierra Leone, and Liberia) and Cape Verde. To further promote regional integration in the Economic Community of West African States, countries are seeking to implement a common West African currency (the Eco) by 2020.

4 This section draws from a blog post I wrote with Mariama Sow, "Four Questions on the State of the West African Economic and Monetary Union and Implications for Other Regional Economic Communities" (Sy and Sow, 2016b).

The WAEMU has an institutional arrangement with France in which the CFA franc is pegged to the euro (currently at a rate of CFA 655.957 per euro), and the French Treasury (Compte d'Opérations) provides an unlimited convertibility guarantee. In exchange for this guarantee, the central bank of the WAEMU, the Central Bank of West Africa States, is required to deposit part of its foreign exchange reserves in an account with the Compte d'Opérations. Currently, 50 percent of the central bank's foreign exchange reserves are held in the Compte d'Opérations and are remunerated at the European Central Bank's marginal lending facility rate. These peculiarities of the WAEMU raise questions for Africa observers.

Discussions about the WAEMU are often limited to the degree of overvaluation of the real effective exchange rate and the level of remuneration of the central bank's foreign exchange reserves. These are valid questions, especially as they relate to competitiveness and the opportunity cost of leaving foreign exchange reserves at the Compte d'Opérations. But they are not the only ones. In Sy and Sow (2016b) we explored a number of other questions to provide a greater insight on the nature of regional economic communities in Africa:

1. *To what extent does the WAEMU encourage trade and financial integration?* The literature finds that belonging to a currency union leads to increased trade levels with other members of the currency union (Frankel and Rose, 2000; Glick and Rose, 2001; Tsangarides, Ewenczyk, and Hulej, 2006). The WAEMU has typically had the largest level of intraregional exports in sub-Saharan Africa. However, since 2009, the share of intraregional exports in the Southern African Development Community has surpassed that of the WAEMU. Still, the region continues to have relatively high and growing intraregional exports. When looking at overall trade (combining import and exports), the WAEMU has the second-highest level of intraregional trade, behind the Southern African Development Community.

Even though the WAEMU was only created in 1994, countries in the region have been sharing a common currency since 1945, when they were French colonies (this excludes Guinea-Bissau, which was a Portuguese colony). Sharing a currency, a central bank, a regional real-time gross settlement system (a funds transfer system for high-value transactions), and a regional automated clearing house has reduced transactions costs, thus promoting intraregional trade. Additionally, in 1996, the WAEMU countries removed tariffs and quantitative restrictions on intraregional trade.

Despite having some of the highest levels of intraregional trade in sub-Saharan Africa, those levels are relatively low compared to customs unions around the world. Whereas the Association of Southeast Asian Nations and the EU's intraregional trade amounts, respectively, to around 25 percent and 60 percent of all their trade, that figure is estimated to lie below 15 percent for the WAEMU.

Many nontariff barriers impede intraregional trade in the region. Such barriers include costly border procedures, weak governance, inadequate transport infrastructure, poor business environments, and irregular implementation of WAEMU rules of origin (certifying products as being of WAEMU origin and tariff-free).

2. *How do the WAEMU countries compare to other sub-Saharan African countries in terms of macroeconomic stability?* Having a fixed exchange rate pegged to the euro has enhanced macroeconomic stability in the WAEMU. Indeed, the countries in the CFA franc zone outperformed fellow sub-Saharan African countries in terms of macroeconomic stability. Importantly, whereas some WAEMU countries suffer from political instability and weak governance, the CFA franc has historically provided a stable monetary institutional framework.

Similarly, this steadiness was quite noticeable during the 2009 financial crisis, when the peg served as a stabilizing factor. Recently, as several countries in sub-Saharan Africa with floating exchange rate regimes—notably Nigeria and South Africa—have seen their currencies depreciate in the face of a deteriorating external environment, the CFA peg to the euro has provided macroeconomic stability to the region. A legitimate question, however, is whether stability has been achieved at the expense of a loss of competitiveness.

3. *Has the WAEMU's fixed exchange rate regime impeded competitiveness?* As noted above, having a fixed exchange rate regime has truly benefited the WAEMU when it comes to achieving macroeconomic stability. Still, a well-known conclusion from the academic research on currency regimes is that competitiveness is more challenging to achieve with a fixed exchange rate regime compared to a flexible one. In spite of the 50 percent exchange rate devaluation in 1994, the WAEMU region is still

relatively less competitive when compared to other regional economic communities in sub-Saharan Africa. Nevertheless, the lag in competitiveness witnessed in the region cannot be solely attributed to the fixed exchange rate regime.

One explanation is that structural barriers in the region, such as a relatively poor institutional environment and underdeveloped infrastructure, have contributed to its inability to attract capital and diversify the economies. In terms of ease of doing business, the WAEMU is performing relatively worse than the African region as a whole. WAEMU countries tend to rank far lower than the Asian and African benchmarks, illustrating this trend. While the fixed exchange rate system has contributed to the lag, structural factors have taken a toll on competitiveness in the region.

4. *How has the WAEMU promoted economic convergence among member countries?* Convergence—defined as the reduction of disparities in economic indicators—that is, inflation, growth levels, and per capita income—is one of the key goals of currency unions. The idea is that, if achieved, convergence makes countries react in a similar way to common shocks, which makes a common macroeconomic policy to manage such shocks more effective for all countries. For example, to adopt the euro as their currency, EU member states are required to meet the Maastricht criteria, which require economies to meet certain macroeconomic benchmarks relating to price stability, budget deficit, and debt-to-GDP ratio.

Despite the WAEMU's adoption of convergence criteria (which were revised in 2015 so as to be achieved by 2019), member countries have not converged toward similar growth levels. Rather, as portrayed in a 2013 study, two groups of convergence have emerged: one with Senegal and Côte d'Ivoire converging toward growth levels exceeding the union average and one with Guinea-Bissau, Niger, and Togo converging toward a level lower than the WAEMU average (African Development Bank, 2013b). International Monetary Fund (2015c) estimates show that WAEMU countries will continue to face difficulties in meeting convergence criteria. Some member countries do not meet (or are not projected to meet) the convergence criteria adopted by the WAEMU. For example, none meets (or is projected to meet) the domestic revenue mobilization convergence criteria that states that the tax revenue to GDP ratio should be 20 percent at a minimum.

GOING BEYOND A COMMON CURRENCY: THE NECESSITY OF STRUCTURAL TRANSFORMATION AND MACROECONOMIC STABILITY

WAEMU member countries face potential benefits (macroeconomic stability and increased trade and financial integration) and challenges (limited competitiveness). The common currency is only one tool among many, and more needs to be done to reduce nontariff barriers and comply with convergence criteria, especially on the fiscal front (including that convergence criteria should be well calibrated).

To increase competitiveness, countries will need to not only ensure macroeconomic stability but also improve the business climate, reduce the hard infrastructure gap, and invest in soft infrastructure such as skills and technology. Structural transformation is needed, and the example of Côte d'Ivoire, which has increased agriculture yields, reaching two tons per hectare, should be emulated. To do so, countries will need to invest in rural infrastructure and adopt policies to increase regional and global trade. Increasing farmers' productivity will require strengthening training and extension programs. Structural transformation will also require industrialization policies to go beyond investment climate reforms and promote exports with both regional and global value chains, build capabilities of domestic firms, and foster industrial clusters. Last but not least, structural transformation will require a better understanding of the services sector and the factors that shape it. It will require leveraging the success in the information and communication technology sector to increase productivity and access to finance. Finally, in preparation for the planned integration with the West African Monetary Zone—which includes Nigeria, a major oil exporter—regional trade, financial ties, and domestic macroeconomic frameworks will need to be strengthened.

BIG DATA AND SUSTAINABLE DEVELOPMENT IN DAKAR, SENEGAL

To help achieve the Sustainable Development Goals, hope surrounds the potential of big data—volumes of data (such as cell phone GPS signals, social media posts, online digital pictures and videos, and transaction records of online purchases) so large they are difficult to process with traditional database and software techniques. The United Nations even calls for using the ongoing data revolution, the explosion in quantity and diversity of big data, to inform development analysis, monitoring, and policymaking. In fact, the United Nations (2014a) believes, "Data are the lifeblood of decision-making and the raw material for accountability. Without high-quality data providing the right information on the right things at the right time; designing, monitoring and evaluating effective policies becomes almost impossible." The United Nations even held the Data Innovation for Policy Makers conference in Jakarta, Indonesia, in November 2014 to promote use of big data in solving development challenges.

Big data has already played a role in development: early uses of it include the detection of influenza epidemics using search engine query data and the estimation of a country's or region's GDP from satellite data on night lights (Henderson, Storeygard, and Weil, 2012). Work is also under way by the World Bank to use big data for transport planning in Brazil.

During the Data for Development session at the 2015 NetMob conference at MIT, Thiemo Fetzer and I (Fetzer and Sy, 2015) presented work on using mobile phone data to assess how the opening of a new toll highway in Dakar, Senegal, is changing how people commute to work in this metropolitan area. The new toll road is one of the largest investments by the government of Senegal, and expectations for its developmental impact are high. In particular, the new toll road is expected to increase the flow of goods and people into and out of Dakar, spur urban and rural development outside congested areas, and boost land valuation outside Dakar. The study is a first step in helping policymakers and other stakeholders determine the toll road's effect on these objectives, which will help policymakers benchmark the performance of their investment and better plan the development of urban areas.

The Dakar Diamniadio Toll Highway

The twenty-mile Dakar Diamniadio Toll Highway (in black in figure 6-1), inaugurated on August 1, 2013, is the first section of a broader project to connect the capital, Dakar, via a double three-lane highway to a new

FIGURE 6-1 Dakar Diamniadio Toll Highway and Affected Suburban Areas

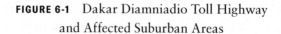

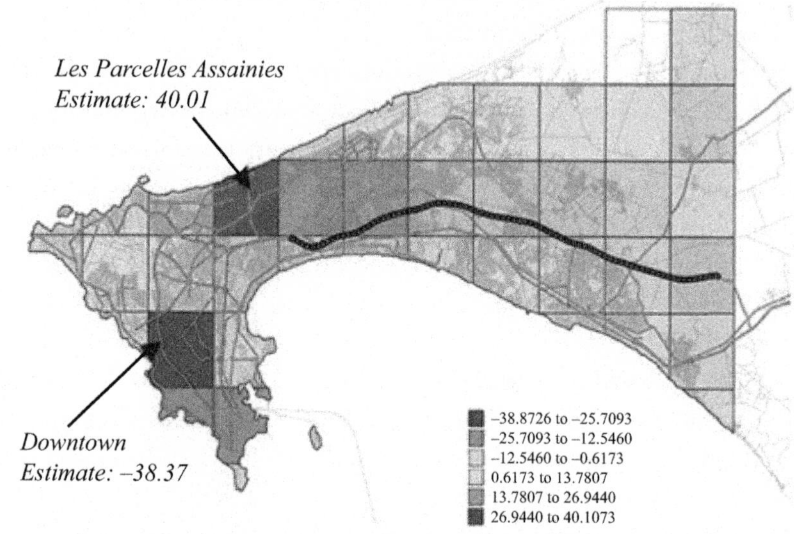

Note: The numbers relate to mobility within each grid cell and were used to calculate the percentage increase in mobility.

airport (Aeroport International Blaise Diagne) and a special economic zone, the Dakar Integrated Special Economic Zone, with the rest of the country.

The cost of this large project is estimated to be about $696 million (380.2 billion CFA francs, or 22.7 percent of 2014 fiscal revenues, excluding grants), with the government of Senegal having already disbursed $353 million. The project is one of the first toll roads in sub-Saharan Africa (excluding South Africa) structured as a public-private partnership and includes multilateral partners such as the World Bank, the French Development Agency, and the African Development Bank.

We asked whether the new toll road led to an increase in human mobility and, if so, whether particular geographic areas experienced higher or lower mobility relative to others following its opening. Using mobile phone usage data (big data), we performed a statistical analysis to approximate where people live and where they work. We then estimated how the reduction in travel time following the opening of the toll road changes the way they commute to work.

As illustrated in figure 6-1, we found some interesting trends:

- Human mobility in the metropolitan Dakar area increased on average by 1.34 percent after the opening of the Dakar Diamniadio Toll Highway. However, this increase masks important disparities across the different subareas of the Dakar metropolitan areas. Areas in dark gray in figure 6-1 are those for which mobility increased or decreased the most after the opening of the road toll.
- In particular, the Parcelles Assainies suburban area benefited the most from the toll road, with an increase in mobility of 26 percent. The Centre Ville (downtown) area experienced a decrease in mobility of about 20 percent.

These trends would have been difficult to discover without big data. Now, researchers need to parse the reasons these trends might have occurred. For instance, the Parcelles Assainies area may have benefited the most because of its closer location to the toll road, whereas the feeder roads in the downtown area may not have been able to absorb the increase in traffic from the toll road. Or people may have moved from the downtown area to less expensive areas in the suburbs now that the toll road shortens their commute.

The Success of Big Data

From these preliminary results (the study is a work in progress, and we will be improving its methodology), we are encouraged that our method and use of big data has three areas of application for a project such as this:

- ***Benchmarking***: This method can be used to track how the impact of the Dakar Diamniadio Toll Highway changes over time and for different areas of the Dakar metropolitan areas. This process could be used to study other highways in the future and inform highway development overall.

- *Zooming In*: Our analysis is a first step toward a more granular study of the different geographic areas within the Dakar suburban metropolitan area. Perhaps it will inspire similar studies around the continent. In particular, it would be useful to study the socioeconomic context within each area to better appreciate the impact of new infrastructure on people's lives. For instance, to move from estimates of human mobility (traffic) to measures of accessibility, it will be useful to complement our analysis with an analysis of land use, a study of job accessibility, and other labor market information for specific areas. Regarding accessibility, questions of interest include the following: Who lives in the areas most or least affected? What kinds of jobs do they have access to? What type of infrastructure do they have access to? What is their income level? Answers to these questions can be obtained by combining satellite information with land prices, survey data (including through mobile phones), and public data collected by the government. Regarding urban planning, questions include the following: Is the toll diverting traffic to other areas? What happens in those areas? Do they have the appropriate infrastructure to absorb the increase in traffic?

- *Zooming Out*: So far, our analysis is focused on the Dakar metropolitan area, and it would be useful to assess the impact of new infrastructure on mobility between the rest of the country and Dakar. For instance, the analysis can help assess whether the benefits of the toll road spill over to the rest of the country and even help differentiate the impact of the toll road on the different regions of the country.

This experience tells us that there are major opportunities, but also limitations in converting big data into actionable information. In our case, the use of mobile phone data helped generate timely and relatively inexpensive information on a large transport infrastructure and human mobility. On the other hand, it is clear that more analysis using socioeconomic data is needed to get to concrete and meaningful policy actions. Thus, I think that making such information available to all stakeholders has the potential not only to guide policy action but also to spur it.

UNDERSTANDING THE ECONOMIC EFFECTS OF THE 2014 EBOLA OUTBREAK IN WEST AFRICA

From 2014 to 2016, more than 11,000 people died from the relentless spread of the Ebola virus throughout the West African countries of Guinea, Sierra Leone, Liberia, and Nigeria.

Despite the heroic efforts of the humanitarian and medical professionals in these countries, crumbling public health systems—which were notoriously weak even before the current outbreak began—and a lack of facilities, equipment, and medical staff were unable to stem the virus for well over a year. Distrust of the government—fueled by decades of civil war—also prompted attacks on health workers by fearful groups, which further undercut crucial outreach and educational interventions aimed at sensitizing communities to the virus and breaking the chain of transmission.

Before the Ebola outbreak intensified, these countries were making remarkable economic progress—particularly Sierra Leone and Liberia, which experienced rapid economic growth in recent years after overcoming decades of civil strife. In 2013, Sierra Leone and Liberia ranked second and sixth among countries with the highest GDP growth in the world (albeit their base levels of GDP were very small to begin with). Guinea, while growing more slowly at 2.5 percent in 2013, had high expectations for growth resting on its Simandou iron ore project, which international investors Chinalco, Rio Tinto, and the International Finance Corporation signed on to. However, the iron mining sectors in Sierra Leone, Guinea, and Liberia have been hit both by declining prices and the Ebola outbreak, calling into question the expected profitability of these projects, hurting investor confidence in the region, and hindering contributions to future growth. At the beginning of the year, the IMF forecast that GDP growth in 2014 would amount to 11.3 percent, 5.9 percent, and 4.5 percent, respectively, for Sierra Leone, Liberia, and Guinea. In mid-August, as a result of these factors, the IMF revised these estimates to 8.0 percent, 2.5 percent, and 2.4 percent, accordingly.

Economic Effects of the Outbreak

In addition to the enormous and tragic loss of human life, the Ebola epidemic had devastating effects on these West African economies in a variety of essential sectors: halting trade, hurting agriculture, and scaring investors.

Mobility restrictions, trade, and transport. To halt the spread of the virus, the countries most affected by Ebola implemented quarantines in areas where risk of infection was high, and neighboring countries such as Côte d'Ivoire and Senegal imposed restrictions on the movement of people and goods, including border closures. These measures, in turn, reduced internal and regional trade, transport, and, of course, tourism. But because official trade statistics do not capture informal trade—including cross-border trade that could range from 20 to 75 percent of GDP for West African countries—the estimated impact proposed by the World Bank may overlook the large reduction in informal trade from mobility constraints (Afrika and Ajumbo, 2012). While these actions aim to break the chain of transmission, the president of Sierra Leone has called them an economic blockade that resulted in scaled-back production and revenues for the government.

Agriculture. According to World Bank data, agriculture accounts for 57 percent of Sierra Leone's GDP, 39 percent of Liberia's, 20 percent of Guinea's, and 22 percent of Nigeria's. Disruptions from the outbreak during the planting season were not helpful for the harvests of staple crops of rice and corn during the harvest season, between October and December. The price of the staple crop cassava in some places in Liberia more than doubled during the crisis (increasing by 150 percent) according to the Food and Agriculture Organization. Food price shocks such as these often lead to inflation: according to IMF estimates, in Liberia the inflation rate climbed to 9.9 percent in 2014 from 7.6 percent before the Ebola crisis first broke. Overall, inflation did not exceed the high teens, but this was still a significant effect.[5]

Mining and investment. Mining activity (which constitutes 14 percent of Liberia's economy and approximately 17 percent of Sierra Leone's) de-

5 See the World Bank database at https://data.worldbank.org/indicator/NV.AGR.TOTL.ZS.

creased in Liberia and Sierra Leone following restrictions on nonessential travel and repatriation of personnel. Voice of America reported that investor confidence has dropped since the escalation of Ebola cases (Eagle, 2014). China Union and Arcelor Mittal scaled down iron ore mining operations in Liberia. Some miners in Sierra Leone and Liberia were afraid to enter high-risk districts, and several firms (including Australian mining firm Tawana Resources and Canadian Oversea Petroleum) suspended operations or sent foreign workers home. Investments were postponed and some even canceled because the perceived risks were too great.

Fiscal challenges. Fiscal revenues declined as limited economic activity reduced revenues from taxes, tariffs, and customs duties. Yet at the same time, resolving the crisis and meeting the greater health and security needs of their people meant government expenditures needed to rise. Avoiding the impact on the poorest and most vulnerable will also necessitate more transfers. The World Bank (2014c) reported during the Ebola crisis that "short-term fiscal impacts are also large, at $93 million for Liberia (4.7 percent of GDP); $79 million for Sierra Leone (1.8 percent of GDP); and $120 million for Guinea (1.8 percent of GDP)" (p. 2).

The financial sector. Although the financial sector had been largely excluded from the narrative of the outbreak, it is worth noting that the possibility of large depositors withdrawing funds meant banks needed to be concerned they would face serious liquidity problems. Similarly, if some big creditors missed payments, the number of nonperforming loans could increase, eventually leading to some defaults. So liquidity management also had to be a priority, as banks' bad loans portfolio needed to be monitored carefully. Ultimately, loss of confidence in the financial system was the main risk factor to avoid. Finally, capital flight was an additional risk to the financial system, especially as exchange rates became more volatile. The World Bank (2014c) reported that many wealthier Guineans and expatriates left the country and that uncertainty and risk aversion in Sierra Leone prompted a rise in capital outflows (p. 2).

Tourism. Airlines such as British Airways, Emirates, Air France, Asky Airlines, and Arik Air banned some flights to and from the most affected countries. The African Union asked for these bans to be lifted and for proper screening mechanisms to be put in place at airports. CEOs of eleven firms operating in West Africa said that some measures, including these travel restrictions, were doing more harm than good and may well have contributed to the humanitarian crisis by blocking crucial trade flows, thereby pushing up the prices of essential foods and medicines (Dosso, 2014). There were also some concerns that an indirect consequence of the Ebola outbreak would be diminished tourism throughout the African continent: the Ebola outbreak dominated headlines in the U.S., African, and international press, even overshadowing the U.S.-Africa Leaders Summit. Misconceptions about the transmission of Ebola and the risk of travel in Africa could have served to further reduce tourism to and within the continent.

Fear of Contagion Curbs Economic Activity

What is striking about the Ebola outbreak's effects on the economies of West Africa is that the most influential factor constraining economic activity there was fear (Specter, 2014). As stressed by the World Bank,

> The largest economic effects of the crisis are not as a result of the direct costs (mortality, morbidity, caregiving, and the associated losses to working days) but rather those resulting from aversion behavior driven by fear of contagion. This in turn led to a fear of association with others and reduces labor force participation, closes places of employment, disrupts transportation, and motivates some government and private decision-makers to close sea ports and airports. (World Bank, 2014b)

The World Bank also noted that behavioral effects were responsible for as much as 80 to 90 percent of the total economic impact of the SARS epidemic of 2002–04 and the H1N1 flu epidemic of 2009. The World Bank estimated that because of Ebola, economic activity may have been drastically affected in both the short and the medium term.

A Collective Response to a Global Threat

During the outbreak, the United Nations stated that $1 billion would be needed to contain the Ebola outbreak, whereas the World Bank estimated that containment and mitigation would require several billion dollars for humanitarian support, fiscal support, screening facilities at airports and seaports, and strengthening of surveillance, detection, and treatment capacity of health systems. According to the Centers for Disease Control and Prevention (2016), in total around $3.6 billion was spent to fight the epidemic by the end of 2015.

International donors including the World Bank and IMF provided financing for emergency response and medium- and long-term recovery in the most affected countries. The United States also provided financial support to help train nurses and establish emergency treatment facilities in Liberia. China committed doctors to Sierra Leone and $37 million in assistance to West Africa. Cuba provided the largest medical team of any country to assist the region.

Many African countries made contributions in the fight against Ebola as well; for example, under the UN Mission for Emergency Ebola Response, Ghana served as a logistical hub for medical professionals in the region. Senegal helped set up an air corridor to facilitate transportation of medical personnel to Ghana. Through the African Union Support to Ebola Outbreak in West Africa mission, Uganda—a country that has dealt with Ebola crises in the past—provided medical experts to advise regional efforts, as did the Democratic Republic of the Congo. The WAEMU gave approximately $1 million to reinforce preventive measures aimed at stemming the spread of Ebola throughout West Africa. In addition, South Africa established an Ebola diagnostics lab in Sierra Leone.

The considerable support from African countries and institutions, as well as the international community, highlighted the recognition that Ebola was not just a West African problem. It was and is not an African problem. It is a global problem that needs to be addressed at all levels (national, regional, and international) as swiftly and completely as possible. In this sense, it was important that a coordinated and united African and global response was achieved in the short term, but it will also be important to consider how to integrate investment in health systems into regional development plans in the medium to long term so that public health crises like the Ebola outbreak can be addressed more quickly (or averted entirely) in the future. The good news is that the people of Guinea, Liberia, and Sierra Leone are resilient. The same strength that allowed them to endure and rebuild from past devastating conflicts, in conjunction with international support, helped them to rebuild after the outbreak and to establish new heights of political and macroeconomic stability in recent years.

INNOVATION IN SUB-SAHARAN AFRICA

The words *Africa* and *innovation* are not often found in the same sentence. But, in fact, much is happening in Africa. And the benefits are likely to be dramatic.

Mobile Money Transfers

Africa is already a global leader in mobile money transfer services. Mobile money services such as M-Pesa in Kenya (*pesa* means "money" in Kiswahili) started by enabling people to send money to their parents in their home village. But it gradually evolved into a platform for savings and loans, and the payments platform is now crucial for the business model of numerous start-ups across Nairobi. More recently, Paga in Nigeria is following in M-Pesa's footsteps.

Financial Inclusion

There has been rapid progress in broadening financial inclusion. Over 70 percent of Tanzanians now have access to financial services, compared to just 20 percent in 2009. Rwanda and Uganda are not far behind. And it is not only about money transfers. M-Shwari (*shwari* means "calm" in Kiswahili)—a savings and loan product—enables Kenyans to access a bank account through their mobile phones, and M-Akiba (*akiba* means "savings" in Kiswahili) offers them the opportunity to purchase government bonds using the same technology. I would not be surprised if Kiswahili becomes once more a lingua franca, but this time in the technology sector!

Technology is also reducing inequality. Greater financial inclusion is helping reduce poverty and empower women.

Innovation in Agriculture

Innovation in the agricultural sector has huge potential in Africa. Digital financial services increase smallholder farmers' access to weather and market information and help them decide when and which crops to plant and where to sell those crops. The Tigo Kilimo SMS-based application (*kilimo* means "agriculture" in Kiswahili), launched in Tanzania in 2012, provides up-to-date weather and agronomic information, and the Connected Farmer program in East Africa sends up-to-date market prices to farmers' mobile phones, allowing them to select the best markets and best times at which to sell and receive digital payments and receipts.

Financial Technology

In fragile and conflict-affected states, financial technology has played an instrumental role. In Sierra Leone, the government turned to mobile wallets to help fight the Ebola virus outbreak. The United Nations finds that mobile payments to emergency workers dramatically shortened the payment times and minimized fraud during the outbreak. In Liberia, mobile payments to health and education workers who work in areas isolated during the rainy season have helped maintain critical social services. Financial technology is also increasingly being harnessed to improve tax collection, thereby contributing to domestic revenue mobilization, a key objective in many African countries.

Health Sector Innovation

Innovation has also benefited the health sector. In Rwanda, the government has partnered with a U.S. company (Zipline) to use drones guided by mobile phone location services to deliver lifesaving medical products to rural health clinics within thirty minutes, rather than several hours by road delivery—if the roads are passable. Payment by mobile phone makes this possible.

Infrastructure Deficit

New technology also has the potential to help address Africa's infrastructure deficit. M-Kopa Solar in Kenya (*kopa* means "borrow" in Kiswahili) sells solar home systems on a payment plan, with an initial deposit followed by daily payments for up to one year. After completing payments, customers own the product outright. M-Kopa elegantly solves two problems simultaneously: it accelerates rural electrification, a big challenge in sparsely populated African countries, and it provides consumer credit to rural households who would never have qualified for a loan from a traditional bank. And an unanticipated benefit is that the lightbulbs powered by M-Kopa have also boosted education outcomes in rural areas, as schoolchildren no longer have to do their homework in the dark.

KEY BOTTLENECKS TO FINANCIAL SECTOR DEVELOPMENT: CHALLENGES AND SOLUTIONS

We should recognize that there has been some progress in many areas such as the advent of pan-African banks, an increased use of payment system tools such as debit and credit cards, and a very robust growth in mobile payments in many countries. Still, the data show that sub-Saharan Africa's financial systems suffer from several limitations and are not contributing enough to much-needed sustainable and inclusive economic growth.

Financial Inclusion

The advent of mobile payments has been a game changer in many countries and has the potential to increase financial inclusion in others. Still, questions remain. Why has mobile payment not grown in some regions as much as in East Africa? Do regulatory or other issues limit the growth of mobile payments in those regions? For instance, "know your customer" and "know your customer's customer" requirements are difficult to meet when identification of users is not achieved (for example, in the Democratic Republic of the Congo). Can biometric identification technology offer solutions when large segments of the population do not have any form of identification? The key distinction between access and usage also remains important. Users may have an account but use it infrequently.

At the same time, the microfinance sector is increasingly relying on mobile payments and other tools to reduce existing inefficiencies. Such a sector has grown rapidly in sub-Saharan Africa but has faced challenges, including from fraud and other poor corporate governance practices. Mobile payments and financial technology (FinTech) have the potential to address such challenges.

Access to Finance

The cost of credit risk assessment remains high in sub-Saharan Africa. Banks must deal with poor or unreliable accounting and financial information, lack of credit bureaus, and poor legal framework. Small and medium enterprises cite access to financing as their main challenge. This has gender equality implications, as woman-owned businesses are even more limited in getting access to credit.

Big data and machine learning, for instance, have the potential to reduce the cost of credit risk assessment by using a broad range of information such as mobile phone usage data and payment data. Lower cost of credit risk assessment will attract new entrants in the provision of credit, including (nondeposit taking) financial technology firms (peer-to-peer and other platforms) with implications for competition and the use of personal information by third-party players.

Competition and Efficiency

The competitive landscape of sub-Saharan Africa's financial systems has been evolving with the entry of pan-African banks in a market traditionally dominated by state-owned banks, foreign banks, and small banks. Issues of cross-border supervision have come to the fore recently, and the rise of financial technology will challenge regulators and supervisors.

Capacity building will be needed, and there the trade-offs between safety and efficiency will need to be assessed quickly. The merits of different models, such as the one used by the Central Bank of Kenya, where regulation did not hamper the growth of mobile payments, or a sandbox approach, such as the one used by the Bank of England, where regulators allow and learn from innovation, should be considered.

Cross-Border Flows, Remittances, and Cross-Border Relations

Cross-border flows, including those related to trade and remittances, are being challenged in many countries by the loss of cross-border relations. The current model for cross-border relations is also expensive, as sub-Saharan African respondent banks need to maintain liquidity (prefunding) at correspondent banks and enter in a credit relationship with them (for overdrafts). Such a model also entails long payment chains and is dominated by transactions in U.S. dollars.

Efforts to develop central bank digital or cryptocurrencies are under way in mature economies (Bank of Canada–Monetary Authority of Singapore and potentially the Hong Kong Monetary Authority, European Central Bank–Bank of Japan), and the IMF has recently mentioned the idea of a crypto–Special Drawing Right. Cryptocurrencies eliminate the need for prefunding, the existence of a credit relationship, and verifying counterparty identities, which results in shorter waits for payments. This is also the case for virtual currencies in private payment networks, such as Ripple.

The cost of sending remittances to sub-Saharan Africa is the highest globally (as per World Bank 2017b data) in part because of the oligopolistic nature of the industry. Regional trade and financial integration is relatively low in the region because of high transaction costs, multiple currencies, and inefficient payment systems for intra-African cross-border payments. Financial technology has the potential to reduce transaction costs with positive effects on remittances to sub-Saharan Africa and regional integration.

Financial Sector Development

There is a need to develop financial markets in sub-Saharan Africa beyond the banking sectors and the payment systems because capital markets, insurance companies, pension funds, and other financial institutions and instruments remain limited. The level of financial literacy remains relatively low in sub-Saharan Africa.

Efforts are under way in the region to use financial technology for making insurance premium payments (Lesotho), receiving pension payments (Ghana), and purchasing government securities (Kenya). Financial technology tools can also help support financial literacy programs (electronic wallet, education at the primary school and higher levels).

Governance, Corruption, and Trust

Countries in sub-Saharan Africa rank among the lowest in the World Governance Indicators[6] (which capture six dimensions of governance: of voice and accountability, political stability and lack of violence, government effectiveness, regulatory quality, rule of law, and control of corruption), and in particular, corruption remains an important constraint to business and finance.

Blockchain technology, which enables a list of records to be linked and secured simultaneously using cryptography, seeks to reduce such constraints. Private payment networks and smart contracts are gaining traction globally. Smart contracts, for instance, are computer protocols that facilitate, verify, or enforce contract negotiations or performance. Given the central role of the government in sub-Saharan African economies and the ambitious increase planned for public investment, potential gains from improved procurement and contracting could be significant.

Macroeconomic Issues

Policy issues from mobile payments are not restricted to financial sector issues. Several macroeconomic issues will have to be revisited.

- The growth of mobile money and the possible adoption of cryptocurrencies such as Bitcoin challenge the traditional view of money as a medium of exchange, a store of value, and a unit of account. For instance, recent studies in East Africa show the increased difficulty in forecasting the velocity of money as use of mobile payments grows (Simpasa and Gurara, 2012; Weil, Mbiti, and Mwega, 2012; Adam and Walker, 2015). Central banks will need to revisit their traditional liquidity forecasting and more generally the impact of such innovations in the implementation of monetary policy and its transmission.

6 The World Governance Indicators are produced by Daniel Kaufmann, Natural Resource Governance Institute and Brookings Institution, and Aart Kraay, World Bank Development Research Group. See http://info.worldbank.org/governance/wgi/#home.

- Potential gains in strengthening governance and improving public finance, financial technology, and associated innovations can have macroeconomic gains for sub-Saharan African countries. Increased and more efficient financial intermediation can increase growth (according to the finance and growth literature pioneered by Ross Levine [2005] and others), especially if access to credit by small businesses is increased.

- In economies dominated by the informal sector, new technologies can increase the incentives to join the formal sector (for instance, electronic payment of taxes in exchange for inclusion in a pension system).

- In addition to real economy effects, innovation can help make growth more inclusive by targeting subsidies through electronic payments.

- More broadly, in the context of rapid demographic trends and urbanization, unemployment of youth and women needs to be reduced. By 2035, more than half of those entering the global labor market will be in sub-Saharan Africa, and technological innovation and infrastructure development can play key roles in allowing the continent to transform its demographic dividend into jobs, growth, and rising living standards for all, but education and skills for the new digital economy in sub-Saharan Africa need to be implemented early on.

In sum, sub-Saharan African policymakers will in many instances have to face issues similar to those faced by their counterparts in other regions. At times, the speed of adoption of technology will be even faster in the region, as in the rapid growth of mobile payments. Efficiency considerations include choices regarding competition and coordination (for example, whether to push for interoperability), the likely impact on business models and profitability, and cost and inclusion issues. They will also have to manage risks to stability and security (including cyber risk), possible consequences to monetary policy implementation and transmission, and financial stability issues (such as licensing and regulatory perimeter).

7

Africa's Partners

Africa has a variety of partners working with it to help implement its vision, both at the continental and the national levels. Traditional partners like members of the European Union (EU) and the United States, and newer partners like China, Japan, and India, are important in helping Africa achieve its vision for growth and development, whether it be through trade, foreign direct investment (FDI), or development assistance. This chapter makes policy observations and examines key recommendations for these partners' relationship and engagement with Africa.

While at Brookings, my colleagues at the Africa Growth Initiative and I focused a great deal on U.S. policy toward Africa. One of our main goals was to bring African voices and policymaking perspectives to Washington. This section takes a look back at commentary I made about a variety of U.S.-Africa issues. It includes an overview of the Bill Clinton and George W. Bush administrations' Africa policy and initiatives, the progress of the Obama administration's economic development goals in Africa, and the priorities of the U.S. Treasury under the Obama administration. This section also examines in depth the historic and first U.S.-Africa Leaders Summit and U.S.-Africa Business Forum, events that will likely continue to influence the United States' relationship with Africa.

The final part of the section examines a potential side effect of the U.S. African Growth and Opportunity Act and what it signals for policymakers in the future.

EXAMINING THE OBAMA ADMINISTRATION'S ECONOMIC DEVELOPMENT GOALS FOR AFRICA

Barack Obama made his last trip as president to sub-Saharan Africa in July 2015, just after hosting newly elected Nigerian president Muhammadu Buhari at the White House. This happened after what some called a slow start with regard to Africa (associated in part with the 2008 financial crisis), but the Obama administration initiated a formidable list of new U.S. government programs in sub-Saharan Africa, with a high point occurring when President Obama convened the first-ever U.S.-Africa Leaders Summit. A defining feature of all the Obama administration's activities in Africa was the great emphasis the president placed on improving the U.S.-African commercial relationship and supporting broader, more inclusive economic growth throughout the region. Each of his signature programs consistently included a prominent role for the business community, with Obama's Power Africa initiative reportedly leveraging an astounding $20 billion in commitments from the private sector to support badly needed electricity generation and access in the region.

In many ways, all these efforts began when the Obama White House published the U.S. Strategy toward sub-Saharan Africa in 2012, a unique document that set out key policy areas to guide all U.S. government efforts in the region. Not surprisingly, the strategy prominently featured improved economic growth, business, and trade, with five actions identified as primary goals for U.S. federal agencies. The former president's last trip to Kenya and Ethiopia offers an opportunity to assess how African countries progressed on the Obama administration goals during the president's two terms in office. A quick review of relevant indicators reveals that progress has been mixed, so presenting this data might also help African and U.S. policymakers in using this moment to address areas in need of attention and leverage successes to date.

First, though, it should be acknowledged that assessing this type of information is a challenging task. Movement against each of the U.S. government's strategic focus areas depends on complex push and pull factors. External (or push) factors include the president's initiatives but also involve trends far outside his control, like the evolution of commodity prices. In contrast, pull factors are domestic variables, which are under the control of African policymakers and to some extent the business community and civil society in the region. These internal dynamics include time-intensive regional efforts to improve macroeconomic and political governance, as well as African initiatives to support competitiveness and economic transformation, among others. Ultimately, Africans are the ones who have to implement initiatives to support growth, whether they are backed by the United States or homegrown.

Goal 1: Promote an Enabling Environment for Trade and Investment

Better policies to enable business and trade could support growth and promote an expansion in the benefits of the region's economies. Accordingly, the Obama administration committed to encouraging legal, regulatory, institutional reforms that contribute to an environment that enables greater trade and investment in sub-Saharan Africa. The White House further stated that this focus built on U.S. participation in programs like the Extractive Industries Transparency Initiative and the Open Government Partnership. Many sub-Saharan African countries have also prioritized creating an enabling environment for trade and investment; however, the Heritage Foundation, in its "2015 Index on Economic Freedom," which includes ten measures of regulatory, fiscal, and rule-of-law restrictions, reports that the region at the time hosted nine of the world's twenty-six "repressed economies."

When measured by a subset of Heritage's freedom ranking on open markets (trade, investment, and financial freedom), sub-Saharan African countries were fairly static throughout Obama's terms in office but did record some modest progress. On Heritage's scale of 0 to 100, sub-Saharan African countries on average have improved their score from 47 to 51 since 2008, an increase of approximately 9 percent. Big gains do not really register in other regions around the world either, though, with

East Asia and the Pacific having an increase of 5 percent and Latin America an increase of 8 percent (Heritage Foundation, 2015).

Goal 2: Improve Economic Governance

Somewhat relatedly, the former president's strategy on U.S.-Africa relations also identified strong public financial management as a key means to increase transparency and effectiveness in government operations and broaden the revenue base. Several U.S. programs for engaging sub-Saharan Africa emphasize these areas, including the Millennium Challenge Corporation's[1] government effectiveness focus and the work of the U.S. Treasury's Office of African Nations. However, the Mo Ibrahim Foundation's "2015 Ibrahim Index of African Governance" notes that scores for "sustainable economic opportunity" have generally "stalled," and their ranking of African countries on "public management and accountability" shows a similar middling performance (Mo Ibrahim Foundation, 2015).

Goal 3: Promote Regional Integration

African countries have historically traded with each other far less frequently than their counterparts trade with each other in other regional groupings like Latin America and western Europe. Acknowledging this deficiency, President Obama prioritized supporting greater regional integration in Africa, highlighting intra-African harmonization as a key point in his strategy toward the region and backing that up with new programs like Trade Africa, which aims to increase coordination between countries in East Africa. This emphasis is consistent with the great priority African leaders have also placed on these issues, with twenty-six nations committing just last month to a new Tripartite Free Trade Area, a critical stepping-stone toward the ambitious goal of creating an Africa-wide economic community by 2018.

1 The Millennium Challenge Corporation is a U.S. government foreign aid agency based on the principle that aid is most effective when it reinforces good governance, economic freedom, and investments in people.

These policy commitments might have started to make a difference, as there were big increases in intra-African trade during the president's terms in office. Trade within sub-Saharan Africa increased by 66 percent since 2008, and trade within the regional group the Southern African Development Community increased by 95 percent. Africa's other major regional economic communities mostly showed gains too. (I must note that this is based on figures for formal trade—if informal trade were included, growth in this area might be even higher.) Additionally, trade data in sub-Saharan Africa can be unreliable, so changes require some healthy skepticism.

Goal 4: Expand African Capacity to Effectively Access and Benefit from Global Markets

In addition to intraregional trade, the Obama administration supported improved African capacity to engage with the international markets. Perhaps most significantly, Obama in 2015 signed the renewal of the African Growth and Opportunity Act, which provides eligible African countries with preferred access to U.S. markets and is a linchpin for trade-capacity building and expanded, worldwide market access for African countries. However, this important milestone comes at an incredibly turbulent time for African exporters, who historically have relied predominantly on the sale of raw materials, like unprocessed oil and gas. Dramatic recent fluctuations in the prices of commodities have prompted associated decreases in Africa's international exports. President Obama's strategy also sought to support a diversification of exports beyond natural resources. Raw material exports decreased by 65 percent from 2008 to 2015, while intermediate goods (those that involve some processing) saw a 14 percent increase in the same period.

Goal 5: Encourage U.S. Companies to Trade with and Invest in Africa

Helping U.S. businesses identify and pursue opportunities to trade with and invest in sub-Saharan Africa was a key focus of the Obama administration. This area is also one in which Obama had perhaps the greatest potential to positively influence growth, given the control he had over the many federal agencies mandated to support American commerce. In this regard, the U.S. Strategy toward sub-Saharan Africa announced a "Doing Business in Africa Campaign" in which the Commerce Department led eleven U.S. agencies and a private sector panel in efforts to connect American business with African partners. These initiatives corresponded with increases in U.S. exports to Africa, but there was and still is significant room for improvement: there was also a 22 percent increase in U.S. exports to developing countries in Africa from 2008 to 2015, but this was accompanied by a 42 percent increase in exports to developing countries in the Americas and a 38 percent increase to those in Asia. Unfortunately, African imports to the United States—still largely concentrated in commodities—also saw a sharp decline as the American domestic energy production capacity advanced.

FDI inflows to sub-Saharan African countries were also more positive, with a 19 percent increase from 2008 to 2015. Regarding greenfield FDI trends (in which FDI enters the region to support new projects), the United States stood out. The 2015 Ernst & Young Africa Attractiveness Survey reports that American companies were the largest source of greenfield investment in Africa in 2014. Since 2007, American businesses initiated over 700 FDI projects in Africa, "pouring in US$52.7b[illion] and creating nearly 98,000 jobs" (Ernst & Young, 2015). This is a significant standout area for President Obama's goals.

Movement around each of these areas is mixed and inconsistent. This is understandable given that the Obama administration's goals really cannot be assessed in a unified way—the institutional change required to support improvements in public financial management is a slow and daunting challenge, whereas the technological breakthroughs, those in hydraulic fracturing, for example, can alter a business calculus almost overnight. Rather than showing lack of progress, perhaps the mixed results of this quick exercise indicate that attempting to improve progress on each of these items should be a source of consistent attention, and reviewing the data can be a helpful guide to areas in need of special focus.

It also seems that many U.S. programs are positioned to support positive change around areas of slow progress. The president's Power Africa initiative, for example, aims to create infrastructure improvements, which enable better business performance and could help increase trade, ultimately adding to advancements around measures of competitiveness. It would be tempting therefore to recommend a focus on implementation of this initiative, Trade Africa, and the many other U.S. government programs. However, project implementation must occur alongside work on the broader underpinnings of economic growth in Africa. In addition, while the African Growth and Opportunity Act was renewed, much can still be done to strengthen the program, and important proposals could be pursued to consolidate gains.

AFRICAN PRIORITIES AND THE U.S. TREASURY GLOBAL AGENDA

The United States plays a leadership role when it comes to framing the agenda on global economic and financial policy, and it is important for African policymakers to be aware of what is at stake for the continent.

On December 3, 2014, U.S. Treasury Undersecretary for International Affairs Nathan Sheets outlined the top priorities of the Treasury's global economic agenda in his debut speech at a Brookings Institution event I attended (Sheets, 2014).

Sheets led the formulation of U.S. policy in the decision-making bodies of the World Bank and the International Monetary Fund (IMF). Because the United States is the largest shareholder and practically has veto power in both institutions, the U.S. Treasury's agenda typically serves as a guide for their strategies. In turn, the IMF and World Bank have immense influence when it comes to low-income African countries. As a result, Sheets helped formulate these institutions' strategy toward Africa. So I am betting that these U.S. priorities will become much more important for Africa in the years to come.

Sheets spoke on the six core pillars of the Treasury's strategy: (1) strengthening and rebalancing global growth, (2) deepening engagement with emerging market giants, (3) framing a resilient global financial system, (4) facilitating access to capital, (5) promoting open trade and investment, and (6) enhancing U.S. leadership at the IMF.

These mutually reinforcing objectives aim to strengthen economic performance at the global level, but also have specific implications for the African continent: Stronger global economic growth helps sustain the current GDP growth many African countries are currently experiencing, boosts financial and investment flows to the continent, and potentially deepens local financial markets. An increasingly resilient international financial system would insulate Africa from disruptive crises and provide a supportive environment for the continent's growth. Improved U.S.-China relations could yield a fruitful trilateral partnership with Africa by ensuring complementarity in investments, as both the United States and China are increasing their commercial engagement with the continent. Giving a greater voice to emerging markets through reform of the IMF is also a good step toward improving relations with these countries and supporting the good governance of international institutions.

The U.S. Treasury's Approach to African Challenges

In addition to these global objectives, in his speech Sheets specifically highlighted African issues two times. First, he named the West African Ebola virus epidemic one of the foremost challenges facing global economic policymakers as they seek to achieve the Group of Twenty leaders' objective of "strong, sustainable and balanced global growth." Second, he identified Africa as one of the focal regions of one of the "core pillars" of the Treasury's strategy "facilitating access to capital":

> Expanding access to financial services for the over 2 billion unbanked people in the world promises to open new possibilities as the financial wherewithal in these population grows. Expanding access to finance and deepening financial markets in Africa, the Middle East and other developing regions will support businesses, empower entrepreneurs, boost household incomes, and ultimately help fuel growth across developing economies. This is why we are working with the G-20 and with other partners to broaden access for developing countries and to make access to capital within these countries more inclusive. (Sheets, 2014)

The Treasury's focus on expanding access to capital and enhancing capital markets in Africa is a welcome step, as nearly a quarter of adults in sub-Saharan Africa lack access to formal financial services. Moreover, Africa requires substantial inflows of capital to the region in order to finance transformative projects in infrastructure across the continent—

estimated to cost $100 billion a year. However, to meet this ambitious target, the U.S. Treasury will need to coordinate with international and African stakeholders to leverage sufficient public and private sector investment and bolster African capital markets.

The U.S. Agenda to Expand Access to Capital and Deepen Capital Markets for Development

Five elements are integral to financing the region's development projects as enumerated in Sheets's speech:

1. *Blended financing.* Sheets called on multilateral development banks, including the World Bank, to "use their balance sheets to catalyze private investment." Development finance institutions can help guarantee investments and mitigate risks posed in unstable institutional and economic environments. In doing so, development institutions provide private sector investors with a safety net, which can reduce risks and spur investment. They will need to innovate to come up with new instruments and arrangements that can facilitate private investment in Africa.

2. *Domestic private financing.* African governments and private sector leaders must collaborate to generate a stable regulatory environment conducive to the growth of financial markets and bolster financial intermediation. Indeed, small- and medium-enterprise financing is still in short supply. Developing local capital markets and broadening the domestic institutional investor base will help raise long-term finance.

3. *International private financing.* In the past decade, international investors have increasingly looked toward Africa for high returns on investment. Maintaining sound economic policy and addressing potential destabilizing risks are crucial to continuing to attract these investments.

4. *Remittances.* Remittances to Africa amounted to approximately $33 billion (about 2 percent of the continent's GDP) in 2016. These resources are key to Africa's development, especially improving the

livelihoods of the region's poor. Yet excessive money transfer fees cost the region close to $1.8 billion a year. Increasing the efficiency of money transfers by reducing fees is a crucial step to getting the most value from these important development resources.

5. *Climate financing.* Providing financial support to promote the use of low-carbon technologies is another major facet of the U.S. Treasury's strategy that will benefit African countries by increasing the region's renewable energy supply while also spurring employment opportunities in this sector. In 2014, the Obama administration pledged $3 billion to the Green Climate Fund, which serves as a channel for private funds supporting efforts related to climate adaptation and mitigation.

Aligning U.S. and African Economic Priorities: What Does the U.S. Agenda Mean for Africa?

The U.S. Treasury's international agenda converges with African priorities in several key areas. Its agenda is also broadly in line with current thinking on financing for development, which was covered in 2015 when world leaders met in Addis Ababa, Ethiopia, for the third International Conference on Financing for Development. The U.S. agenda's focus on remittances is apt, especially considering that flows of remittances are increasingly becoming comparable to levels of official development assistance on the continent. The U.S. proposal to encourage competition among money transfer operators and strengthen remittance markets can help public and private sector leaders maximize the value of this major development resource. The U.S. focus on climate financing is also a noteworthy area, given that public-private partnerships are driving growth in the renewable energy sector.

One thing that struck me during Sheets's remarks, however, was the absence of infrastructure finance in the U.S. Treasury's priorities. At the 2005 Group of Eight Gleneagles Summit on development assistance, world powers made a special commitment to financing infrastructure improvements. And given the centrality of improving energy infrastructure in President Obama's Power Africa initiative, this omission seems to be a significant oversight when it comes to U.S.-Africa policy. On another note, there was some indication of U.S. policy toward the BRICS (Brazil, Russia, India, China, and South Africa) Development Bank. Sheets showed some skepticism toward the group and noted that, to be effective, the BRICS bank needs to (1) show its complementarity and additionality with existing institutions and (2) include the hard-learned lessons of development finance: good governance, debt sustainability, adequate procurement, and ability to address environmental issues.

Another area where the U.S. Treasury can help support U.S.-Africa trade and investment policy is in financial regulation. Indeed, the U.S. dollar remains the centerpiece of global trade. Intra-African trade and the fast-growing trade between China and Africa are typically settled in U.S. dollars. SWIFT, the financial messaging services firm, released figures that indicate that about 50 percent of intra-African import and export settlements involve a bank outside Africa. In particular, U.S. dollar clearing banks are becoming more important as trade and investment within Africa (about 23 percent of total trade according to SWIFT data) and with China and other emerging markets is increasing. Know-your-customer, anti-money-laundering, and combating-financial-terrorism regulations increase compliance and other transaction costs. At times, foreign banks decide to simply close correspondent accounts with some African banks for fear of the scale of potential fines for breaking sanctions. Thus, there is room for regulatory cooperation and other policies that can help safeguard the objectives of U.S. financial regulation and, at the same time, help its objective to increase trade and investment with Africa (Chilosi and others, 2013).

Finally, climate financing is definitely an important global issue, and Africa can be at the forefront. Indeed, the International Energy Agency forecasts the share of renewables in Africa's total power capacity to more than double, reaching 44 percent by 2040. In fact, recent data on public-private investment from the World Bank indicate that the renewable electricity sector is growing. In 2013, the top deals in sub-Saharan Africa included projects worth \$1.6 billion for an open-cycle gas turbine project and a wind farm in South Africa, as well as a \$440 million thermal power expansion project in Ghana.[2]

2 See the World Bank's Private Participation in Renewable Energy Database at http://ppi-re.worldbank.org/data.

This said, in terms of global warming and climate change, the Commission on Growth and Development[3] argues that it makes economic sense for developed countries to bear some of the costs of developing-country investments that would cut carbon emissions to safe levels. Since 2013 the United States and other governments pledged $10 billion toward the new Green Climate Fund for both mitigation and adaptation and to catalyze private sector investment in clean technologies and climate resilience. African countries need to ensure that climate investments are aligned with their overall infrastructure and development strategy.

LOOKING BACK AT THE U.S.-AFRICA LEADERS SUMMIT AND BUSINESS FORUM

In the following I compare the first-ever U.S.-Africa Leaders Summit with similar summits that have taken place with Africa and the EU, China, and Japan, and look at the different relationships of those regions with Africa. It is notable that Ebola attracted much of the media's attention—more than the summit itself. This analysis provides interesting insights into the way Africa is viewed by the media and how difficult it is to showcase the continent through a business, investment, or political collaboration lens. I also examine the similarities and differences between the policies of the administrations of Donald Trump and Barack Obama.

Building a Strategy Together with Africa

In 2013, while visiting Cape Town in South Africa, President Obama announced plans for the first continentwide U.S.-Africa Leaders Summit, to be held in August 2014. The summit provided an opportunity for the Obama administration to open a new chapter in U.S.-Africa relations, moving from interaction on the bilateral level to a continentwide engagement. Obama had been criticized for not reaching the same level of

3 The Commission on Growth and Development, or the "Growth Commission," chaired by Nobel laureate Michael Spence, was established to examine those economies that did achieve high growth in an attempt to draw out lessons for lower-growth economies.

engagement with Africa as Presidents Bill Clinton and George W. Bush, but his second term coincided with an effort to ramp up U.S.-Africa relations. In June 2012, Obama launched a strategy for sub-Saharan Africa, and the president's budget for 2015 showed his support for the region. The U.S.-Africa summit, however, allowed the United States an unprecedented opportunity to build a strategy together with Africa.

The Brookings Institution's Africa Growth Initiative (AGI) reviewed the components—organization, frame, and communications strategies—of three long-standing Africa summits to inform the designers of the U.S. version. In this comparison, AGI chose China, the EU, and Japan, some of Africa's other key trade and investment partners. AGI also compared the position of the United States and those partners in terms of trade, FDI, and other engagement with African countries, which is highlighted in the sections that follow.

Obtaining a maximum level of foreign policy action and results from a two-day summit with nearly all of the African heads of state in attendance is an enormous undertaking. However, the other summits have had plenty of time to work out the kinks. Thus, they provided excellent examples of successful summits for the U.S. organizers.

Important Summit Design Features and Recommendations

The features of those summits that could strengthen the U.S.-Africa partnership are frequency, sustainability, inclusivity, transparency, and accountability.

Design Feature 1: Frequency and Sustainability. The United States is playing catch-up in terms of using a continentwide leaders' summit to frame its strategy with Africa. Japan, China, and the EU have maintained long-running Africa summits. Japan's Tokyo International Conference on African Development (TICAD) started in 1993 and has met every five years since. China's Forum on China-Africa Cooperation (FOCAC) and the EU-Africa Summits of Heads of State both started in 2000. FOCAC meets every three years, and the EU-Africa summits have taken place three times since the first gathering (see figure 7-1). Other countries and a continent have held similar summits, including India, Brazil, South Korea, South America, and Turkey. While the United States deserves credit for its yearly Africa Growth and Opportunity Act trade ministerial,

FIGURE 7-1 African Leaders' Summits Time Line

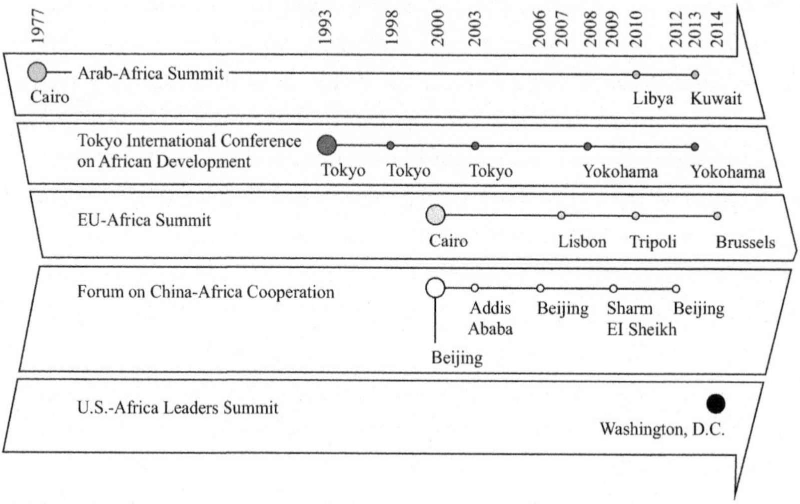

Note: Larger dots represent first conference meeting.

which alternates between the United States and an act-eligible country in Africa, it covers fewer themes than the EU-Africa, FOCAC, and TICAD summits. For the first U.S.-Africa summit, the theme was "Investing in Africa's Future."

The ultimate goal of the China, EU, and Japan summits has been to frame a sustainable, lasting engagement with Africa. The main products of each of the summits are a joint summit declaration and a joint summit action plan. China, the EU, and Japan hold meetings every three to five years and are able to regularly review and update action plans and commitments.

Recommendation: The United States should prioritize the sustainability of the U.S.-Africa Leaders Summit. The first priority for the summit should be to build a framework for a U.S.-Africa partnership that will stand the test of time. The most important products are the declaration and the action plan; these documents should present a clear plan of how the United States will engage Africa going forward (through further summits or otherwise). A joint communiqué should contain action items that will be measurable and trackable for substantial progress by the *next* summit, including the announcement of a date and location for the next leaders' summit, a joint follow-up committee, and a date for the first follow-up committee meeting. The U.S.-Africa Summit Policy Liaison Office of the State Department is a logical entity to manage future summits and could transition into a permanent entity similar to the TICAD secretariat.

China, the EU, and Japan have all learned to start planning for the next summit three to five years ahead of time, with multiple joint meetings and preparatory work between summits. More preparatory time helps them bring greater perspective and more voices to the table, which leads us to the next key summit design feature.

Design Feature 2: Inclusivity. As shown by the numbers in figure 7-2, a major challenge is inviting all African leaders to the summit so that they can be included in the discussions. Another challenge is including the multitude of voices from outside the leadership—civil society, businesses, youth leaders, and women. Both China and the EU have foreign policy challenges with African countries that have affected summit attendance. For example, China does not invite the leaders of African countries that recognize Taiwan as a sovereign nation to FOCAC (this includes Burkina Faso, São Tomé and Príncipe, Swaziland, and previously, the Gambia). Early in 2014, the European Union faced a backlash for its summit invitation list. Ahead of the EU summit, the African Union proposed a boycott of the event after hearing that Morocco, not a member of the African Union, was invited, whereas the leader of Sudan (an African Union member) was excluded because of human rights abuses. However, only Zimbabwe's president, Robert Mugabe, followed through with the proposed protest, although South Africa's president, Jacob Zuma, also did not attend the summit, vaguely citing other commitments. President Mugabe's boycott was ultimately for more personal reasons. His wife, Grace Mugabe, was slated to accompany the president to the summit but was denied a visa.

The United States faced challenges similar to the EU and China. The United States invited fifty of the fifty-four countries in Africa recognized by the UN to the summit but excluded the Central African Republic, Eritrea, Sudan, and Zimbabwe from the list. Why? The White House stated that it selected members that were in good standing with the African Union and the United States. Here are some more details on country standings: first, the Central African Republic is currently suspended

FIGURE 7-2 Key Statistics on Inclusion at Summits with African Partners

China—2012 FOCAC V

50/54 African countries represented*

•• **2** Main preparatory events

African countries not represented:
Burkina Faso, Gambia, São Tomé and Príncipe, and Swaziland

European Union—2014 4th EU-Africa Summit

50/54 African countries represented*

•••••• **6** Main preparatory events

African countries not represented and/or restricted persons:
Central African Republic, Guinea-Bissau, Libya, Zimbabwe, and Head of State of Sudan (a representative from Sudan attended)

Leaders that were invited but did not attend the recent summit:
South Africa (sent a representative) and Zimbabwe (did not send a representative)

Japan—2013 TICAD V

51/54 African countries represented*

•• **2** Main preparatory events

African countries not represented:
Central African Republic, Guinea-Bissau, and Madagascar**

United States—2014 African Leaders' Summit (forthcoming)

50/54 African countries invited*

TBD Main preparatory events

African countries not invited:
Central African Republic, Eritrea, Sudan, and Zimbabwe

* The United Nations recognizes fifty-four African countries. The Western Sahara, a disputed territory, is not one of them (though it is recognized by the African Union [AU]). At the time of this post, the AU has suspended the Central African Republic. Morocco is not a member of the AU.

** At the time of the TICAD V, Madagascar was suspended from the AU.

from the African Union; second, the United States has concerns about the status of democracy in Eritrea; and third, the leaders and government officials of Sudan and Zimbabwe currently face U.S. sanctions. In total, fifty-one delegations attended, which included fifty heads of state and the African Union chairperson.

Beyond the guest list, past summits have used other techniques to build a sense of partnership and inclusiveness among African nations. Joint preparatory events that include African senior officials and ministers have been used by China, the EU, and Japan to prepare and consult on the key themes and issues that will be discussed at the summit. Preparatory events help the host countries cover more summit themes by allowing more time for discussion with ministers, senior officials, diplomats, and other stakeholders. The fifth summits, FOCAC V and TICAD V, used at least two preparatory events, and the EU summit held at least six meetings The U.S. joint ministerial meeting on energy June 3–4, 2014, was a good start for the U.S.-Africa partnership.

In addition, China, the EU, and Japan all chaired their summits jointly, with typically the host country or region at leader level and either the African Union president or chairperson of the African Union Commission. Japan also cochairs with the other TICAD organizers, which include international multilateral organizations. Bilateral meetings have taken place at all three summits, but these can offend countries not scheduled to meet the president. Prime Minister Shinzo Abe notably met with all heads of state and government who attended the TICAD V summit, and the EU provides a channel for the European Parliament to engage with African leaders at the Pan-African-European Parliamentary summit.

Recommendation: The United States should include as many African voices as possible to build the credibility of U.S.-Africa engagement: The U.S.-Africa summit is an opportunity to shift from having a strategy toward Africa to having a strategy together with Africa, its leaders, and other stakeholders. If the United States cannot invite a country's leader for political reasons, it should strive to give the country at least some representation at the forum. The United States can use the EU summit as an example of how to manage invitations to ministers or other non–head of state representatives. For example, while Omar al-Bashir was subject to EU sanctions, Minister of Foreign Affairs Ali Ahmed

Karti was able to represent the Sudan at the summit. Given the last U.S. administration's efforts to help resolve the crisis in the Central African Republic, inviting representatives from the capital, Bangui, is an example of what could help continue the dialogue.

Given that most of Africa's leaders are men, it is important to strive for gender balance at such a summit. Among the invited African leaders at the 2014 summit, only two were female (Ellen Johnson Sirleaf of Liberia and Nkosazana Dlamini-Zuma, chairperson of the African Union Commission), and of the U.S. cabinet and cabinet-rank positions there were six women out of twenty-two positions. One proposal AGI had for the summit was to acknowledge the gender imbalance in the summit declaration and make a commitment to improve, with tangible benchmarks for the next forum.

Design Feature 3: Transparency and Accountability. In order to increase transparency, the fourth EU-Africa Summit and FOCAC V used economic and social stakeholder meetings before their summits to allow a review of themes and action plans. The TICAD summit took a different approach to civil society engagement and allowed stakeholders to register to attend the summit plenary events. In addition, TICAD V held official, public side events and information booths. Well ahead of the summit, Amnesty International USA, Freedom House, Front Line Defenders, Open Society Foundations, and the Robert F. Kennedy Center for Justice and Human Rights hosted a U.S.-Africa Civil Society Forum on June 18–20. Other civil society groups and Washington-based think tanks also planned events around the summit, including AGI.

In terms of press access, China uses official press conferences to convey information about the summit discussion (information on press access is difficult to find on the FOCAC website). The EU and Japan, on the other hand, have readily available press guides on their websites. They allow registered press to access scheduled media opportunities (for example, arrivals and departures of leaders, opening discussions, and press conferences).

After the summits, follow-up mechanisms increase the participation of African nations and hold all countries (host or otherwise) accountable to commitments. Joint follow-up meetings are used by all three summits. Japan has a TICAD secretariat, managed by the Ministry of Foreign Affairs' director general for Foreign Affairs. The secretariat is a permanent department that manages the summit and follow-up actions. China has a similar mechanism, the FOCAC Chinese Follow-up Committee, composed of twenty-seven Chinese ministers. In addition to joint meetings, the Chinese and Japanese summits were followed by presidential visits to the African Union and African countries. Each of the summits uses a results-based framework to guide the action items from the summit declaration. Japan is the only summit that has a progress report website, which allows the public to track the progress of the TICAD implementation matrix. Summit websites store summit information and documents for access by the public after the event. Currently, Japan has the most information available across two websites (the Ministry of Foreign Affairs TICAD page and the conference page). The EU also provides a lot of public information, again on two websites (EU Council and EU-Africa Partnership), while China's information is mainly limited to official statements.

Recommendation: The United States should participate in stakeholder forums and provide public information and progress reports to hold the United States and summit participants accountable: Washington, D.C., civil society has taken on the task of organizing a civil society forum. The White House should consider any suggestions that result from the discussion.

The United States can foster transparency by developing a summit website, one location where civil society, press, and other stakeholders can learn more about the event. The web designers should consider how best to consolidate information into one central location on the web and include links to the additional forums and events (such as the yearly African Growth and Opportunity Act trade ministerial, the Young Africa Leaders Initiative gathering, and the business forum). The other summits often do not consolidate information and have multiple summit sites, so the United States would be leading the way. In addition, creating a permanent summit site as Japan did that houses a progress chart for action items that is updated on a regular basis would be a great model to follow.

The long-running EU-Africa, FOCAC, and TICAD summits set a high benchmark for the first U.S.-Africa Leaders Summit. While President Obama should be commended for taking on the endeavor of the first one, these recommendations can aid in continuing to improve such a summit's design and implementation together with African counterparts.

FOREIGN DIRECT INVESTMENT IN SUB-SAHARAN AFRICA: TRENDS AND HIGHLIGHTS

Foreign Direct Investment in Africa is a very important topic, with a lot of discussions focusing on the role of China on the continent. With assistance from AGI, I completed a review and comparison of economic relations between sub-Saharan African countries and some of their major commercial partners: the United States, China, the EU, and Japan.

FDI to sub-Saharan Africa has increased substantially, in part driven by China, but remains low compared to other regions (see figure 7-3). Global FDI stock in sub-Saharan Africa has increased dramatically, from over $27.3 billion in 2001 to $246.4 billion in 2012. According to AGI analysis of the United Nations Conference on Trade and Development's (UNCTAD) Bilateral FDI Statistics (United Nations Conference on Trade and Development, 2014a), the EU, China, Japan, and the United States accounted for approximately 54 percent of FDI in the region in 2012. South–South investment was also important and included partners such as South Africa (9 percent), Singapore (6 percent), India (5 percent), and Mauritius (5 percent).

FDI in sub-Saharan Africa from the EU, China, Japan, and the United States grew by nearly five times between 2001 and 2012, from $27.2 billion to about $132.8 billion. This growth was primarily driven by China, whose FDI grew at an annual rate of 53 percent, compared with 29 percent for Japan, 16 percent for the EU, and 14 percent for the United States. China's contribution amounted to $18.2 billion in 2012.

Four EU member countries—France (38 percent), the United Kingdom (31 percent), Germany (8 percent), and Belgium (8 percent)—accounted for 85 percent of the EU's share of FDI in the region. While the EU is considered the largest of the four partners in terms of FDI, when the EU is disaggregated by country, the United States and France were the largest sources of FDI for sub-Saharan Africa in 2012 at $31 billion each, followed by the United Kingdom with $25 billion. Yet, even though the United States is one of the top contributors of FDI to sub-Saharan Africa, less than

FIGURE 7-3 Sub-Saharan Africa: Share of FDI Stock, 2001 and 2012, and FDI Flows, 2001–12

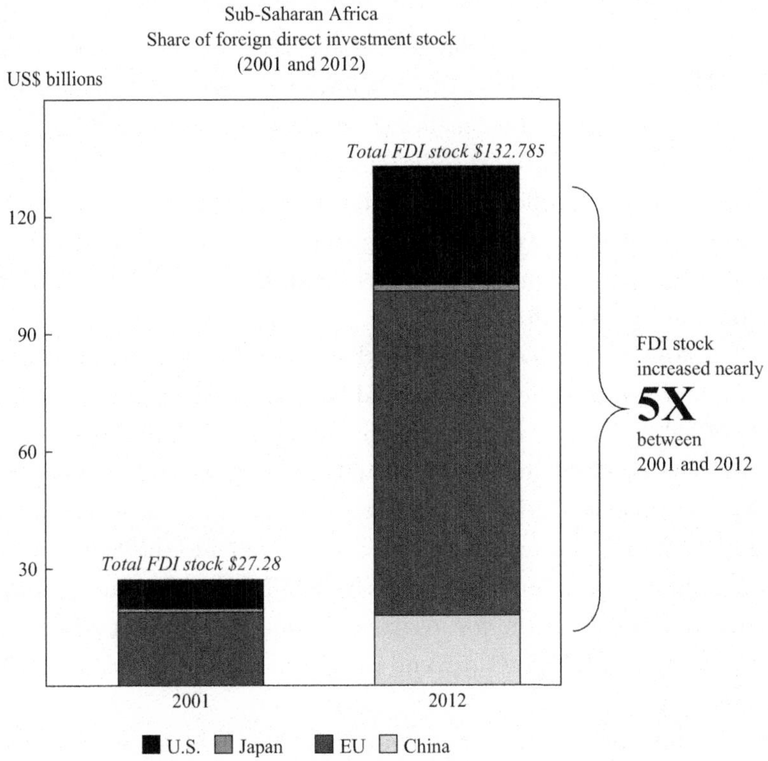

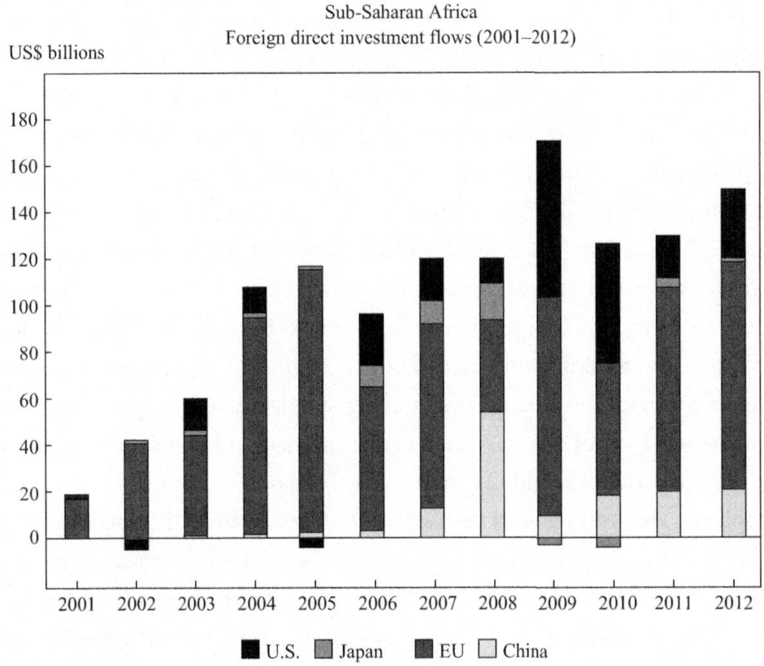

Source: Copley, Rakotondrazaka, and Sy (2014).

1 percent (0.7 percent) of the U.S. global FDI is destined for the region. The United States has primarily invested its $367 billion of FDI in Europe (55 percent), Latin America (13 percent), Canada (8 percent), and other developed countries such as Australia, New Zealand, Israel, and Japan (13 percent collectively). Similarly, the EU and Japan, respectively, directed only 0.8 and 0.2 percent of their FDI toward sub-Saharan African countries. China, on the other hand, invested 3.4 percent of its FDI in the region in 2012.

FDI flows to sub-Saharan Africa have been highly concentrated in only a few countries; South Africa and Nigeria have been the top recipients of sub-Saharan Africa FDI from China, the EU, and the United States. The top destinations for U.S. FDI in the region have been Nigeria (37 percent), South Africa (17 percent), and Mauritius (16 percent). For the EU, South Africa received 68 percent of its FDI to sub-Saharan Africa, and for China, South Africa received 35 percent. For Japan, South Africa has also been the top recipient (at 68 percent), but Mauritius (22 percent) and Liberia (7 percent) each have received sizable shares as well (see figure 7-4).

Predominantly resource-rich countries—South Africa with its precious metals and minerals and Nigeria with its oil reserves—have received a majority of FDI, indicating that natural resources remain a significant factor in attracting investors to the continent. For example, the main sectors in which the United States and China invested in sub-Saharan Africa were the mining and extractive industries, making up approximately 58 percent and 30.6 percent, respectively, of each country's FDI in the region in 2011. However, financial services, manufacturing, and construction also received notable FDI from both countries. China's reported FDI was more diversified than that of U.S. FDI, with 19.5 percent in financial services, 16.4 percent in construction, 15.3 percent in manufacturing, and the remaining 18.2 percent in business and tech services, geological prospecting, wholesale retail, agriculture, and real estate. U.S. FDI was 12 percent in finance and insurance, 5 percent in manufacturing, and 25 percent in other industries. Despite this emphasis on mining and extractive industries in 2012, according to UNCTAD's *World Investment Report 2014* (United Nations Conference on Trade and Development, 2014b), international investors have been increasingly looking to new opportunities in consumer-oriented sectors

FIGURE 7-4 Top Five Recipients of FDI, 2001–12

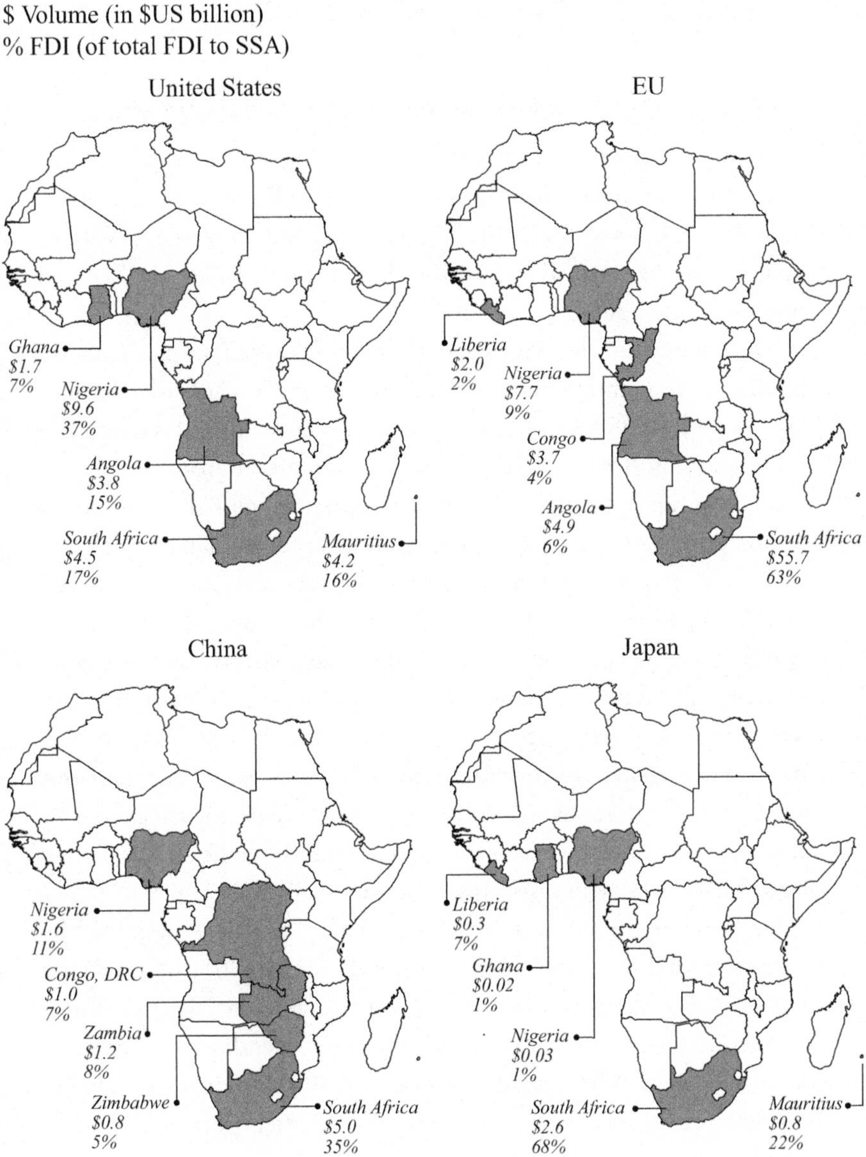

Source: Copley, Rakotondrazaka, and Sy (2014).

(such as information technology, food, financial services, and wholesale retail) that target the region's expanding middle class.

Investors' Pledge for Good Governance in Sub-Saharan Africa

Along with the appetite for mineral resources, energy, and other returns that drew massive investment into Africa, my colleagues and I (Copley, Rakotondrazaka, and Sy, 2014) compared the status of the quality of governance in the countries where the United States, Japan, the EU, and China invested in 2012.

Investing in countries with relatively higher governance performance can reflect at least three concerns: (1) the investors' level of risk aversion, (2) the pursuit of democratic principles or a nonideological relationship based on noninterference, and (3) the level of pressure from global consumers, who increasingly make choices along the global value chains based on governance indicators, such as respect for human rights.

We used the World Governance Indicators for 2012, produced by Kaufman, Kraay, and Mastruzzi (2011), which cover six dimensions of governance: voice accountability, rule of law, government effectiveness, political stability, regulatory quality, and control of corruption (see figure 7-5). The governance index ranges from −2.5 (weakest) to 2.5 (strongest governance performance). In 2012, Botswana and Mauritius topped the list with respective scores of governance performance of 0.71 and 0.66, and Zimbabwe and the Democratic Republic of the Congo were at the bottom with respective scores of −1.35 and −1.74.

Our computed levels of average governance indicators (weighted by the share of total FDI in the host countries between 2001 and 2012) are comparable across the EU, the United States, and China. Japan's investment is concentrated in South Africa, where the overall governance performance is high. When we disaggregate the EU by individual member countries, France has the largest share of investment in countries with the lowest levels of governance.

Given its focus on oil-producing countries with low governance levels, the United States is comparable to other regions. Importantly, however, the U.S. Dodd-Frank Act requires public disclosure of payments at the project level from listed companies involved in extractive industries. Other initiatives require companies to eliminate conflict minerals from

FIGURE 7-5 Governance Indicator of Recipients of FDI by Partner Country

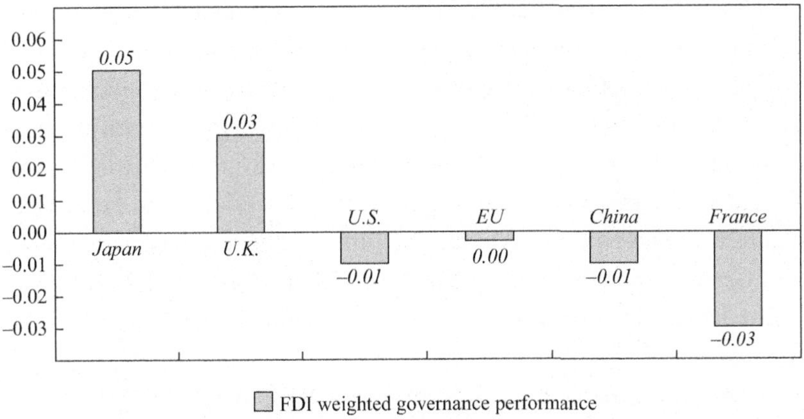

Source: Copley, Rakotondrazaka, and Sy (2014).

their supply chains. For instance, the use of coltan originating from the Democratic Republic of the Congo and neighboring countries is effectively banned. UNCTAD data actually show no record of U.S. investment stock in the Democratic Republic of the Congo from 2007 onward. The EU has a similar set of policies manifested in its Accounting and Transparency Directives. Furthermore, the United States, along with China, the EU, and Japan, is a participant in the Kimberley Process, which has banned the sale of "blood diamonds." Other transparency initiatives supported by the United States have included the Extractive Industries Transparency Initiative, the International Tropical Timber Organization, and the International Chamber of Commerce Rules on Combating Corruption.

Engagement through Bilateral Investment Treaties

Bilateral investment treaties (BITs) are agreements signed between countries aiming to promote FDI by ensuring certain guarantees—against expropriation, for example—for investors in unstable business environments. BITs are low-cost options to encourage business climate reform while simultaneously signaling investor commitment to host countries and providing them with policy space to design and implement their development agendas. These BITs and other international investment arrangements have proliferated over the past fifty years: the total number of BITs globally reached 2,902 in 2013, with the number of sub-Saharan Africa BITs accounting for at least 300 of these treaties.

Sub-Saharan Africa's partners vary significantly in the number and distribution of BITs with the continent. China has BITs with twenty-seven sub-Saharan African countries, signing ten in the past ten years. For the EU, member countries negotiate BITs bilaterally, and France has eighteen in sub-Saharan Africa, the United Kingdom has twenty-one, and Germany has thirty-nine. The United States has six, and Japan has only one. So why is the United States so far behind in the number of BITs it has enacted?

According to Benjamin Leo from the Center for Global Development, it is in part due to the United States' limited "negotiating capacity"—it has only a few foreign commercial officers on the ground to negotiate these treaties, whereas the EU and China have distributed delegations of commercial attachés at offices and embassies in nearly all African countries. The United States has also focused its efforts on establishing trade and investment framework agreements in the region, which provide a forum for discussions on trade and investment but do not confer protections on investors or indicate a serious commitment to host countries because they are not legally binding. Furthermore, the U.S. BIT model, which it uses in its negotiations, is a very dense and complicated legal document and difficult for many countries to review and discuss without adequate legal support (which some lack). These compounding factors hinder the United States from establishing mutually beneficial investment agreements with countries in sub-Saharan Africa (Leo, 2014).

Policy Recommendations

There is ample scope to expand the U.S. investment strategy with Africa. The United States funnels less than 1 percent of its FDI into the region, and it invests mostly in only a few countries and sectors. While the perceived risks of investing in Africa have historically been high, rates of return have also proved to be high, averaging 11.4 percent on inward FDI for the period from 2006 to 2011 (compared with 5 percent for developed countries). The United Nations Conference on Trade and Development's *World Investment Report 2013* also reported that four of the top twenty economies with the highest rates of return on inward FDI in 2011 were in sub-Saharan Africa.

One way the United States can increase FDI to sub-Saharan Africa is through the promotion of BITs. African countries are seriously engaging in the negotiation of BITs: among the most active countries at concluding BITs in 2013 (globally) were Mauritius and Tanzania, each concluding three BITs. The United States should reciprocate this engagement by focusing its efforts on implementing sustainable development–oriented, legally binding BITs rather than trade and investment framework agreements; providing technical assistance to reform business environments and reduce the cost of doing business; and establishing BITs with strategic countries like Nigeria. With China and the EU continuing to sign BITs, the United States risks being locked out of certain markets and industries.

So-called blended initiatives, such as Power Africa, offer another useful model to increase investment through partnerships between the African private sector, U.S. government agencies, African governments, and other partners like multilateral institutions such as the African Development Bank. At the same time, African policymakers should engage the U.S. authorities and its private sector to do the following:

- Get more transfer of knowledge and skills from FDI. For example, policymakers can provide incentives for investors to include local businesses in the value chain and invest in education and training;
- Reduce illicit financial flows from tax evasion, the underpricing of concessions, and trade mispricing; and
- Strengthen African common institutions. For instance, the Africa Investment Initiative of the New Partnership for Africa's Development and Organization for Economic Cooperation and Development aims to raise the profile of Africa as an investment destination while facilitating regional cooperation and has led to a number of investment policy reviews in four South African Development Community countries (Mozambique, Botswana, Tanzania, and Mauritius).

THE U.S.-AFRICA LEADERS SUMMIT: FAR FROM "BUNGLED"

As the clock ticked down to the first U.S.-Africa Leaders Summit, the level of expectation was ramping up as to what the summit would deliver. *Foreign Policy*'s Gordon Lubold (2014) distilled views from Africa experts in an article that did not make for encouraging reading. But while the article did a good job of building a discussion around this important event, it makes the common mistake of focusing too heavily on China's engagement with the continent and ignores the key successes of the summit in the process.

Here is where I disagree with *Foreign Policy*:

Argument 1: African Leaders Will Compare Their Treatment at the U.S. Summit with the Way They Are Received by China's Leadership

It is true that, unlike his Chinese counterpart, President Obama did not have one-on-one meetings with his African guests. Holding bilateral meetings would have been a "first-best" solution, but it will not be a deal breaker. African leaders came to Washington, D.C., because they saw the benefits in engaging the U.S. administration on key economic and political issues. Furthermore, the format of the Summit Leader Meetings allowed a broad, constructive dialogue that helped President Obama play his role as a welcoming host. AGI and I had suggested that, in addition, bilateral meetings with the leaders of the African Union and the Regional Economic Communities would be important.

Argument 2: The United States Is Too Late, and China Is Winning

It is true that China has been holding summits with African leaders since 2000. But the United States coming late to the summit game does not mean it is losing the continent. In fact, the loss of U.S. competiveness relative to China is often blown out of proportion. China is very active on the continent, and most of the recent growth in aid, trade, and investment to Africa can be attributed to China. China is now Africa's largest bilateral trade partner. But the United States has a long-standing economic relationship with the continent. The potential for more U.S. FDI is huge, given that less than 1 percent of U.S. global FDI is destined for the region. While China invested 3.4 percent of its FDI in the region in 2012, that accounts for only $18 billion (or up to $21 billion, depending on the data source) compared to the United States' $31 billion in FDI.

Argument 3: The Business Forum Will Not Lead to Major Deals and Therefore Is of Limited Value

I also did not expect the major deals that were pledged, but the United States had an opportunity to shape how the U.S. private sector could engage the continent. Obama's Power Africa initiative aimed at strengthening the role of the U.S. private sector in energy projects on the continent. At a time when the aid community is recalibrating its model toward more blended programs that leverage the public sector's role to partner with the private sector, Power Africa is a welcome innovation. In addition, commitments from the U.S. and African private sector have already been announced. The U.S.-Africa Leaders Summit was not the beginning of a process but rather another important step in ongoing U.S. engagement with Africa. It built on a number of meetings such as the U.S.-Africa Energy Ministerial in Addis Ababa or Commerce Secretary Penny Pritzker's visit to the continent in 2014. President Obama's scheduled presence at the business forum showed its importance for the U.S. administration.

Argument 4: African Leaders Will Resent the U.S. Message on Human Rights

I find this argument difficult to digest. First, the United States has been consistent in its message to strengthen governance, defend human rights, and promote democracy, so this should come as no surprise to African leaders. Secretary of State John Kerry's visit to the Democratic Republic of Congo is a good illustration of the U.S. stance on such matters. But why focus only on how African leaders may feel? How about African citizens, civil society organizations, and members of opposition political parties? The U.S.-Africa Leaders Summit was an opportunity to have a genuine conversation about difficult and sensitive issues. Future generations of Africans deserve such a debate. And while China may have no qualms doing business with countries with dubious human rights records, it refuses to invite countries that recognize Taiwan to its summit.

THE U.S.-AFRICA LEADERS SUMMIT: FINAL THOUGHTS

In Obama's speech to the Ghanaian parliament in Accra in 2009, he mentioned a need for a true partnership "grounded in mutual responsibility and mutual respect." My colleagues and I recommended, similarly, that the first U.S. summit be designed to create a sustainable policy tool that is inclusive and accountable. Indeed, Africa is a region that is increasingly gaining mutual respect from world partners. The real GDP in sub-Saharan Africa grew at a much faster rate than the GDP for the rest of the world over the ten years prior to the 2014 U.S.-Africa Leaders Summit. Africa has made great strides in reducing poverty and mortality indicators—which was reflected in the proposed U.S. official development assistance budget for fiscal year 2015, in which the priorities for assistance shifted from health and education to peace, security, governance, and economic growth. The United States has increased its military presence in Africa, and there is demand for foreign intervention to halt terrorism across the region; however, Americans are fatigued by interventions in Afghanistan and Iraq. Thus, the summit had a key role to play in helping Americans overcome their military lassitude to focus on governance, peace, and security priorities in Africa.

In his Accra speech, Obama mentioned that the United States can do more to promote trade and investment in African countries. U.S. investors face an evolving landscape of foreign investment in Africa, though total FDI to Africa is still relatively low compared with world FDI totals in Asia. Now, China and other emerging market countries are driving growth in FDI to Africa. Meanwhile, compared to China, the United States has a small presence of trade facilitation support on the ground in Africa. However, the U.S. trade preferences extended under the African Growth and Opportunity Act (AGOA) have produced increased trade and investment in some African industries, such as textiles. The summit also housed the U.S. AGOA forum, a yearly event during which African leaders and U.S. officials review enhancements for the trade preference program and discuss a more cohesive strategy for AGOA in the future.

As stated by the late Brookings AGI director Mwangi Kimenyi (2013), it is necessary to define the parameters of a successful U.S.-Africa summit before holding the event. One indicator of particular importance to AGI that my colleagues and I highlighted is fruitful participation of Africa's leaders in the summit. The U.S.-Africa summit is an unprecedented opportunity to transform U.S. strategy toward Africa into a mutually beneficial U.S.-Africa strategy.

THE U.S.-AFRICA LEADERS SUMMIT: MAJOR TRENDS IN MEDIA COVERAGE

The historic U.S.-Africa Leaders Summit, held August 4–6, 2014, resulted in some remarkable achievements, including investment deals totaling a massive $33 billion and a new peacekeeping partnership with six African countries. While the summit garnered some attention over the course of the week, the tragic Ebola outbreak (and other international events, including the violence in Gaza, Iraq, and Ukraine) also captured public attention and dominated media headlines.

To understand the extent to which dynamic, global events such as the Ebola outbreak may have influenced or even overshadowed media coverage of the first-ever U.S.-Africa Leaders Summit, the AGI team conducted a brief study examining headlines of major newspapers as well as overall tweets during the week of the summit.

The top five keywords in the headlines of Africa-related articles (that is, articles with the word "Africa" or one of its variations in the headline or leading paragraph) of thirty major U.S., African, and international publications were "Ebola," "United States," "summit," "Obama," and "leaders."

Variation in Coverage among U.S., International, and African Publications

Of the 698 Africa-related articles published by our selected sources, U.S., international, and African newspapers, respectively, published 366, 161, and 171 articles. Table 7-1 shows the top five keywords in the headlines of the U.S., African, and international publications.

"Ebola" was the most widely used keyword across all publications, with U.S., international, and African sources, respectively, mentioning it in 36, 31, and 17 percent of the headlines for the week. "Summit," on the other hand, featured prominently in approximately 14 percent of U.S.

TABLE 7-1 Top Five Keywords in Percent of All Headlines of Select U.S., African, and International Sources, August 3–8, 2014

U.S. Press	International Press	African Press
Ebola (36%)	Ebola (31%)	Ebola (17%)
Summit (14%)	China (11%)	Summit (6%)
United States (13%)	United States (11%)	United States–Africa (6%)
Leaders (9%)	Help (4%)	Nigerian (6%)
Obama (9%)	Virus (4%)	Leaders (4%)

headlines but showed up only in 6 percent of African and 3 percent of international headlines. "China" was the second-most frequently cited keyword in headlines published by the international press—in 11 percent of headlines, with a few more mentions than "U.S."—however, "China" appeared in less than 1 percent of U.S. headlines and not at all in the African headlines, both of which appeared to prioritize stories on the United States and U.S.-Africa relations. African sources on the other hand highlighted "Nigerian" in 6 percent of their headlines. Across all publications, "trade" and "investment" appeared hardly at all, in 2 percent or less of headlines that were examined, despite trade and investment being the central pillars of the summit.

Did Business-Focused Publications Cover the Summit Differently than General Publications?

In the three business-focused sources—the *Wall Street Journal* (United States), the *Financial Times* (United Kingdom), and *Business Day* (South Africa)—I found 159 articles related to Africa during the week of the summit. Although these business-focused publications covered Ebola slightly less than non-business-centric publications (focusing more on Ghana's debt and IMF loan instead), Ebola-related headlines still made up over a quarter of the headlines written in business-focused publications that week. (Although "virus" features prominently in the business-focused publications, in only one case was the word not paired with "Ebola," meaning it does not significantly increase the number of articles covering the disease.)

FIGURE 7-6 Number of Tweets per Day Using Africa, Ebola, and Summit-Related Hashtags, July 15–August 13, 2014

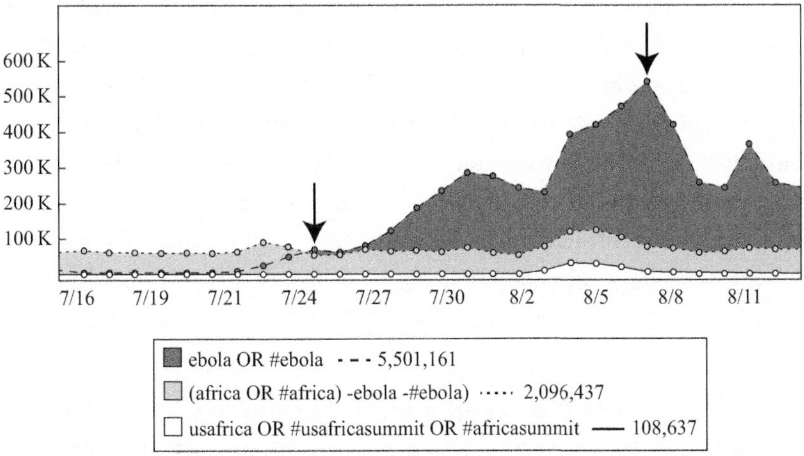

Analytics by TOPSY

"Africa, but not Ebola" tweets peaked at about 100,000 tweets per day during the U.S.-Africa Leaders Summit, starting their ascent approximately the Sunday before the three-day event. Hashtags associated with the summit exhibited a brief peak (at less than 50,000 tweets per day) that started their rise on the Sunday before the event. On the Thursday after the summit, "Ebola" tweets were increasing to a peak of over 500,000 tweets per day, but "Africa, but not Ebola" tweets and summit hashtags were already decreasing. The Monday after the summit (August 11, 2014), the "Ebola" tweets peaked again at nearly 400,000 tweets per day, while "Africa, but not Ebola" tweets and summit-related hashtags returned to pre-summit levels.

Changes in the Public's Attention on Africa during the Summit

Looking at tweets related to the U.S.-Africa Leaders Summit, Ebola, and Africa in the weeks before and after the summit, we see that tweets mentioning "Ebola" did not surpass tweets mentioning "Africa, but not Ebola" until July 25, 2014, when a U.S. citizen, Patrick Sawyer, died of Ebola in Nigeria (see the leftmost arrow on the time line in figure 7-6). In addition, around this time, two Americans working for Samaritan's Purse contracted the Ebola virus.

Concluding Thoughts

During the week of the U.S.-Africa Leaders Summit, media coverage of Africa-related news did not highlight issues of trade and investment as much as the summit's organizers might have hoped. Nor did the summit have the staying power to outlast the unfolding story of the Ebola outbreak. Since the Obama administration planned for a recurring U.S.-Africa Leaders Summit to serve as a key policy tool for future engagement and dialogue with the continent, extending the dialogue past the end of the summit when it was clouded by the Ebola outbreak was of utmost importance.

THE U.S.-AFRICA BUSINESS FORUM: ASSESSING PROGRESS AND CONSIDERING THE STAKES

Two years after the first U.S.-Africa Leaders Summit and the U.S.-Africa Business Forum brought together U.S. and African CEOs in addition to heads of state and government, the United States convened a second U.S.-Africa Business Forum on September 21, 2016, in New York City. Co-hosted by Bloomberg Philanthropies and the U.S. Department of Commerce, the forum emphasized opportunities for expanding U.S.-Africa business, trade, and investment ties in key sectors positioned for growth, such as finance and capital investment, infrastructure, power and energy, agriculture, consumer goods, and information communication technology. At the inaugural forum in 2014, nearly 150 CEOs from U.S. and African companies announced more than $33 billion in new deals—thus highlighting Africa as a strategic business and investment destination. In 2016, the forum delved further into the question "How do you effectively do business in Africa?" It also served as an opportunity to assess how far the United States has come in fulfilling its commitments from the last forum to the continent.

Progress in U.S.-Africa Trade and Investment Initiatives

So where did U.S.-supported economic goals in Africa stand two years after the inaugural forum? To answer this question, my colleagues and I examined some of the commitments made at the 2014 forum and discussed their progress and outcomes to date.

Translating the energy and positivity from the first U.S.-Africa Business Forum into concrete trade and investment gains was no doubt an arduous task. Many of the initiatives stemming from the first forum required immense political or technical lifts to be operationalized. For example, common roadblocks to large infrastructure—including energy projects—are standards, procurement, taxes, and project financing, which require technical expertise and coordination with local partners and sometimes regional and multilateral stakeholders. Implementation has been notably slow in some respects, as various U.S. government agencies are attempting to simultaneously address multiple, complex, and mutually reinforcing facets to doing business in Africa. Ultimately, implementation of these projects depends not only on U.S. leadership but largely on support from national systems and local political will too. Despite the slowdowns, however, there is still a general acknowledgment among U.S. business leaders that the conditions for doing business in Africa are progressively improving and there is "money to be made" in the continent.

Several important achievements have been reached: For instance, as a part of the Trade Africa initiative, the United States signed a cooperation agreement, "Trade Facilitation, Sanitary and Phytosanitary Measures, and Technical Barriers to Trade," with the East African Community in February 2015. This agreement aims to advance East African Community partner states' ability to meet international quality and safety standards by improving the countries' technical regulations, standards, testing, and certification systems. Furthermore, in June 2015, President Obama signed the AGOA Extension and Enhancement Act of 2015 into law, extending the act for ten years. The act builds on the 2015 AGOA to allow the Millennium Challenge Corporation to make regional compacts possible and encourage regional trade-capacity-building efforts in Africa. So far, it seems progress has been made in implementing policies to meet trade-oriented goals, including both demand-side (tariffs, quotas, and so on) and supply-side constraints (trade capacity, international standards, and so on). Power Africa, another key initiative of the Obama administration, has continued expanding energy access on the continent with some promising results, and with the enactment of the Electrify Africa Act in February 2016, U.S. support for ending energy poverty in Africa has become law.

On the business front, the U.S. Department of Commerce doubled its presence in sub-Saharan Africa: It established new offices in Angola,

Tanzania, Ethiopia, and Mozambique; expanded its operations in Ghana; and reinstated a position at the African Development Bank. In turn, it increased the number of foreign commercial service officers in the region who provide crucial support to U.S. and African firms, including counseling and technical assistance. It also held a number of events across the continent and in the United States—including the Trade Winds Business Forum and trade missions in eight African countries—to connect U.S. firms with local decisionmakers and business opportunities. Meanwhile, the Department of Commerce's Presidential Advisory Council on Doing Business in Africa led a fact-finding mission to Nigeria and Rwanda to learn from local stakeholders how U.S. government programs and policies can better support economic engagement between the United States and the region. From these visits, as well as several council meetings, the group compiled a series of in-depth reports, identifying the key successes and gaps of U.S.-Africa business relations and providing guidance on future engagement.

From Action to Outcomes: A Complicated Picture

These notable policy achievements, however, are not necessarily reflected in the latest figures on trade outcomes between the United States and Africa. According to the IMF Direction of Trade Statistics,[4] exports from the United States to African countries *decreased* overall, from $25.1 billion in 2014 to $17.5 billion in 2015, mostly due to huge declines in U.S. exports to Nigeria, South Africa, Angola, Togo, and Kenya. The drop in U.S. exports to Africa could be somewhat explained by the lower-growth environment in the region, generally reducing demand for exports. Similarly, African imports to the United States decreased from $26.7 billion in 2014 to $18.8 billion in 2015, with the largest declines in imports from oil exporters Angola, Nigeria, and Chad. Over the same period, the United States began shifting away from importing oil from African countries in favor of domestically produced oil. While these declines might seem to signal bad news for U.S.-Africa trade, U.S. exports to and imports from other areas of the world (excluding the region) also declined from 2014 to 2015 as did global trade, indicating a broader

4 See www.imf.org/en/Data.

slump across the international trading system, resulting from lower commodity prices as well as China's diminished growth and import demand.

In terms of investment, according to Ernst & Young's 2016 Africa Attractiveness Program, the United States was the largest investor on the continent in terms of number of greenfield FDI projects in 2015, retaining its top position from the previous year—despite a 4 percent decline in projects. Unfortunately, taking a more granular look at the projects and specifically attempting to track the progress of deals reached during the 2014 forum is extremely difficult, except when individual companies choose to publicize their follow-up or they receive coverage from business reporters. For example, at the last forum, Coca-Cola announced that it would invest $5 billion over the next six years in Africa to fund new manufacturing lines and to create additional jobs across the supply chain. In June 2016, the firm opened a bottling plant in Mozambique, and later that month, in a merger with SABMiller and Gutsche Family Investment (Coca-Cola Beverages Africa), it announced that the new African company will expand services to fourteen African countries and create more than thirty bottling plants throughout the continent. As the case of Coca-Cola shows, firms are implementing their promises across the continent, although it is difficult to gauge to what extent companies have followed through on their stated commitments.

Expectations and Recommendations for the Second U.S.-Africa Business Forum

The U.S.-Africa Business Forum series provides an excellent platform for launching a conversation, but it requires concrete follow-up from all stakeholders to initiate action. Given the brevity of the forum, it is important for both U.S. and African partners to come to the table prepared—with strategies highlighting their key requests and the mutual benefits afforded to all partners—in order to take full advantage of their time together. Moreover, presenting updates on the investments and deals made at the inaugural forum in 2016 and publishing them on the forum website would provide greater transparency on these initiatives and allow U.S. and African companies to benefit from the lessons learned in various country- and sector-specific contexts.

It is also important for the right mix of leaders to connect during the forum in order to achieve the specific goals outlined by the administration through its Doing Business in Africa campaign—one of which includes job creation in the United States and Africa. While it was expected that the usual suspects from large African multinationals would attend, it was not clear whether African small and medium enterprises would be adequately represented at the forum. Considering that 66–80 percent of the formal employment in the region is in small and medium enterprises and that 50 percent of job creation comes from enterprises with fewer than 100 employees, it is crucial that these players be considered active and vital contributors to Africa's thriving business community and invited to the forum as well. That being said, it is worth noting that the United States does recognize the value of African small and medium enterprises through other means, including a wide array of development programming and the Global Entrepreneurship summit for business leaders and entrepreneurs, which was held in Kenya in 2015.

Lastly, ensuring adequate support for U.S. investors and firms in Africa is imperative if the deals reached at the forum are to be successfully implemented. A larger presence of foreign commercial service officers, commerce specialists, and similar embassy support throughout the continent could facilitate many of the issues related to deal flow, legal regulations, and customs that currently are bottlenecks to greater U.S. business investment. Providing targeted support for deals related to the Power Africa initiative and ensuring coordination with the regional Southern Africa Trade Hub and the East and West Africa Trade and Investment Hubs would help simultaneously achieve U.S. and African business and development objectives.

In conclusion, irrespective of our expectations for beyond the forum, U.S. administrations should keep building on the momentum behind U.S.-Africa business and investment promotion and follow through on the expert recommendations identified by the President's Advisory Council on Doing Business in Africa.

THE AFRICAN GROWTH AND OPPORTUNITY ACT

The African Growth and Opportunity Act is a trade preference that has been in place since 2000 and that gives preferential access to the U.S. market to sub-Saharan African countries if they are eligible with respect to democracy, governance, and so on. The legislation, originally signed into law by President Bill Clinton, was extended for ten years in 2015 by President Barack Obama.

Here I examine one example of the potential trade effects of AGOA, taking a slightly different look at how the trade preference is designed and how it could affect the economic diversification and growth of different export sectors. The policy analysis is useful as African countries attempt to better use the legislation and as the United States considers any changes or revisions to the trade preference.

The African Growth and Opportunity Act and Dutch Disease: Madagascar

The suspension of Madagascar's AGOA privileges following its 2009 coup offered a natural experiment that allows analysts to study the effect of a tariff preference program on the recipient developing country and its subsequent removal. The situation provides two distinct but comparable states: One with preferential access (2001–09—the "AGOA years") and the other without (2010–14—the "sanction years").

Using readily available bilateral trade data from the U.S. Department of Commerce and the U.S. International Trade Commission to investigate Madagascar's export performance in each of those two periods generates a number of useful and interesting insights.

My coauthor, Soamiely Andriamananjara and I (2015) find, not surprisingly, that Madagascar's total exports to the United States declined following the loss of AGOA eligibility. However, a closer look at the composition of total exports shows that not all sectors were negatively affected by the sanctions. In particular, textile exports to the United States, which surged under AGOA, fell abruptly, while nonapparel and clothing exports gradually increased.

The evolution of Madagascar's exports to the United States during the AGOA years, can be summarized as follows:

- The preferential access to U.S. markets, enhanced by the generous rules of origin, led to a boom in textile exports.
- As the textile industry boomed, productive resources were drawn away from the rest of the economy and to the textile export processing zones.
- At the same time, the local currency (the ariary) started to appreciate, thereby hurting the competitiveness of the rest of the economy.
- As a result of the reallocation of resources and the real appreciation, nonapparel exports (such as other manufactured products or coffee, tea, and spices) declined significantly, leading to a decline in overall exports between 2004 and 2009.

During the sanction years, the textile sector drastically shrank, and it seems that the resources and factors of production (labor) were reallocated to the rest of the economy. As a result, although total exports to the United States fell immediately following the loss of access to U.S. markets for the textile sector, they gradually expanded as nontextile exports started to increase after 2010.

These sectoral dynamics during both periods are reminiscent of the "Dutch disease," which afflicts economies that experience a sharp inflow of foreign currency following booming exports in one sector, such as oil, leading to a currency appreciation and loss of export competitiveness in other sectors. Let me elaborate: As one would expect, the trade sanctions had negative impacts on the Malagasy economy. Madagascar's total exports to the United States dropped significantly—by 56 percent—following the loss of AGOA eligibility. Exports decreased from an average of $312 million per year during the AGOA years to an average $136 million during sanction years, without AGOA. In addition, thousands of jobs were lost as individuals were laid off.

The data also reveal that, during the AGOA years, only 70 percent (an average of $216 million) of Madagascar's yearly exports actually entered the United States using preferential tariffs. The remaining 30 percent entered on a most favored nation basis (that is, no preferences).

The quasi-totality of the Malagasy exports that entered the United States under AGOA preferences was composed of articles of apparel and clothing accessories. This concentration was strongly facilitated by the third-party-fabric rule of origin, which allows least-developed AGOA beneficiaries to use yarn and fabric from any country. It is not surprising that when Madagascar lost its privileges, its apparel and clothing exports to the United States dropped sharply—by 85 percent. This sectoral concentration of benefits has some important economic implications.

While the drop in the clothing exports is quite predictable and intuitive, it is the evolution of sectors other than apparel and clothing that illustrates an interesting trend. In fact, at first glance, the data seem to suggest that by generating a boom in the Malagasy apparel and clothing sector, AGOA might have inadvertently caused other important sectors to shrink. The boom has, at least partially, led to an appreciation of the ariary during the AGOA years and hurt the competitiveness of those other sectors. Actually, it is possible that AGOA may have caused some kind of Dutch disease in Madagascar.

While apparel and clothing exports boomed during the AGOA years, exports in other sectors actually decreased sharply in both absolute and relative terms. Other sectors' exports dropped from $119 million to $36 million between 2002 and 2009, and their share of total exports decreased from 57 percent to 15 percent. This change could have been caused by various factors, but one obvious suspect is the shift toward the booming sector, away from the (possibly more efficient) rest of the economy. As a result, total exports decreased between 2004 and 2009.

One can also find some complementary evidence of this resource movement by looking at the sanction years. Total exports more than doubled, from $103 million in 2010 to an estimated $213 million in 2014, while the sanctions were in place. Decomposing this trend reveals that the jump in total exports was driven by exports in sectors other than apparel and clothing, which increased by 300 percent, from $48 million in 2010 to an estimated $194 million in 2014 (admittedly, this was also driven by the new nickel exports). During that period, exports of apparel and clothing dropped by 65 percent. This change suggests that when Madagascar lost its AGOA privileges, some resources and factors of production released by the shrinking textile sector may have moved to other (possibly more efficient) sectors in the rest of the economy.

One obvious policy implication of the case of Madagascar is that trade preferences should be as comprehensive and inclusive as possible in terms of sectors. The discussion suggests that the impact of AGOA, while broadly positive, has been concentrated in too few sectors. The current focus on apparel and clothing (boosted by the third-party rules of origin) can lead to perverse effects if excessive resource shifts and significant real exchange rate appreciation results. The boom of the beneficiary sectors may have had some unintended negative consequences on other nonbeneficiary sectors in the economy—possibly a Dutch disease–type of impact, which can lead to undesirable overall outcomes.

THE IMPORTANCE OF THE U.S. EXPORT-IMPORT BANK FOR SUB-SAHARAN AFRICA

The Export-Import (Ex-Im) Bank of the United States is the nation's official export credit agency and finances the export of U.S. goods and services to foreign markets. The bank operates under a renewable general statutory charter and is thus authorized through congressional legislation. When the bank's most recent charter was up for renewal in 2014, there was a great deal of controversy regarding its role. Some opponents called it corporate welfare, claimed it cost too much, or said it was no longer needed and the private sector could fill its role. Mike O'Hanlon and David Petraeus (2014) made a noteworthy rebuttal to these claims. While its mandate was reauthorized through September 30, 2019, it may again face a similar reauthorization debate at that time, making the takeaway from the following particularly relevant to consider in future policy discussions.

What the Ex-Im Bank Means for U.S. Businesses in Sub-Saharan Africa

When the Ex-Im Bank was up for reauthorization it attracted an unprecedented amount of controversy in Congress. The Ex-Im Bank, which finances the export of U.S. goods and services to foreign markets, is critical and relevant for supporting U.S. trade—now more than ever in the increasingly competitive global market. It is particularly relevant when doing business with emerging markets, where export and import credit is hard to come by or insufficient for some large-scale projects. And it's especially important to U.S. businesses working in regions like sub-

Saharan Africa, where there is a global rush to do more business. Sub-Saharan Africa is, in fact, one of the three congressionally mandated areas of focus for the Ex-Im Bank. Thus, the bank's role in supporting U.S. business in Africa and, through this, African development, should be taken into consideration as its reauthorization is debated.

To give a broad overview, most leading economies have export credit agencies (ECAs) playing a similar role to that of the Ex-Im Bank. For example, the Berne Union, which is a global union of export credit and investment companies, has forty-nine member companies from all around the world. The Ex-Im Bank in particular serves as an especially effective example of an ECA: It does not cost U.S. taxpayers money, given its low delinquency rates, and it received the highest award among global ECAs for the second time in 2013 from the magazine *Trade Finance*. The Ex-Im Bank, in fact, earns money for the U.S. government; over the last five years it has earned $2 billion for U.S. taxpayers and has supported the existence of 1.2 million jobs.

> The Bank has financed the sale of more than $200 billion in U.S. exports over the last six years [2009–14] supporting over 1.3 million private-sector American jobs, including 164,000 jobs in Fiscal Year 2014 alone. Last year, Ex-Im financed the sale of $27.5 billion in exports through more than 3,700 transactions, including nearly $16.6 billion in manufacturing exports—and jobs supported by exports are good jobs, paying up to 18 percent more on average than other jobs. (White House, Office of the Press Secretary, 2015)

In the same announcement, the White House also countered the argument that Ex-Im is corporate welfare, explaining that of the 7,500 businesses supported by the bank, two-thirds of them are small businesses. Similarly, in fiscal year 2014, 90 percent of the bank's transactions directly supported American small businesses.

Trade experts are similarly mystified as to why many in the private sector want Ex-Im to go away. As quoted in the *Washington Times*, Miriam Sapiro, a nonresident senior fellow with Brookings, noted that getting rid of the bank makes "little sense as a cost-saving measure because it is funded by the interest it receives from its loans" (quoted in Johnson and Howell, 2014). In addition, she added, the Treasury Department receives any extra money at the end of the fiscal year. And default rates? They stand at just over 0.175 percent. And what of American competitiveness? Sapiro noted that getting rid of Ex-Im could hurt American competitiveness, stating, "China would be delighted to see Ex-Im go away." Even Chinese officials have admitted so.

What the Ex-Im Bank Means for Sub-Saharan Africa

When it comes to Africa, the Ex-Im Bank's efforts on the continent are ever expanding; in 2013, it financed a record 188 transactions in Africa with authorizations totaling over $600 million supporting exports in thirty-five of forty-nine sub-Saharan African countries. In 2014, fiscal year 2014 the Ex-Im Bank authorized $2.0 billion for sub-Saharan Africa, a historical high (this figure dropped to $38.2 million in in fiscal year 2017) (Export-Import Bank of the United States, 2017). Its website notes that the majority of its authorizations for sub-Saharan Africa benefit "small-business exporters of spare parts, consumer goods and other products" through short-term export credit insurance, which is contrary to notions that the Ex-Im Bank supports only big businesses.

The Ex-Im Bank works across a range of sectors on the continent, with many large-scale transactions supporting needed infrastructure and construction work, including exports geared at transportation, power, and port-related equipment. Highlights from its most recent annual report include authorizations of $155 million toward exports needed for a hospital expansion project in Ghana; $108 million for locomotive kits for a rail, port, and pipeline company in South Africa; and $15.7 million for firefighting trucks to Nigeria. In 2012, almost $300 million in authorizations went to small-business-supported exports.

Thus, the work the Ex-Im Bank is doing is important not only to U.S. companies looking to export to the continent but also to the communities buying U.S. goods. The bank's 2013 annual report goes into detail about the loan to Ghana to finance American exports for a hospital expansion project in the capital, stating that the hospital will serve as the primary hospital for greater Accra and be "among the most advanced medical facilities in West Africa" (Export-Import Bank of the United States, 2013).

Moreover, the Ex-Im Bank works with multiple U.S. government initiatives focused on U.S.-Africa business and African development. It is part of the U.S. Department of Commerce's Doing Business in Africa campaign, which is working to enhance U.S.-Africa business, and also part of the U.S.-Africa Clean Energy Development and Finance Center, which is a coordinated interagency approach to promote development of clean energy on the continent. The Ex-Im Bank has also played an important role as part of President Obama's Power Africa initiative, where it works with other U.S. agencies—the U.S. Agency for International Development, the U.S. Trade and Development Agency, the Overseas Private Investment Corporation, the Department of State, and the Department of Energy—with the goal of doubling sub-Saharan Africa's access to electricity.

If the Ex-Im Bank ceased to exist, it is possible that some projects couldn't proceed or would be delayed because of unavailability of financing or similar constraints, but what is more likely is that one of the many big players outside the United States would be the partner of choice instead. During the reauthorization debate, Tom Donohue, president and CEO of the U.S. Chamber of Commerce, and Jay Timmons, president and CEO of the U.S. National Association of Manufacturers, issued a statement that said, "If Ex-Im is not reauthorized, products of all shapes and sizes, from planes to medical equipment, will still be purchased overseas. They just will not be produced in the U.S. by American workers" (Donohue and Timmons, 2014). The Ex-Im Bank is facilitating partnerships with U.S. and African businesses that could not exist or be financed without U.S. government support.

As Congress questioned whether to reauthorize the Ex-Im Bank, one question was and will be key: Does the United States want to have the capability to be a partner of choice to emerging markets like those in Africa, home to some of the fastest-growing economies in the world, or does it want to stand on the sidelines while the continent continues to rise without it?

CAN THE PRIVATE SECTOR REALLY REPLACE THE EX-IM BANK? BEWARE OF THE MISSING MIDDLE

U.S. small and medium enterprises (SMEs) probably would have faced more challenges in obtaining financing for their exports if Congress had not reauthorized the bank's charter. The argument for not renewing the eighty-year-old Ex-Im Bank's charter centers on its support for large U.S. companies to the detriment of SMEs, in some kind of crony capitalism. According to this reasoning, the private sector will pick up the tab after Ex-Im Bank ceases to exist. This outcome seems to make perfect economic sense. After all, why should the government support the private sector (even if Ex-Im Bank makes money in the process)?

One problem with this argument is that when it comes to helping U.S. SMEs export their products, there may actually be a role for the government to work with the private sector. This is because SMEs typically face problems obtaining financing from commercial banks for export purposes.

A recent survey of seven ECAs by the Berne Union (Mancuso and Vinco, 2014) highlights the challenges that SMEs face and how ECAs try to address them. For the purpose of the survey, SMEs are defined as companies with less than $69.4 million in revenues or fewer than 250 employees. The results of the survey indicate that most ECAs are being asked to support SMEs and have started to develop tailored products. The top challenge that SMEs face in accessing foreign markets is obtaining financing, either for their buyers or to support their own growth. Others include understanding market opportunities and conditions; navigating the complexity of market regulation, taxation, and legal issues; lack of support in determining and managing the risks of exporting; and grasping the cost of doing business, including double taxation and trade agreements.

Reasons for timidity by banks include new banking regulations such as Basel III (international measures developed by the Basel Committee on Banking Supervision after the 2007–08 global financial crisis) and know-your-customer requirements. But perhaps a better explanation is that the relatively high risks and transaction costs banks incur when financing small transactions are why banks are less involved in the business of helping SMEs export their products and services abroad. In less economically advanced countries, the dearth of SME finance is called the missing-middle problem because, unlike SMEs, very small firms can get microfinance loans and large firms have access to bank loans.

It is therefore unlikely that the missing-middle problem will be solved by the private sector alone. Rather, solutions will probably involve schemes in which ECAs like the Ex-Im Bank will work together with commercial banks. For instance, in the Berne Union survey, experts identified solutions, including insurance, financing, and guarantees tailored to the SME segment. It is true that not all ECAs are state sponsored, but private ECAs such as AIG and Zurich Global Corporate in North America (whose CEO is the former president of the Berne Union) are not commercial banks but private insurers. If private banks are unable to do the same job alone, then it is likely that the public sector will have to remain a partner. At a time when new exporting countries (think China) are stepping up their game and ECAs are working to cater more to SMEs, it is wise to continue to renew the Ex-Im Bank's charter to support SMEs.

FAILURE TO REAUTHORIZE THE EX-IM BANK: EFFECTS ON SUB-SAHARAN AFRICA?

The Ex-Im Bank is mandated to focus on three regions, one of which is sub-Saharan Africa. The commonly cited high growth rate of so many African countries in Africa (sub-Saharan Africa has averaged 5.2 percent since 1995) is just one of the many reasons the United States should continue its commercial relationship with the continent. With AGOA reauthorization, U.S. businesses will continue to be ensured special preferences when investing on the continent. Thus, continuation of AGOA gives promise to U.S. businesses looking to Africa.

However, there is no doubt there are risks to working in Africa and myriad obstacles for businesses, such as weak institutions and poor infrastructure. For these and other reasons, SMEs typically have difficulty obtaining financing from commercial banks for export purposes (and this problem is not exclusive to sub-Saharan Africa). Without ECAs like the Ex-Im Bank, these businesses would struggle to get the financing they need to grow. In addition, the Ex-Im's other financial products, such as its export credit insurance, which protects businesses against the risk of foreign-buyer or other foreign-debtor default for political or commercial reasons, encourage businesses to look to Africa.

So where do we go from here? The role the Ex-Im Bank plays for small business in the United States and the potential it offers for sub-Saharan Africa cannot be understated. The president and the Hill need to preserve the Ex-Im Bank's function.

EU-AFRICA VERSUS U.S.-AFRICA

The engagement strategies of the EU and the United States with Africa during the Obama administration converged in several key areas, and additional coordination would improve their mutual outcomes in Africa.[5] Despite the United States now having a new president, this section still provides useful comparisons of the two different approaches to Africa across a number of areas, including trade, aid, and security.

Trade

In the past decade, the United States and the EU have experienced dramatic transformations in their trade relations with Africa. According to IMF data, the EU more than tripled its total trade with Africa, from $66.6 billion in 2000 to $200.5 billion in 2013. Meanwhile, U.S. trade with Africa has increased more gradually, from $29.4 billion to $63.0 billion, with imports from Africa ($39.5 billion) accounting for nearly double its exports to Africa ($23.5 billion) in 2013. However, in 2011, U.S. imports from Africa had reached a relative peak of $75.7 billion. In the two following years, the United States experienced nearly a 50 percent decline in African imports. In addition, U.S. exports to Africa, after remaining stagnant at approximately $20 billion since 2008, have fallen to about $14 billion in 2016 and 2017, in stark contrast to the EU's growth in trade with the continent.

To increase its commercial engagement with Africa, the United States has pursued a multifaceted trade strategy, distinguished by the AGOA preference, which enables African exporters of nearly 6,000 eligible products to access the U.S. market duty-free, and aided by the Generalized System of Preferences. The U.S. Agency for International Development has established three regional trade hubs to support African exporters seeking to take advantage of U.S. trade preferences. They are located in West

5 This section is adapted from Lesser and others (2014).

Africa (with offices in Ghana and Senegal and in fifteen resource centers throughout the region), East Africa (Kenya), and Southern Africa (Botswana).

Several other key U.S. programs, including the Trade Africa initiative and Doing Business in Africa Campaign, have aimed to increase Africa's commercial ties with the United States and within the African continent. A small number of U.S. foreign commercial service officers are already stationed in Ghana, Kenya, Nigeria, and South Africa to assist U.S. exporters targeting African markets. However, their numbers are expected to grow in line with the U.S. Department of Commerce's pledge to double its presence in Africa and open new offices in Angola, Tanzania, Ethiopia, and Mozambique (Schneidman and Lewis, 2014). The U.S. Trade and Development Agency and Overseas Private Investment Corporation also stated that they would be introducing new personnel to work on U.S.-African trade and investment issues in Africa.

The EU's trade promotion strategy has focused on expanding the coverage of Economic Partnership Agreements (EPAs) across the African continent. EPAs are similar to the AGOA preference in the sense that they allow partners to have duty-free access to European markets. Yet they are reciprocal agreements, so they not only give African countries preferential access to European markets but also give EU countries preferential access to African markets. While the reciprocal nature of these agreements has helped secure the EU-Africa trading partnership and provide cheaper products for African consumers because of the duty-free conditions, it has also come under fire for undermining African regional trade and integration, in addition to depriving African governments of potential revenues by eliminating export taxes. According to a report released by the Mo Ibrahim Foundation (2014, p. 21), EPAs will orient trade toward Europe rather than internally on the continent because they "have rules of origin that differ from those in the RECs [regional economic communities], which are simpler and have lower value-added requirements." The first EPAs signed between the EU and African regions were concluded in July 2014 and included six of the fifteen countries in the Southern African Development Community, the Economic Community of West African States, and Mauritania, indicating the EU's interest in pursuing these policies on a large scale. Considering the impact that these EPAs will have on U.S. and African trade and development strategies, the U.S. government will have to consider how to react to their implementation.

Aid

In 2012, the total net official development assistance (ODA) to Africa amounted to over $51.4 billion, according to Organization for Economic Cooperation and Development (OECD, 2014) figures. The top five bilateral and multilateral donors of ODA to Africa were the United States with $9.1 billion, EU institutions with $7.1 billion, the World Bank's International Development Association with $4.7 billion, France with $4.1 billion, and the United Kingdom with $3.4 billion. Since 1975, the United States and France have alternated between being the continent's first- and second-largest donors of bilateral ODA. However, in 2004, the United States surpassed France as the largest bilateral donor to Africa and has since steeply increased its contributions so that it more than doubles France's annual contributions.

France and other EU member countries have reduced their ODA to Africa, and growth in their overall bilateral ODA has generally stagnated since 2005. This is, in part, due to the 2008 onset of the global financial crisis and the EU debt crisis (United Nations Economic Commission for Africa, 2012). For example, some of France's ODA contributions are linked to its GDP, so as GDP growth slows, so too do its ODA disbursements. Yet despite the slowdown in bilateral ODA, multilateral ODA contributions from EU institutions to Africa have been on the rise. In 2004, EU institutions' ODA disbursements to Africa exceeded even those of the World Bank, making the EU the largest multilateral donor to Africa at present.

The increase in ODA from EU institutions to Africa, and the concurrent reduction in bilateral ODA from individual EU member countries to Africa, may reflect member countries' preferences in channeling aid through the multilateral EU system, as well as their commitments to expanding ODA to the continent. In 2010, EU member countries contributed, on average, 19 percent of their bilateral ODA budgets to EU institutions; top donors by volume were Germany ($2.9 billion), France ($2.7 billion), and the United Kingdom ($2.1 billion) (Organization for Economic Cooperation and Development, 2012). Furthermore, EU institutions have committed to "increasing [their] financial assistance for sub-saharan Africa by collectively allocating at least 50 percent of the agreed increase in ODA resources to the African continent," although they currently fall short of this target (ONE, 2013). Still, growth in EU funding may offset losses in bilateral funding.

The United States expended 54 percent of its disbursements to Africa on social sector programming in 2012, with specific allocations to populations and reproductive health (30 percent); basic health (8 percent); government and institutions (8 percent); and education, water supply and sanitation, and other infrastructure (8 percent). It also contributed nearly 25 percent of its ODA to humanitarian aid, and the remaining 21 percent was allocated to economic and production assistance (11 percent) and multisector, general programming, and debt relief (10 percent). The considerable proportion of ODA focusing on populations and reproductive health can be attributed to spending for the President's Emergency Plan for AIDS Relief (PEPFAR), which provides resources to combat HIV/AIDS to fourteen countries (Ingram and Rocker, 2013).

On the basis of the U.S. government's fiscal year 2015 budget request, the U.S. ODA budget to Africa is expected to shift, increasing assistance in governance and economic growth-related programming, while slightly reducing funding for health programming (Ingram, 2014).

EU institutions, on the other hand, concentrated 50 percent of their funding on economic and production-oriented activities in 2012. The sectors receiving sizable contributions were energy (17 percent); transportation and communications (11 percent); industry, mining, and construction (11 percent); and agriculture, forestry, and fishing (9 percent), with the remaining 2 percent allocated to banking and other business services. Social sector disbursements accounted for 29 percent of EU institutions' ODA, and only 3.2 percent of ODA was allocated to humanitarian aid. However, individual donors such as the United Kingdom and France both allocated nearly 22 percent of their bilateral disbursements to humanitarian aid, demonstrating their preference to pool funding for strategic economic programming but to operate on a bilateral basis with respect to humanitarian assistance.

Security

The United States and the EU are major partners with the African continent in its diverse national and regional security efforts. They make significant contributions to African peacekeeping and military operations through the UN system, although they also provide additional funding to countries on a bilateral basis. The United States is the single largest financial contributor to UN peacekeeping, funding 28.4 percent of the total budget in 2013 (United Nations, 2015a). The twenty-eight EU member states in aggregate contributed 36.8 percent of the budget ($2.7 billion), with France (7.2 percent), Germany (7.1 percent), and the United Kingdom (6.7 percent) funding the largest proportions of the EU contributions (Tardy, 2013). Whereas these substantial financial contributions amount to nearly 65 percent of the total UN peacekeeping budget, the number of troops contributed to UN peacekeeping operations by the United States and EU member states, along with other top donors such as Japan, Canada, and Australia, accounted for less than 6 percent of all UN peacekeeping troops by mid-2013—revealing a preference for both donors to commit financial but not troop support to these missions.

European foreign policy has long been concerned with the security challenges on the African continent given the involvement of former European colonial powers (specifically, France and the United Kingdom) in the region's social and economic development, as well as the significant number of European citizens and strategic commercial assets in Africa. Over the past century, African security initiatives have been pursued by individual European powers in their traditional spheres of influence. However, since the early years of the twenty-first century, with the establishment of the Common Security and Defense Policy allowing for pooled European military and defense resources, the EU has become a growing African security actor, providing funding, equipment, and troops to UN- and African-led military operations. As of July 2014, the EU is supporting nine ongoing military and civilian operations in Africa—two per country in the DRC, Somalia, and Mali; one each in Niger, Libya, and the Central African Republic; and maritime training missions in five countries and the Western Indian Ocean (European External Action Service, 2014).

In 2004, the EU established the African Peace Facility, a mechanism of the European Development Fund that channels collective EU funding for military interventions in Africa. This mechanism was updated in 2007 with the establishment of the EU's first-ever Peace and Security Partnership with Africa through the Africa-EU Joint Strategy (Africa-EU Partnership, 2007). The Peace and Security Partnership's primary objective is to "achieve the effective functioning of the [African Union's] African Peace and Security Architecture to address peace and security challenges in Africa" (European Commission, 2014). It expanded the role of the African Peace Facility to not only support military and peacekeeping operations but also to fund conflict prevention and stabilization efforts as well as coordination and logistical support during conflicts. At the end of 2013, the African Peace Facility had provided nearly $791 million to support the African Union Mission in Somalia and approximately $66 million to support the African-led International Support Mission to Mali; by the end of 2012 it had also provided roughly $132 million to support the African-led International Support Mission to the Central African Republic and the Economic Community of Central African States Peace Consolidation Mission in the Central African Republic. All of these are African Union–led peacekeeping missions (Balthasar and Barrios, 2014).

Independently of the EU, France and the United Kingdom have their own military footprints in Africa. France has military bases in Dakar, Libreville, and Djibouti, and it is conducting security operations across the continent, including Operation Unicorn in Côte d'Ivoire, Operation Sparrowhawk in Chad, and Operation Boali in the Central African Republic (Operation Serval in Mali concluded in July 2014) (Hansen, 2008). On August 1, 2014, it also launched Operation Barkhane, which called for 3,000 troops to be deployed across five countries in the Sahel (Burkina Faso, Chad, Mali, Mauritania, and Niger) to support African counterterrorism and regional securitization efforts (Larivé, 2014). As of the end of 2017, there are 4,000 French soldiers involved in this operation. Furthermore, France addresses issues of African peace and security through its role on the UN Security Council and has led military interventions under a UN mandate or with support from African and UN troops. The United Kingdom also has bases in Sierra Leone and Kenya, which focus mainly on providing training to the Sierra Leonean and Kenyan security forces, but which also, in the case of Kenya, provide the armed forces with training on safe landmine clearance practices through its International Mine Action Training Center (Alexander, 2013).

Compared to the EU, the U.S. presence on the continent is relatively limited. It coordinates all of its operations from its Africa Command in Stuttgart, Germany, and has only one official African base (in Djibouti, although it also has established drone bases in Niger and Ethiopia as well as unofficial bases in Uganda and Burkina Faso [Taylor, 2014]). However, as a part of its African security strategy, the United States has reached a large number of countries through its distributed network of specialized technical training programs, intelligence programs, and logistical support. For example, the United States has spent $241 million on its Africa Contingency Operations Training and Assistance program since 2009, which "has trained more than 248,000 peacekeepers from 25 partner countries across the continent, prior to their deployment to UN and [African Union] peacekeeping operations" (White House, Office of the Press Secretary, 2014b). The United States has also provided training and equipment to police forces through its support of the International Police Peacekeeping Operations Support program, which has worked with over 1,100 African police before their deployment to UN peacekeeping operations in Darfur, South Sudan, and Mali.

At the U.S.-Africa Leaders Summit in August 2014, the Obama administration announced a new security initiative: the African Peacekeeping Rapid Response Partnership, which will focus on "build[ing] the capacity of African militaries to rapidly deploy peacekeepers in response to emerging conflict" (White House, Office of the Press Secretary, 2014b). Through the program, the U.S. government will invest $110 million per year for three to five years to provide military training, equipment, and institutional support to six countries initially: Senegal, Ghana, Ethiopia, Rwanda, Tanzania, and Uganda. In 2013 the United States and the EU partnered through the Global Counterterrorism Forum to support the work of the Horn of Africa Region and Sahel Region Capacity-Building Working Groups (White House, Office of the Press Secretary, 2014a). They are also specifically funding and providing technical expertise to the Dutch-Moroccan Foreign Fighter Project to prevent and prosecute foreign fighters in the Maghreb and Sahel countries.

STRATEGIES WITH AFRICA

U.S Strategies

Following the 2014 U.S. and EU summits, both partners laid out their approaches and themes for further engagement with Africa. At the U.S.-Africa Leaders Summit, the following issues were emphasized as strategic areas for sustained engagement with Africa: (1) investing in Africa's future, (2) advancing peace and regional stability, (3) governing for the next generation, (4) investing in women for peace and prosperity, and (5) providing skills and opportunities to youth (White House, Office of the Press Secretary, 2014c). To achieve these objectives, the Obama administration proposed the following activities:

1. *Investment.* Investments in public health, agriculture ($10 billion through the New Alliance for Food Security and Nutrition), and energy ($26 billion through Power Africa) were highlighted as critical to the development of the African continent and will receive continued support from the government. The United States also seeks to expand trade and increase investment by renewing and updating AGOA and mobilizing partnerships with the private sector.

2. *Regional stability.* The United States will address regional peace and security in Africa by contributing to UN peacekeeping operations and implementing its own capacity-building initiatives, the African Peacekeeping Rapid Response Partnership and the Security Governance Initiative, which focus on training, equipping, and providing institutional support to partner militaries and civilian organizations.

3. *Governance.* The United States committed to continuing the dialogue on African governance by creating a joint high-level working group on illicit financial flows and corruption.

4. *Women.* Fuller participation of women in business and government was recognized as a crucial step toward unlocking the potential of African societies and economies. The United States will increase financial and technical assistance to female entrepreneurs, support their integration into peacebuilding processes, and support parliamentary efforts to advance women's rights.

5. *Youth.* The United States pledged to expand its engagement with African youth through the Young African Leaders Initiative by doubling the number of youth leaders participating in the Mandela Washington

Fellowship, establishing African regional leadership centers, and creating online educational tools for professional and vocational education as well as resources for young entrepreneurs.

EU Strategies

The five pillars of the 2014–17 Roadmap for the Joint Strategy are based on the following joint priorities between the EU and Africa: (1) peace and security; (2) democracy, good governance, and human rights; (3) human development; (4) sustainable and inclusive development and growth and continental integration; and (5) global and emerging issues (Africa-EU Partnership, 2014). According to the map, these priorities will be operationalized through the following actions:

1. *Security.* On African security initiatives, the EU has predominantly worked through the African Union's African Peace and Security Architecture to build institutional and troop capacity, especially the African Standby Force, and it will continue to prioritize the capacity-building of these structures and forces. It also highlights key areas where additional attention and cooperation would be needed, including the protection of civilians, especially women and children in conflicts, as well as "terrorism and related threats and transnational organised crime including trafficking in human beings, drugs, arms trafficking, and illegal trade in wildlife" (Schneidman and Lewis, 2014).

2. *Governance and human rights.* The EU will work to reduce corruption and promote accountability and transparency through relevant conventions; assist in the national (and regional) ratification of key treaties, including the African Charter on Democracy, Elections, and Governance; and provide technical and financial assistance in the monitoring of elections.

3. *Human development.* The EU's human development–oriented activities will fall under three general categories: science, technology, and innovation (promoting joint Africa-EU research synergies); higher education (providing scholarships and fellowships to African students and scholars, reinforcing existing exchange programs, and developing centers of excellence through the Pan-African University); and mobility, migration, and employment (reducing the cost of remittances, improving migration management, and upholding the human rights of migrants).

4. *Economic development and integration.* Promoting sustainable, inclusive development and economic integration are the core features of the EU's commercial strategies. The EU's multifold approach to achieving these goals includes strengthening public-private partnerships; supporting the accession of African countries to the WTO; expanding EPAs while simultaneously working to increase intercontinental trade; maintaining the annual EU-Africa Business Forums; prioritizing strategic investments in the fields of energy, transport, water, and information and communication technologies; and implementing the agriculture, food security, and safety strategy through the Comprehensive Africa Agriculture Development Program.

5. *Global issues.* The EU has also committed to working with African leadership in the areas of climate change, the post-2015 development agenda, arms and weapons of mass destruction proliferation, and reform of international governance structures in their respective international fora.

Opportunities for EU-U.S. Cooperation in Africa

The EU and the United States align on many points regarding their strategies with Africa. Both the United States and the EU agree that promoting regional integration and expanding Africa's external trade are essential for the continent to reach its full economic potential. Equally, they recognize the importance of mobilizing the private sector to collaborate with African investors and governments in order to develop key sectors such as energy, agriculture, and infrastructure.

However, the EU and the United States differ in their approaches to achieving these objectives. For example, while the United States seeks to promote trade through AGOA, a nonreciprocal agreement, the EU is pursuing its agenda using reciprocal EPAs. Because these EPAs have been criticized for deterring intra-African trade and integration and blocking U.S. access to African markets, it is essential that U.S., EU, and African leaders have a frank discussion to reexamine how their policies affect African and international trade dynamics. Meanwhile, the United States could benefit from following EU member countries' lead regarding the proliferation of bilateral investment treaties as development tools, because its current trade and investment framework agreements are doing little to promote investment on a comparable scale.

With respect to aid and security policies, there are also commonalities between the United States and the EU, especially in terms of supporting women in business, government, and peace processes, and combatting terrorism globally and in Africa. Yet they often use different channels for achieving the same goal. For instance, the United States channels its peacekeeping funding through the United Nations while the EU finances the African Peace and Security Architecture of the African Union. The United States and the EU both provide funding bilaterally to countries as well. The United States' new African Peacekeeping Rapid Response Partnership and Security Governance Initiative, and the EU's involvement in Mali and the Central African Republic show they are both committed to expanding these initiatives. While the United States has worked to eliminate violent extremism in the Sahel and the Horn of Africa regions through building security and intelligence organization capacity, the EU has focused on strategic countries such as Mali and Niger (through its EU Capacity Building Mission in the Sahel civilian missions) to achieve the same objectives. Equally, France launched Operation Barkhane in 2014, which will boost the number of French troops in the Sahel and allow for additional resources and programming in security sector reform. As leaders in countering violent extremism around the globe with similar strategic interests in the countries of the Sahel and Horn of Africa, the United States and the EU should coordinate closely to reduce duplication of their efforts, optimize how they allocate their resources, share leading counterterrorism practices, and improve their communications with relevant African Union bodies. The lessons learned from the U.S. and EU experiences in countering violent extremism throughout Africa and internationally could inform African counterterror strategies as crises unfold, such as in Nigeria.

The United States prioritizes aid for public health and other social programming, while the EU focuses its multilateral ODA more on economic programming and its bilateral aid from its member states on social programming, including humanitarian aid. Achieving complementarities such as these is vital to creating a holistic approach to addressing African security and development challenges. Meanwhile, both partners have begun to shift the focus of their economic agendas and international development activities from aid to trade. Trade and investment in Africa, however, could become a divisive issue for the EU and the United

States if the conflicting agendas of the reciprocal EPAs and nonreciprocal AGOA preferences are not resolved. Both partners must coordinate to maximize the scope of their social investments in infrastructure, education, and health systems across the continent, because trade and investment alone will not necessarily yield the inclusive economic opportunity and growth that African leaders are working toward. Moreover, promoting good governance and creating secure and inclusive political and commercial environments must remain core pillars of each partner's commitments to the continent. These principles can be upheld through relevant transparency mechanisms such as the Extractive Industries Transparency Initiative, the International Tropical Timber Organization, and the International Chamber of Commerce, of which both partners are already members, and through collective enforcement by the partners, while also supporting African governments in ratifying relevant accountability treaties and enhancing the voices of civil society organizations.

Conclusion

As long-standing partners with the African continent, the EU and the United States are renewing their commitment to addressing security, economic, and human development concerns. African leaders appear to welcome the opportunity to forge closer partnerships with the United States and the EU to contend with these challenges at the bilateral and regional levels. Particular strategies in which increased cooperation between the EU and the United States would benefit both partners' relations with Africa include joint counterterrorism efforts—which both partners have been supporting for more than a decade—and promoting trade and investment in Africa as a means of advancing economic and social development.

However, for any common agenda to yield effective and sustainable results, Africa's economic and political integration will need to be strengthened and accelerated. Increased African economic integration would create larger markets for global trade and investment. Stronger African political integration will help prioritize the policy agenda and would also help African countries better coordinate their policy response and implement key policies. For EU and U.S. efforts at supporting regional integration in Africa to have a bigger impact on the lives of

Africans, deepened engagement should start with regional economic communities and the African Union. Regional economic communities and the African Union would benefit from funding and capacity building, such as for the design, implementation, and monitoring of common African policies. Building strong institutions would help lay the basis for faster and better African integration, which in turn would help ensure better cooperation with European and U.S. partners.

AFRICA'S NEW PARTNERS: CHINA AND OTHER NONTRADITIONAL PARTNERS

Africa has newer partners, meaning those that are not its historical partners like the United States and the EU member states. China's relationship with Africa is a hot topic in policy circles of late, but Japan and India are engaging with the region as well.

Chinese Premier Li Keqiang's Visit to Africa: A (Rail)road to Success in Sino-African Relations?

Chinese premier Li Keqiang conducted an eight-day, four-country tour of Africa on May 4–11, 2014. His visits to Ethiopia, Nigeria, Angola, and Kenya focused heavily on expanding economic ties with the continent and resulted in dozens of agreements on trade, energy, investment, and development. A highlight of his trip was his appearance at the World Economic Forum on Africa in Abuja, Nigeria, on May 8. In a special address at the plenary session of the meeting, he laid out the grand strategy of China's aid plan, calling for "more investment and financing, and expanded cooperation in infrastructure projects" ("China to Expand Cooperation," 2014).

His words reflected a pledge he made earlier in the week to increase Chinese aid to Africa by $12 billion: $10 billion in loans and $2 billion for the Chinese Africa Development Fund. With this commitment, China has extended a total of $30 billion in credit to the continent and $5 billion in development assistance. Moreover, in response to the kidnapping of over 200 schoolgirls in Nigeria, Li made a promise to support rescue operations to recover the missing girls. In general, he also pledged to "assist Africa's capacity-building in such areas as peacekeeping, counterterrorism and anti-piracy" ("China to Expand Cooperation," 2014). These commitments fall in line with the general trends exhibited by the Africa policy of President Xi Jinping's administration, which has emphasized peace and security as well as economic cooperation.

The trip culminated on a high note in Nairobi, where Li signed agreements with Kenyan president Uhuru Kenyatta and other East African leaders to construct a $3.6 billion, 380-mile railway line linking Nairobi to the important Kenyan port of Mombasa. This line is part of a regional railway system that extends through Rwanda, Uganda, Burundi, and South Sudan. Construction began in October 2014 and was completed in June 2017. The Export-Import Bank of China funded 90 percent of the project, and the Kenyan government covered the remaining 10 percent.

The railway project represents a major opportunity to promote trade among East African countries, where costs of transporting goods and people are generally very high. The new railway line is expected to be significantly more efficient and reliable than Kenya's existing, colonial-era lines, reducing journey times and the costs of shipping freight—from twenty cents per ton per kilometer to eight cents—according to President Kenyatta. These gains in efficiency have serious implications for expanding access to markets and taking advantage of economies of scale, especially for farmers who lose an estimated half their crops in transport annually. It may also spur foreign investment, because investors often consider poor infrastructure a major deterrent to investment.

On the other hand, critics of the project argue that, in the past, Chinese infrastructure projects have sourced much of their labor from China, failed to train African workers, and neglected labor laws in host countries. Concerns over the increase of Kenya's national debt by nearly one-third and the increase in interest payments on external debt by 50 percent have also been raised. Furthermore, questions over the funding necessary to maintain the railroad after it is built still remain. As this railway project and other Chinese-funded projects such as the $13.1 billion railway project in Nigeria get under way, it is important that discussions between African and Chinese leaders focus on ensuring that Chinese funds benefit Africa as much as they do China.

Transparency over financing and other terms of Chinese engagement in African countries will benefit everybody in the long term. Transparency will help African voters better assess the expected costs and benefits of the deals and know how much future generations will have to pay for them. If the projects are successful, other foreign investors will be able to better assess the political risk and other risks associated with large infrastructure projects and will participate in future ones. And China will have the satisfaction of playing a leadership role in the development of infrastructure in Africa.

Perception of China: Views from Africa

According to the survey by the Pew Research Center (2014), nowhere is public opinion more positive about China than in Africa. This result should not be surprising, as China's engagement with Africa comes at a time when the continent is developing and pursuing its agenda for economic transformation and is in need of strong economic partnership.

Indeed, after a long delay in the postindependence era, African countries were able to restart growing their economies only in the 1990s, and they did so at a robust pace. Some African countries such as Angola, Mozambique, Ethiopia, and Rwanda have even joined the club of growth miracles, with 7 percent or more GDP growth for twenty-five years or longer. But to reach Asian levels of income, African states need to transform their economies to achieve a more sustainable and inclusive growth. This agenda starts with addressing Africa's large infrastructure gap.

This context for Africa's growth is important for understanding why perceptions of China are so positive. Indeed, China's economic engagement with the continent through bilateral trade and foreign investment has increased dramatically in recent years. Some countries, such as Angola, which exports half of its oil to China, rely heavily on this new economic partner for trade. Chinese investments go to a relatively broad range of sectors (not just natural resources) and to a broad range of countries (from fragile to middle-income countries). China is also a major financer of African infrastructure and the only player in some sectors such as railroads.

China's rising economic engagement with Africa has, however, not been without criticisms. For instance, concerns about violations of labor rights, investments with relatively low local content, and insufficient transparency in loans to African countries (especially when they are in exchange for natural resources) have been trumpeted by the global press.

Africa is in need of economic partnership, and China is engaging the continent on the economic front at an unprecedented scale and scope. As a result, Africa is becoming increasingly globalized through China. These factors all contribute to the rather positive perception of China on the African continent.

What Do We Know about the Chinese Land Grab in Africa?

There is a consensus in Africa that agriculture is one of the keys to achieving sustainable and inclusive growth there. Most of Africa's population and its poor depend on agriculture, so this sector can provide potentially significant gains. Agriculture also has the potential to become one of the growth engines of the continent, help Africa's industrialization through agro-processing and agro-business, and reduce dependence on the services sector, which is currently the main driver of growth. Because of these advantages and despite its current low production, its high poverty, and the looming threat of climate change, Africa is uniquely placed to be a rising agricultural leader.

Indeed, Arezki, Deininger, and Selod (2012) find that a country's attractiveness to foreign investors correlates directly to its amount of uncultivated land with the potential to generate significant output. Now, where on planet Earth would we find such a treasure? Well, Africa accounts for about 60 percent of the world's arable land, and most of its countries do not achieve 25 percent of their potential yield. No wonder, therefore, that there has been increased interest in large-scale investment in agriculture in Africa, especially by China.

In light of this opportunity, China—with an already rapidly growing economic interest in the continent—has been accused of an abundance of land grabs in Africa. But is China really planning on greedily exploiting African agriculture? Have these land grabs been as widespread as some critics imply? What might be the detriment to Africa? In her book *Will Africa Feed China?* (2015), Deborah Brautigam discusses these questions and debunks myths around China's interest in African land and agricultural resources as well as enters the larger discussion: How do we increase investment in African agriculture?

Will Africa Feed Africa?

Africa has not yet achieved its green revolution, or jump in agricultural productivity, and because of low cereal yields—the lowest in the world—it is experiencing a food deficit. In fact, from 2012 to 2016 the region's food trade deficit was around US$30 billion annually, and it accounts for only 6 percent of global food imports and 4 percent of such exports (Fundira, 2017). For every $1 it earns today in agricultural exports (mainly coffee, cotton, and cocoa), the region spends nearly $2 on agricultural imports, mainly food. Africa has a serious problem, which some countries like Ethiopia, Kenya, Niger, and Nigeria among others are addressing. Senegal has created a program that creates communal farming areas and equips 74,131 acres of farmland with infrastructure for water retention, electricity, roads, and other essentials. Côte d'Ivoire has surpassed three tons per hectare in cereal yields, which could be a very big deal.

Will Africa Feed China?

Let's assume for a moment that Africa's green revolution happens, and that the region can feed itself. Will it then be able to feed China? The answer is that Africa will then face a second yield gap to be able to export to China: A second jump in agricultural productivity would be necessary. Indeed, Chinese diets are moving more toward proteins than cereals as people become wealthier. Now, as Brautigam (2015) notes, it takes a lot of grain to generate protein: It takes more than four pounds of grain to produce two pounds of chicken, and the ratio is almost nine pounds for pork, and more than fifteen pounds for beef. As a result, Africa will need to improve agricultural productivity at an even faster pace if it wants to feed China.

Especially since the sharp increase in international food prices in 2007–08, these land grabs have rung alarm bells, as they raise concerns about corruption, large-scale resettlement of populations, and even a new colonization of Africa.

Chinese Land Grabs in Africa: The Fiction and the Facts

Foreign investor interest in African land and the media's coverage of the race to acquire it are at the core of the myths that Brautigam (2015) explores in her book. Clearly, the number of press reports (obtained from the GRAIN database)[6] on land deals in Africa has spiked—but how many really translate into actual land acquisitions by China and other countries?

To separate fact from fiction, Brautigam painstakingly combs through press reports on Chinese land grabs in Africa. She digs deep into data and fieldwork to cross-check the evidence on the extent and scale of the Chinese land rush in Africa, specifically exploring the following questions: Have the Chinese really acquired large areas of farmland in Africa? Is the Chinese government leading an effort to acquire land through its state-owned firms and funds? What can we really say about the assertions in the global press that "the Chinese want to grow food in Africa and send [it] back to China" and that "Beijing plans to send its displaced farmers to Africa"? Brautigam's finds little evidence of massive Chinese state-sponsored land grab.

Regardless of the land grab controversy, what is the best way to drive investment in African agriculture? Whether Africa intends to feed itself or China, a crucial question is how the region will address the serious underinvestment in agriculture. In "Global Land Rush," Arezki, Deininger, and Selod (2012) document two views on the size of the investments that are needed. One view, held by the likes of Paul Collier, favors large-scale investments, often involving transnational purchases of land to create jobs and bring new technology to the sector. The other view favors smallholder farming and points out the risks of cross-border land acquisitions—the so-called land grabs that neglect local rights, extract short-term profits at the cost of long-term sustainability, ignore social standards, and foster corruption on a large scale. Brautigam documents a third view, which is a middle way and involves contract farming in which a large buyer enters into an agreement with smallholder farmers.

But as Brautigam warns in the case of Chinese investment, there is typically a wide gap between interest in large-scale investment in African agriculture and actual investment. The case studies in the book offer lessons for African policymakers and Chinese (and other foreign) investors in African agriculture, including the following:

6 To download the database, see www.grain.org/article/entries/4479-grain-releases-data-set-with-over-400-global-land-grabs.

- Foreign investors can gain from engaging local communities, adopting corporate social responsibility practices, and assessing political risk.
- African policymakers can gain from addressing the formidable challenges arising from land issues and filling the infrastructure gap, especially in rural areas.
- African policymakers should also learn the lessons from China's early experience in its own land in dealing with foreign investors in agriculture, which spurred research and development and led to the development of hybrid seeds, and even China's current forays into the world of commodity trading.

These recommendations nicely complement the ones in Arezki, Deininger, and Selod (2012), who argue that a strategy to attract investors to fill the current yield gaps in Africa and allow local farmers to thrive can generate large benefits, provided local community rights are respected and investors pay a fair price for the land. However, they are quick to point out that translating potential into efficient farming activity is not easy because closing the yield gaps requires government support, including in the area of technology, institutions, and infrastructure. Their analysis also finds that countries with weak land sector governance (measured in the Institutional Profiles Database)[7] are the ones the most attractive to investors. I quickly checked whether Chinese investments in African agriculture went to countries with low governance (using the 2015 Ibrahim Index of African Governance and table 6.1, page 97, in Brautigam's book) and found that that does not seem to be the case.

Though I found *Will Africa Feed China?* enlightening, I found myself wanting more—I would have loved to hear Brautigam's recommendations on how China, the United States, the EU, and other development partners can work together with African stakeholders to address the challenge of food security and nutrition in Africa (Sustainable Development Goal 2 is to achieve zero hunger by 2030), a topic some of my colleagues are working on now.

7 The Institutional Profiles Database provides an original measure of countries' institutional characteristics through composite indicators built from perception data. See www.cepii.fr/institutions/en/ipd.asp.

Japan in Africa: A Rising Sun?

Japanese prime minister Shinzo Abe completed an African tour to Ethiopia, Côte d'Ivoire, and Mozambique in January 2014. His visit was the first tour of Africa by a Japanese leader in eight years and the first visit to a francophone West African country. Thankfully, this low frequency of visits to the continent by Japanese leaders does not do justice to Japan's involvement in Africa.

According to Japan's official aid statistics (which excludes China), Japan is the fifth-largest bilateral ODA donor to Africa, after the United States, France, the United Kingdom, and Germany. Japanese ODA to the continent averaged about $1.8 billion per year in 2008–12—double its 2003–07 level (Japanese Ministry of Foreign Affairs, 2013). These figures do not include Japan's aid to Africa through some multilateral donors such as the World Bank.

For the last twenty years, Japan's main road map for its assistance to Africa has been charted by the TICAD (Tokyo International Conference on African Development). The TICAD is a global forum for Japanese and African heads of state and is held every five years. It is co-organized with the UN, the UN Development Program, the World Bank, and the African Union Commission. In principle, the TICAD advocates Africa's ownership of its development and the partnership between Africa and the global community. It also serves as an accountability framework. Africans have also become familiar with the JICA acronym (Japan International Cooperation Agency) and may have seen young Japanese men and women from the JOCV (Japanese Overseas Cooperation Volunteers). Up until 2013, most of Japan's focus on Africa under TICAD IV was on traditional aid targets (infrastructure, agriculture, water and sanitation, education, and health, as well as peacekeeping operations: Japan has provided 400 self-defense-forces personnel as part of the UN mission in South Sudan).

But Japan's involvement in Africa is now at a crossroads. TICAD V, held in Yokohama in June 2013, added a new element: private sector involvement. As Prime Minister Abe put it in his opening address at TICAD V, "What Africa needs now is private sector investment, and public-private partnership leverages that investment." He committed to support African growth over the next five years, through not only $32 billion in ODA but also $16 billion of "other public and private resources." Abe also promised $2 billion of trade insurance underwriting. These funds will be targeted to areas identified in consultation with African countries, including infrastructure, capacity building, health, and agriculture.

So Prime Minister Abe's 2014 African trip was in line with TICAD V. It is therefore not surprising that business leaders joined the trip and that $570 million in loans to gas-rich Mozambique were announced. With this in mind, it is encouraging to see that two of the stops in the Japanese prime minister's visit took into account regional integration on the continent. In Addis Ababa, the prime minister gave a speech at the African Union headquarters. He focused on the need to maintain peace and security on the continent, and he pledged about $320 million for conflict and disaster response, including $25 million to address the crisis in South Sudan and $3 million to the one in the Central African Republic. Earlier, in Abidjan, Côte d'Ivoire, Abe met heads of state and government of the Economic Community of West African States.

In short, Prime Minister Abe's visit heralds a new type of relationship between Japan and Africa. Japanese engagement with African countries will involve the private sector much more than previously. It is up to African policymakers to seize this opportunity to meet the continent's transformational agenda.

Three Trends in Indo-African Trade and Investment

Heads of state, policymakers, and experts gathered in New Delhi for the third India African Forum Summit on October 26–29, 2015. Key issues included public health, UN Security Council reforms, terrorism, and climate change. Another major area of focus was the growing trade and investment relationship between India and Africa. In preparation for the summit, AGI looked into the big-picture dynamics of Afro-Indian trade and investment.

Indo-African Trade Is Growing but Still Lags behind Other Big Players

The IMF has determined that the value of India's exports (now largely high-end consumer goods) to Africa have increased by over 100 percent from 2008 to 2013—meaning that India has now forged ahead of the United States in African markets. However, although India benefited from Africa's robust economic growth, India's gains do not quite compare to China's astronomical increase in exports to Africa.

The value of India's imports from Africa also grew dramatically from 2008 to 2013—by over 80 percent—compared to the sharp decline in the value of imports from sub-Saharan Africa to the United States. The decrease in U.S. imports from Africa was likely caused by the development of American hydraulic technology, which lessened U.S. dependence on African oil and gas—its major import from the continent.

Raw Materials Still Make Up the Lion's Share of African Exports to India

Despite the impressive growth in trade relations between India and Africa, a substantial imbalance remains in the import-export relationship between the two countries. A vast majority of exports from Africa to India are raw materials such as crude oil, gold, raw cotton, and precious stones. Meanwhile, most exports from India to sub-Saharan Africa consist of high-end consumer goods such as automobiles, pharmaceuticals, and telecom equipment. This imbalance does not necessarily align with Africa's goals to diversify away from natural resource dependence, which is a common issue in Africa's trade relationships with China, the United States, and the EU.

African FDI with India Is Driven Mostly by One Country, Mauritius

Another noteworthy trend is Africa's growing FDI in India. Since 2010, Africa's FDI in India has proved consistently high compared to its FDI in China and the United States. The primary source of FDI to India is Mauritius.

Although India's FDI in Africa has also increased, with an 11 percent jump between 2010 and 2012, Indian investments are concentrated in just a few countries. Once again, Mauritius accounts for much, attracting a high volume of investments from India because of its favorable tax treaty with India.

Overall, the Indo-African economic relationship has made substantial gains, but there is much more room for growth. Of many of our recommendations, my colleagues and I suggest that African businesses should focus on diversifying their exports to India by increasing awareness of preference opportunities—a strategy that could also mitigate the effects of a slowing Chinese economy. India in turn should expand its preferred areas of investment beyond the few countries on which it currently focuses.

MULTILATERAL INSTITUTIONS: KEY PARTNERS IN AFRICA'S DEVELOPMENT

The World Bank, the IMF, and the African Development Bank are critical partners for helping Africa achieve its vision, so it's important to understand the relationships and dynamics they have with the continent.

Top Three African Topics for the World Bank–IMF Spring Meetings

Early spring in Washington, D.C., is cherry blossom season, with its contingents of tourists streaming toward the National Mall. But early spring also brings to the nation's capital another species: delegations from ministries of finance and central banks from around the globe coming to the World Bank–IMF Spring Meetings. You can recognize them as the men and women in black outfits walking briskly on Nineteenth Street or Pennsylvania Avenue on their way to meetings. Some of them will be from Africa, and I am betting that they will be discussing the following three issues:

The Impact of Fed Tapering

The IMF has warned that although the global economy as broadly stabilized in 2014, new obstacles have emerged (International Monetary Fund, 2014a). One of the major roadblocks the IMF has mentioned—the risk of heightened market volatility associated with the tapering of quantitative easing—has already affected some African countries. In a recent blog (Sy, 2014b), I discuss how Ghana, Nigeria, and South Africa are the African countries most at risk from the February market turmoil. These economies are experiencing capital flow reversal and weakening currencies in addition to domestic challenges, such as higher-than-targeted fiscal deficits, an electoral cycle, or structural deficiencies. I now add Zambia to this list, as the country is being hit by portfolio reversal and lower copper prices.

For these countries, discussions with IMF experts about which instruments for managing the effects of capital flow reversal will take center stage. Such discussions will also include macroeconomic and structural policies to address existing longer-term challenges. Now, how about on the other side of Nineteenth Street?

A Bigger World Bank

In 2014, World Bank president Jim Yong Kim announced a $100 billion increase by the bank's lending arm for middle-income countries over the next ten years. This move followed a record $52 billion replenishment of the International Development Association, the bank's fund for the poorest countries, following the IMF–World Bank Annual Meetings in 2013.

Unbeknownst to many, twenty-two sub-Saharan African countries are classified as middle-income countries by the World Bank. These countries all have an annual per capita income between $1,036 and $12,615. Those with a per capita income lower than $4,085 are classified as lower-middle-income countries, and those with a per capita income higher are upper-middle-income countries. Furthermore, African lower-income countries ($1,035 per capita income or less) such as Kenya, Uganda, Rwanda, and Tanzania may become middle-income countries by 2025.

With the bank's increase in lending capacity, these African middle-income countries and soon-to-be middle-income countries may become eligible for new loans, but they should recognize that the loans will come at a higher cost. For instance, the bank is restoring its twenty-five-basis-point commitment fee that it formerly charged on undisbursed balances. This means that a country borrowing $100 million and not using the money will have to pay a fee of $250,000.

Given Africa's large infrastructure funding gap, a bigger World Bank loan program may be good news, as it will bring in not only more financial resources but also more technical assistance. But the World Bank is not the only one with an increased interest in Africa. These days, everybody—from Beijing and Tokyo to Washington, D.C., and Brasilia via Brussels—is interested in Africa. The real issue is, therefore, whether African policymakers will make the best out of this growing interest.

I suggest that during the spring meetings top African policymakers (not the governors and ministers but technocrats such as chief economists and reform team leaders) meet to compare notes and discuss the best way to refine current strategies to transform the continent's economies. At least, meetings along the lines of existing regional economic communities would be useful. My colleague Ernesto Talvi tells me that this has been going on for a while now for Latin American chief economists.

Conflicts

Finally, I suspect that delegations will discuss the dire situations in the Central African Republic and South Sudan. It is not at all premature to start preparing now for the economic engagement of the Bretton Woods institutions once peace resumes. These will require a long-term reengagement of the international community with not only well-targeted technical assistance but also sufficient funding to kick-start the economy and rebuild institutions. The work should not wait for the arrest of hostilities.

There is a consensus on both sides of Nineteenth Street that growth in sub-Saharan Africa will continue at a strong pace in the short term. African governors may therefore be tempted to start the spring meetings with a sense of accomplishment. That would be the wrong attitude. Africa's growth is still jobless, and its youth bulge shows no clear sign of becoming a youth dividend. The current positive growth prospects should be seen as windows of opportunity to lay the basis for a higher, sustainable, and more inclusive growth. The policies to achieve this goal should be homegrown and the spring meetings provide a good opportunity to test them.

THE IMF AND WORLD BANK ANNUAL MEETINGS: AFRICA'S GROWTH LOSING SPEED

Every year, the IMF and World Bank meetings host a discussion on issues related to poverty reduction, international economic development, and finance. Given these two institutions' presence and influence in sub-Saharan Africa, these meetings often deliver a range of policy prescriptions to improve the economic climates of countries in the region. So what are the key takeaways for African countries from IMF and World Bank meetings that were held in Lima, Peru, in 2015?

Whereas in recent years these meetings have focused on the Africa rising narrative, in 2015 they centered on the continent's recent falling GDP growth rate. For instance, the IMF forecast that GDP growth in sub-Saharan Africa would slow to 3.4 percent in 2015, down from 5 percent in 2014, and its slowest pace since 2009. The case of sub-Saharan Africa's two largest economies, which together account for more than half of the region's GDP, is telling. Whereas Nigeria's growth would slow from 6.3 percent in 2014 to 2.7 percent in 2015, South Africa would continue to muddle through with a 1.3 percent growth rate in 2015, about the same as in 2014 (1.5 percent). In addition, given the region's demographic trends, GDP per capita would slow from 2.6 percent in 2014 to 1.4 percent in 2015.

This slowing GDP growth—driven by the deteriorating external environment witnessed in recent months—will noticeably impair the continent's efforts in achieving UN Sustainable Development Goals. It will be important for African policymakers to have a two-pronged approach: they will need to keep calm and manage short-term macroeconomic shocks while maintaining (or even accelerating) progress in medium- to long-term policy reforms.

In light of this larger challenge, other major themes and lessons emerged among policymakers present in Lima:

1. *Falling commodity prices and tightening financing conditions are eroding recent economic gains.* Not surprisingly, oil-exporting countries will suffer the most under lower commodity prices. For example, in Nigeria, where oil and gas exports represent 75–80 percent of government revenues, lower commodity prices have reduced fiscal space (commonly defined as the budgetary room that allows governments to provide resources for public purposes without undermining fiscal sustainability)[8] and weakened the value of the naira. Still, the average growth forecast for Africa masks disparities among countries. While GDP growth in oil-exporting countries would fall from 5.9 percent in 2014 to 3.6 percent in 2015, continued infrastructure investment, coupled with strong private consumption, has allowed growth in low-income countries on the

8 See, for instance, World Health Organization, "What Is 'Fiscal Space' and Why Does It Matter?" (www.who.int/health_financing/topics/fiscal-space/why-it-matter/en/).

continent to reach 5.9 percent, down from 7.4 percent in 2014. Middle-income countries would grow at about the same pace as in 2014 (2.6 percent in 2015 versus 2.7 percent in 2014). However, without South Africa, growth in middle-income countries would reach 4.6 percent in 2015, down from 4.7 percent in 2014.

2. *Fiscal and current account deficits—especially for resource-rich countries—are increasing, and external borrowing costs are rising.* The period of rapid growth up to 2015 was not coupled with high savings, and countries are now entering this period of slow growth with high fiscal deficits. Tax revenues remain relatively low in sub-Saharan Africa at less than 15 percent of GDP on average and 13 percent of GDP for resource-rich countries. Subsidies continue to take a huge toll on African governments' budgets. For instance, very few water and electricity distribution companies in the region are financially sustainable and can operate without government subsidies. Current account deficits in numerous African countries have been mainly financed by increased influx of foreign investment. This trend could pose problems in the near future, as the deteriorating global financing environment could reduce investment flows to sub-Saharan Africa. Another challenge to GDP growth in Africa is the increasing risk of debt, fueled by the inability to mobilize domestic resources, notably through fiscal means. African countries that have borrowed externally are becoming increasingly exposed to exchange rate risk. Countries that are considering borrowing externally will face higher costs, as global interest rates are increasing, and investors are becoming more risk averse.

3. *Africa's structural transformation agenda is still work in progress.* Trade patterns continue to reveal a dependence on commodities: Growth has been largely driven by external demand, notably through the commodity exports to China. In addition, the continent has grown without structural transformation; in the last twenty years, the value chain has remained unaltered—Africa remains at the global production stage of primary goods exports. With reduced commodity prices, African countries must seek new engines of growth and learn to sustain growth in a context in which commodity prices have significantly decreased. For example, Cape Verde's government is reforming its budget by cutting subsidies and linking the tax structure to its growth engines, such as tourism.

4. *Adequate macroeconomic policies can help ride out the current external shocks.* Fiscal reforms in particular are important for oil exporters—with reduced oil revenues fiscal reforms become necessary. As governments' ability to rely on these exports to fuel government income is reduced, countries must now turn to non-oil fiscal revenues—such as a value added tax—to fuel government revenues. In addition, given the reduction in policy buffers, countries must allow their exchange rates to depreciate in order to absorb economic shocks. This recommendation, however, is not appropriate for countries with a fixed exchange rate, such as the ones in the CFA franc zone. These countries will face a higher fiscal burden as they adjust to these unsettling economic challenges.

5. *Domestic revenue mobilization should be a priority.* African countries, notably resource-rich countries, have struggled with the ability to mobilize domestic resources, notably through fiscal means. Tax evasion and corruption are a major drain on the resources of developing countries. Mobilizing financing as a means to unlock the infrastructure gap and invest in human capital through the promotion of early childhood and STEM (science, technology, engineering, and mathematics) education is essential for spurring growth.

It is difficult to disagree with the economic diagnostic from the discussions in Lima, and I do not expect major disagreements on the policy measures that are needed to address the current challenges. It is now up to African policymakers to go back to the drawing board, consult with their countries' stakeholders, and rapidly make the necessary policy adjustments. Waiting too long could prove disastrous. As of 2015, growth is still in positive territory in spite of the recent shocks, but Africa's room to maneuver has shrunk, and the global environment remains volatile.

DISCUSSING AFRICA'S DEVELOPMENT PRIORITIES AND CHALLENGES WITH DONALD KABERUKA

In 2015, AGI hosted the president of the African Development Bank (AfDB), Donald Kaberuka, for a discussion on his vision for sustaining and expanding sub-Saharan Africa's recent high levels of growth. President Kaberuka had led the continent's premier financial institution since 2005 and was serving his second and final five-year term as president, which ended in September 2015.

The AfDB has a new president now, Akinwumi Adesina, but as he implements a new vision for the AfDB and Africa, it is useful to look back on the policies of Kaberuka while he was in charge, including the reorientation of the institution's lending portfolio to prioritize infrastructure development and regional integration and to extend its reach in supporting global health initiatives, particularly in response to the Ebola epidemic in 2014.

1. *Infrastructure financing and regional integration.* During President Kaberuka's tenure, the AfDB emphasized the role of robust infrastructure in enabling sound, competitive business environments, which in turn encourage foreign and domestic investment, enhance trade and regional integration, and spur private sector–led growth with the potential for broad-based gains. Since the 1990s, when the AfDB's infrastructure investments amounted to less than $500 million a year, its infrastructure financing has grown by more than five times, to approximately $2.6 billion, by 2012. President Kaberuka strengthened the AfDB's role in assessing and funding Africa's infrastructure needs through several key initiatives, such as the Infrastructure Consortium for Africa, the Program for Infrastructure Development in Africa, and the Africa50 Infrastructure Fund, which together study African infrastructure performance and gaps, convene meetings to catalyze investment and design policies conducive to infrastructure development, and disburse funds for infrastructure projects. The AfDB also focused attention on regional infrastructure projects—from 2009 to 2013 it financed more than seventy cross-border operations amounting to $3.8 billion—because it considers effective regional transport and telecommunications networks necessary conditions for regional integration and enhanced competitiveness.[9]

2. *Global health.* As the Ebola epidemic spread through Guinea, Liberia, and Sierra Leone in 2014, the AfDB responded by dispensing $223 million throughout the region, joining with the African Union, the UN Economic Commission on Africa, and private sector actors to create an Ebola Response Fund (which has provided logistical and financial support for African medical corps), and providing an addi-

9 For the AfDB's views on the strategic importance of infrastructure development and its linkages to regional integration, see African Development Bank (2013a).

tional $300 million to fund a regional road transport project aimed at strengthening infrastructure in the three most affected countries. Furthermore, President Kaberuka visited Liberia and Sierra Leone in August 2014 and Guinea in October 2014 to gauge the situation on the ground and provide input to the economic and humanitarian response strategy. He vocally opposed "unnecessary stringent measures" that restricted mobility and trade, including flight bans and border closures, stating, "We need to isolate Ebola, not the countries" (Kaberuka, 2014).

THE IMPORTANT ROLE OF THE PRIVATE SECTOR

The private sector plays a key role in achieving Africa's vision for itself. The investment, job creation, and growth of the consumer base that the Continental Free Trade Area is so focused on all depend on a vibrant private sector that moves Africa forward. Of course, many aspects of the private sector need to be studied and made more effective to ensure that it is promoting growth and sustainable development on the continent. Effective corporate governance works to enhance business climates that support investment, and private investment in the form of FDI is a key to growth that must be analyzed along with the various policies that can be pursued to make such investments more effective.

As noted by the economist Dani Rodrik (2014), sub-Saharan Africa is less industrialized today than it was in the 1980s. Specifically, it is estimated that the contribution of Africa's manufacturing sector was 12 percent of its total GDP in 1980,[10] but as of 2016 it is estimated to be 10.5 percent of its GDP.[11] The UN Economic Commission for Africa indicates that East Asia has remained consistent in the same period, with around 31 percent of its GDP attributable to manufacturing. In addition

10 United Nations Economic Commission for Africa (2013). In the UN report, countries are classified into geographic regions and country groupings. Unless otherwise noted, the data cover fifty-three African countries and exclude South Sudan.

11 World Bank Development Indicators, 2016, sub-Saharan Africa only. This is a World Bank online database accessible at https://datacatalog.worldbank.org/dataset/world-development-indicators.

to Africa's low level of industrialization as a whole, private investment in Africa's modern industries remains too low to sustain structural transformation. In 2016, Africa received only an estimated 3.1 percent of global FDI (United Nations Conference on Trade and Development, 2016). Thus, it is important to understand how and why private investment can be attracted or fail to be attracted.

One reason private investment has remained low is that African companies face serious financing challenges. For example, compared to other regions, bank credit remains low and capital markets remain shallow. Good corporate governance, however, can help remove some of these financing challenges.

As Arthur Levitt, the former chairman of the U.S. Securities and Exchange Commission, once noted, "If a country does not have a reputation for strong corporate governance practices, capital will flow elsewhere. . . . All enterprises in that country—regardless of how steadfast a particular company's practice may be—suffer the consequences" (Levitt, 2000). A number of sub-Saharan African countries have recently developed corporate governance codes, including Ethiopia, Mozambique, and Rwanda (KMPG and ACCA, 2017). Even more countries have recently made revisions to their corporate governance codes.

In October 2013, the Africa Corporate Governance Network was launched with the aim of encouraging best practices and building capacity in corporate governance in Africa.

Building deep capital markets takes time. As a result, standards for good corporate governance in Africa should go beyond the traditional focus on publicly listed domestic companies to include privately held firms, the public sector and foreign firms.

African policymakers and standard setters could address at least three issues:

1. *Strengthening public governance will benefit corporate governance.* In most countries, the government is not just a regulator but also a customer or a business partner. According to a PricewaterhouseCoopers survey (2015), 84 percent of African managers are concerned about "increasing regulatory complexity and scrutiny" and 63 percent said that bribery, corruption, and fraud were threats to their companies' growth prospects. This points to the role of governments in supporting the credibility of corporate governance practices.

2. *Good corporate governance should be a standard for foreign firms too.* FDI often results in large financial outflows from tax evasion, the underpricing of concessions, and trade mispricing. African policymakers should work with developed countries to require full public disclosure of the beneficial ownership of companies and strengthen multilateral rules on taxation.

3. *The role of accountants and auditors as gatekeepers should be encouraged but monitored.* In a context in which boards of directors are often the only institution able to reduce conflicts of interest between shareholders and managers, it is crucial for directors to be able to count on reliable information provided by external accountants and auditors. It is therefore important to uphold high standards of quality on these gatekeepers and provide the proper incentives for their independence.

8

Delivering on the Vision: Making It Happen

This chapter examines ways for taking African destiny into African hands: mobilizing domestic resources, including how that relates to good governance, and leveraging pension funds for funding large-scale infrastructure projects. Use by African countries of existing resources to fund development is, of course, a key part of achieving the continent's vision.

DOMESTIC RESOURCE MOBILIZATION AND EXTERNAL FINANCING: WHEN DOES GOVERNANCE MATTER?

The following offers an overview of related research and policy recommendations from a paper I cowrote with Mariama Sow on the relationship between two global priorities: financing for development and good governance (Sy and Sow, 2016a).

The Addis Ababa Action Agenda of the Third International Conference on Financing for Development identifies domestic revenue mobilization as central to achieving the Sustainable Development Goals. The action agenda also recognizes the importance of international financing in the development process. At the same time, the process leading to the

Sustainable Development Goals has emphasized good governance as a development priority. One of the goals (Goal 16) is solely dedicated to "promot[ing] peaceful and inclusive societies for sustainable development, provid[ing] access to justice for all and build[ing] effective, accountable and inclusive institutions at all levels" (United Nations, 2015b).

But does good governance really matter for mobilizing financing for development? And if it does, do different financing sources respond equally to good governance? In particular, do domestic financing sources respond to good governance in the same way as external financing sources?

The literature has addressed the first question of whether governance matters for mobilizing financing flows. However, relatively little is said about whether domestic financing sources, government revenues in particular, respond to governance in a different way than foreign financing sources.[1] My colleague and I (Sy and Sow, 2016a) used the World Governance Indicators developed by Kaufman, Kraay, and Mastruzzi (2011) to study how good governance relates to financing sources in sub-Saharan African countries. In particular, tax revenue on the one hand and foreign direct investment (FDI) and official development assistance on the other. We also looked at remittances and illicit financial flows in spite of data limitations.

We found that while good governance matters for raising domestic revenues, its effect on external financing sources is mixed.

We conducted three separate tests. First, we used Spearman rank correlations to look at the relationship between World Governance Indicators and the different types of financing sources. Second, we ran panel data regressions in which we controlled for a number of indicators, such as GDP per capita and natural resource rents, which can have an effect on financial flows. Third, we conducted robustness tests using settler mortality as an instrument for governance. The three analyses all point to the same main finding: Good governance does indeed matter for financing development. However, while good governance matters for raising domestic revenues, its effect on external financing sources is mixed. Good governance (except for political stability) does not ap-

1 But note Faria and Mauro (2009), who focus on the external capital structure of countries.

pear to matter much for FDI to oil-rich countries—the largest recipients of such flows to the region. In these countries, good governance can even be negatively correlated to FDI. In contrast, official development assistance to the region is positively associated with good governance.

Our results indicate that the bigger bang for improving governance is at home in the form of increased tax revenue (excluding natural resource rents). This is all the more important as domestic revenues are the largest sources of development financing. Although good governance does not help raise more natural resource rents, it has a positive effect on non-resource government revenues. Improving governance can support African countries' efforts to diversify away from natural resources and increase government revenues coming from the non-resource sector.

Improving governance also appears to attract more official development assistance. In contrast, the inconclusive or negative response of FDI to good governance points to the importance of pursuing efforts on the global agenda for increasing transparency in the natural resource sector (the most important destination of FDI in the region); specifically, identifying policies to improve the link between good governance and FDI in natural resource–rich countries would be useful.

Lastly, corruption was found to be the governance indicator that was the most consistently significant among the six indicators we consider. This result indicates that addressing corruption in the region could yield quick and important gains in terms of raising the much-needed financing for development.

The results also confirm the importance of the Addis Ababa Financing for Development agenda, which aims to increase domestic revenue mobilization to finance the Sustainable Development Goals. The goals point to improvements in governance to complement efforts such as improvements in tax systems and administration and the efficiency of spending.

LEVERAGING AFRICAN PENSION FUNDS FOR FINANCING INFRASTRUCTURE DEVELOPMENT

There is a consensus among African policymakers that the continent's economic growth and transformation is significantly constrained by its limited infrastructure. Inadequate infrastructure—including unreliable energy, an ineffective urban-rural road network, and inefficient ports—is one of the largest impediments to Africa's international competitiveness.

Infrastructure is not only one of the areas in which Africa lags globally the most but also one in which the divide between African countries is the largest (World Economic Forum, 2015). The infrastructure deficit is particularly high for sub-Saharan Africa's less developed countries (LDCs), even when compared to that of other low-income countries.

Improving African infrastructure can benefit the continent through a number of channels, including better performance in the agriculture sector and increased regional and global trade. Increasing investment in rural infrastructure such as irrigation, roads, and energy can help reduce Africa's dependence on rain-fed agriculture, improve access to markets for agricultural produce, and increase resilience to climate change. Through better and more affordable information and communication technology infrastructure, farmers can register their land and have access to credit; use land and water more efficiently; obtain weather, crop, and market information; and trace food and animals.

For instance, better information and communication technology cuts across sectors by allowing the rapid and free flow of information. Similarly, more reliable electricity provision can significantly reduce the cost of doing business for all sectors, in particular the manufacturing sector (World Economic Forum, 2015). Well-connected infrastructure networks can benefit a broad range of sectors by enabling entrepreneurs to get their goods and services to markets in a secure and timely manner and by facilitating the movement of workers. They can also help increase intra-African trade (which currently hovers around 12 percent of total trade) and participation in regional and global value chains.

African policymakers are well aware of the potential for infrastructure to support the continent's accelerated integration and growth, technological transformation, trade, and development. The continent's long-term vision as articulated in the African Union's Agenda 2063 is that, in about fifty years, African infrastructure will include high-speed-railway networks, roads, shipping lines, sea and air transport, and well-developed information and communication technology and a digital economy. The vision plans for a pan-African high-speed railway network that will connect all the major cities of the continent, with adjacent highways and pipelines for gas, oil, and water, as well as broadband cables and other communications infrastructure. Infrastructure will be a catalyst for manufacturing, skills development, technology, research, innovation and development, integration and intra-African trade, investment, and tourism. According to Agenda 2063, building world-class infrastructure and facilitating trade should result in intra-African trade growing from less than 12 percent currently to about 50 percent by 2045 and the African share of global trade rising from 2 percent to 12 percent (African Union Commission, 2015).

Africa's focus on infrastructure is not surprising. Infrastructure is the cornerstone of a country's economic activity, and infrastructure bottlenecks stunt economic growth and increase poverty and inequality. Investing in infrastructure can have three important positive effects on an economy: Infrastructure spending provides a short-term demand stimulus to an economy and boosts output. In the longer term, infrastructure spending can raise the economy's productive capacity and thereby its trend growth rate. Moreover, when financed by debt, the return on investment a country gets from increasing infrastructure investment can be large enough for infrastructure projects to pay for themselves.

Attempts to quantify the macroeconomic effects of scaling up infrastructure investment find significant positive effects. Simulations show that in developing economies, increasing the public-investment-to-GDP ratio from 7 percent of GDP to 14 percent of GDP in about three years and stabilizing it at 9 percent of GDP afterward can substantially increase output by 7 percent over the long term (International Monetary Fund, 2014a). To put things in perspective, a World Bank forecast for sub-Saharan Africa puts real GDP growth at 4 percent in 2015 (World Bank, 2015a, p. 4). However, accounting for the continent's 2.6 percent population growth results in a per capita income growth of only 1.4 percent. The 2017 World Bank growth forecasts of 1.6 percent in 2016 and 2.4 percent for 2017 are even lower than the region's population growth (World Bank, 2017a). As a result, scaling up infrastructure investment in the region could help achieve much needed higher growth.

More and better infrastructure can benefit the economy several ways. Cheaper transport costs can help create new markets and realize the returns to agglomeration, which in turn fosters competition, spurs innovation, lowers prices, and raises productivity, leading to an increase in living standards (Henckel and McKibbin, 2010). Furthermore, transport infrastructure can have a direct effect on economic efficiency of an economy by reducing transport costs and an indirect effect by lowering inventories. As an economy moves up the global value chain, adapting its infrastructure can also help attract foreign investment and contribute to knowledge transfer, leading to more trade with the rest of the world.

The potential benefits of infrastructure are even larger when network and cross-sectoral impacts and synergies are accounted for. The World Bank stresses, for instance, that investments in a platform of urban services may produce economic returns greater than the sum of each individual investment because infrastructure investments may change land usage, productivity levels, settlement patterns, and property values (World Bank, 2014d). Similarly, the World Bank's updated infrastructure plan for fiscal years 2012–15 flags projects that seek to "optimize co-benefits across infrastructure sectors, between infrastructure and environment (green), between infrastructure and social development (inclusive) and heighten spatial benefits (regional)" (World Bank, 2014d). The action plan seeks to identify and prioritize three points of leverage that can unlock a country's growth and development potential: (1) missing links, or infrastructure investments that interconnect two markets or areas such as a bridge within a region or a cross-border power interconnector, international road corridors, or fiber optic links in a region; (2) bottlenecks such as inhibitions to economic activity, laws on competition that reduce the potential of private sector investments, or a lack of clean water, which limits women's ability to participate in economic activity; and (3) ripple effects such as an information and communication technology application that generates data on sector performance with spillover effects in sector accountability and governance, a regional power project that has effects beyond the host country, or a rural infrastructure package that boosts agricultural productivity with effects on rural income and development.

For countries to reap the benefits of infrastructure investment, however, certain conditions are needed. The IMF finds that the short-term effect of increased investment is higher (1) during periods of economic slack and when interest rates are low, (2) in countries with a high degree of public investment efficiency in which new spending is not wasted and goes to projects with high rates of return, and (3) when new investment is financed through debt rather than through higher taxes or lower spending.

Closing much of this efficiency gap could substantially increase the economic dividends for public investment (International Monetary Fund, 2014c). Studies show, however, that public investment spending is particularly wasteful in LDCs. For example, the IMF estimates that about 40 percent of the potential value of public investment is lost to inefficiencies in the investment process. In contrast, the efficiency gap is an average of 30 percent for 134 countries and is lower for emerging markets (27 percent) and advanced economies (13 percent). Closing much of this efficiency gap could substantially increase the economic dividends for public investment. LDCs can do so by strengthening the institutions related to the funding, management, and monitoring of project implementation while all countries will benefit from stricter oversight of public-private partnerships and better integration between national strategic planning with capital budgeting. In addition to the efficiency of public investment, the effects of investment on developing economies depend also on the type of financing, the response of the private sector, and the ability of the authorities to implement fiscal adjustment and manage debt (International Monetary Fund, 2014c).

The shared concern for the infrastructure deficit in Africa has led to a proliferation of initiatives. Among the various multilateral ones are the following:

New Partnership for Africa's Development (NEPAD). Established in 2001 under the African Union, NEPAD supported the Program for Infrastructure Development in Africa (PIDA) in 2011 as one of its flagship initiatives to identify and assess key cross-border infrastructure investments in 2012–40.[2] In the shorter term, PIDA focuses on its priority action plan, which includes fifty-one regional and continental infrastructure projects to be implemented by 2020. These projects are designed to meet Africa's more immediate regional and continental infrastructure needs. To accelerate the implementation of PIDA, African leaders gave their political impetus to eight regional infrastructure projects under the

2 For details on NEPAD, see www.nepad.org/content/about-nepad#aboutourwork. For details on PIDA, see www.afdb.org/en/topics-and-sectors/initiatives-partnerships/programme-for-infrastructure-development-in-africa-pida/.

Presidential Infrastructure Champion Initiative,[3] which was adopted in 2012. In the same vein, African leaders adopted the Dakar Agenda for Action in June 2014 to leverage public-private partnerships and mobilize financing around sixteen infrastructure projects to be realized by 2020 (New Partnership for Africa's Development, 2014). Concrete steps have also been taken by NEPAD to ensure acceleration of infrastructure projects on the continent. For instance, the Africa Global Partnership Platform, a dialogue platform that acts as an umbrella for Africa's rapidly expanding international partnerships, was endorsed by African countries at both the NEPAD Heads of State and Government Committee meeting and the African Union Summit in 2014. The Africa Global Partnership Platform contributes to a greater coherence of Africa's international partnerships and serves as a platform for feeding Africa's interests and perspectives into wider global processes. NEPAD also established the Continental Business Network, which is an African Union Heads of State and Government Committee response to facilitate private sector engagement and leadership in important continentwide infrastructure projects, particularly the regional infrastructure projects under PIDA. The Continental Business Network aims to attain financing and support for infrastructure projects by creating a platform for collaboration between the public and private sectors. The second Continental Business Network High-Level Leader's Dialogue, hosted in May 2016, examined the role of the private sector in removing risks to PIDA projects and paved the way for the subsequent launch of the projects of "NEPAD Continental Business Network (CBN) Report on De-Risking Infrastructure and PIDA Projects in Africa."[4]

Regional Infrastructure Development Master Plan (RIDMP). The RIDMP of the Southern Africa Development Community of 2012 is anchored by the six pillars of energy, transport, information and communication technology, meteorology, transboundary water resources, and tourism (transfrontier conservation areas). The master plan will be implemented over three five-year intervals—short-term (2012–17), medium-term (2017–22), and long-term (2022–27) and first will focus on projects

3 See www.nepad.org/programme/presidential-infrastructure-champion-initiative-pici.

4 See the full report at http://aiswpff.com/wp-content/uploads/2016/07/CBN-RISK-REPORT-THIRD-VERSION-DATED.pdf.

related to capacity building, and regulatory and institutional strengthening. The RIDMP is aligned with PIDA and with the COMESA-EAC-SADC Interregional Infrastructure Master Plan.[5]

Sustainable Energy for All initiative. In September 2011, UN Secretary General Ban Ki-moon launched this initiative to make sustainable energy for all a reality by 2030 by fostering partnerships between governments, business, and civil society. In 2014, the UN General Assembly declared the decade 2014–24 the Decade of Sustainable Energy for All, underscoring the importance of energy issues for sustainable development.

Africa Infrastructure Country Diagnostic (AICD). The African Development Bank (AfDB), in partnership with the World Bank, developed the AICD, which provided a detailed series of infrastructure investment needs by subregion in 2011 (African Development Bank and World Bank, 2011). In 2014, the World Bank launched the Global Infrastructure Fund as a platform for identifying, preparing, and financing large, complex infrastructure projects.[6] This facility thus also covers infrastructure financing in Africa.

Africa50. An infrastructure investment platform promoted by the AfDB, Africa50 aims to accelerate project preparation and financing on the continent. In particular, it seeks to shorten the time between project idea and financial close from a current average of seven years to at most three years. Africa50 held its Constitutive General Assembly in 2015; twenty African countries and the AfDB have subscribed for an initial amount of $830 million in share capital.[7]

New Deal on Energy for Africa. More recently, the New Deal on Energy for Africa put forward by the AfDB seeks to achieve universal access to energy in Africa by 2025. The new deal will be implemented through the Transformative Partnership on Energy for Africa, which is designed to provide a platform to coordinate action among private and public partners and offer innovative financing solutions.[8]

5 Common Market for Eastern and Southern Africa (COMESA); East African Community (EAC); Southern African Development Community (SADC). For the report, see www.sadc.int/files/7513/5293/3530/Regional_Infrastructure_Development_Master_Plan_Executive_Summary.pdf.

6 For details on the Global Infrastructure Fund, see www.worldbank.org/en/topic/publicprivatepartnerships/brief/global-infrastructurefacility.

7 For more on Africa50, see www.africa50.com/.

8 For information on the New Deal on Energy for Africa, see www.afdb.org/fileadmin/uploads/afdb/Documents/Generic-Documents/Brochure_New_Deal_2_red.pdf.

In addition, traditional bilateral and multilateral development flows to African infrastructure have increased overall, and there is a growing amount of traditional (such as from the U.S. Power Africa initiative and the EU-Africa Infrastructure Trust Fund)[9] and nontraditional bilateral flows (from China, Brazil, and India). Finally, substantial opportunities remain because of the BRICS Development Bank (established by Brazil, Russia, India, China, and South Africa), the Asian Infrastructure Investment Bank, and the Silk Road Infrastructure Fund.

Building African infrastructure will, however, require substantial financing. A World Bank comprehensive study estimates that sub-Saharan Africa's infrastructure needs are around $93 billion a year, and estimates are higher when North Africa's financing needs are considered (Foster and Briceño-Garmendia, 2009). According to NEPAD, the PIDA priority action plan projects require an estimated $68 billion for implementation until 2020. An additional $300 billion is needed for the rest of the projects until 2040.

Pension funds could play a particularly important role in financing Africa's infrastructure. A key message is that there is urgency to act now if the significant potential of African pensions to finance infrastructure development is to be leveraged. While sub-Saharan African countries are in a demographic sweet spot, with low dependency ratios, the labor force is rising rapidly. An aging population is not yet drawing on pension systems, and policymakers need to address existing obstacles to pension fund investment in infrastructure. In North Africa, unsustainable pension schemes together with unfavorable demographic and labor trends also point to the need of reforming pension systems.

Apart from countries in southern Africa, such as Botswana, Namibia, and South Africa and a few others such as Kenya and Nigeria, pension assets as a share of GDP are low because pension funds are relatively small and dominated by often poorly performing pay-as-you-go schemes for public sector employees. Even when pension reform has been implemented, as in Nigeria, and assets are available for investment, governance and regulatory obstacles and a dearth of adequate financial instruments limit pension funds' allocation to infrastructure.

9 For more on the U.S. Power Africa initiative, see www.usaid.gov/powerafrica. For more on the EU-Africa Infrastructure Trust Fund, see www.eu-africa-infrastructure-tf.net.

POLICY RECOMMENDATIONS

I now make several policy recommendations to address the obstacles to pension fund investment in infrastructure.

At the National Level

Leveraging political leadership. Leveraging domestic pension funds for financing infrastructure development is only one element of the broader agenda of economic transformation. Economic transformation will generate its own winners and losers because of reforms in a number of sectors. Pension reforms often require trade-offs such as increasing retirement age, cutting pension benefits, or increasing competition in the fund management industry, which can be politically costly in the short term but can ensure the long-term viability of the pension system and the accumulation of resources that can be used to finance infrastructure needs. At the same time, the governance and quality of public investment needs to be improved so as to avoid pension funds seeing losses in their infrastructure investment, which could undermine the benefits of pension reform and trust in the pension system. A minimum of political will and the ability to engage all stakeholders will therefore be necessary to achieve pension reform and reduce obstacles to pension fund investment in infrastructure.

Ensuring a supportive economic environment. Policymakers need to formulate and implement adequate policies to improve the environment for pension funds. Policies that lead to increased formal employment and increase the share of women in formal economic activities can help improve the performance of the pension system. Developing the private sector will help African countries reduce their reliance on social security and civil pension funds and tap the potential offered by its large labor force to effectively contribute to the pension system. At the macroeconomic level, appropriate monetary policy can help avoid high and volatile interest rates and price levels that would complicate the management of pension funds. Adequate fiscal policy will be necessary to address unsustainable pension systems (often supporting civil servants), set up public pension reserve funds, and free up resources for both government and pension fund investment in infrastructure.

Reforming unsustainable pension systems. The sustainability of domestic pension systems is a precondition for pension funds to finance infrastructure development. In some African countries, defined benefit pension systems are constrained by unsustainable structural deficits. Pension funds have accumulated deficits because of inadequate returns on investment, demographic changes, or mismanagement. In such cases, pension reform can pave the way toward a funded pension system with larger assets under management and broader coverage. Given the relatively large size of the informal sector in Africa, micropension schemes for self-employed workers can increase coverage further. Political will is, however, instrumental for maintaining a commitment to the reform of pension systems. Reforming pension schemes will also require strengthening the legal, regulatory, and supervisory environment. Unintended consequences of regulation that could limit infrastructure investment will need to be carefully weighed so as not to compromise the primary objective of pension funds to meet their liabilities.

Strengthening the management of pension funds. It will also be important to build the capacity of pension fund trustees and managers so that they exercise their fiduciary duty adequately. Investment in infrastructure should be consistent with pension fund investment policy as established within a good governance framework. Pension fund managers should assess on a risk-adjusted basis the benefits of different types of infrastructure financing instruments, which range from listed infrastructure companies and infrastructure funds to direct equity investment and debt financing. Pension funds should strengthen their in-house expertise related to the sectors in which they plan to invest, especially in the case of direct participation. Beyond financial obligations, pension funds should consider social, environmental, and governance issues when considering investing in infrastructure.

Developing domestic financial and capital market instruments for infrastructure investment. For pension funds to play a meaningful role in infrastructure development, it will be necessary to develop financial and capital market instruments to channel pension assets into infrastructure investment. Governments will need to ensure an appropriate fiscal policy as well as adequate cash and debt management in order to build a reliable long-dated domestic yield curve. Taking measures to ensure the liquidity of capital markets is a difficult task but is essential for attracting institutional investors. Transparency and appropriate information to ensure adequate pricing of benchmark government instruments is a first step toward deeper capital markets. Adequate market infrastructure, including trading platforms for government bonds, is also necessary to help ensure liquidity. To develop instruments such as project bonds, governments will also need to restructure the infrastructure sector and remove existing bottlenecks in infrastructure financing, including those stemming from the poor governance and financial sustainability of utilities and other parastatals.

Taking innovative measures. In addition, African policymakers will need to consider innovative measures to strengthen the role of domestic pension funds in infrastructure financing. For instance, pension reform can be facilitated through the use of technology such as mobile phones for a unique identification process. Informal sector participation in African pension funds can be increased by including domestic workers in the pension system (as in South Africa).

At the Regional Level

In addition to supporting government and pension funds in implementing the above reforms, regional institutions should focus on the following issues:

Regional financing. Regional development banks should take the lead when it comes to regional infrastructure projects, especially regarding their construction phase, and help finance and catalyze national projects, including through risk mitigation instruments. In addition to conventional financing from regional development banks and other partners, financing tools could consider a blend of multilateral financing (grants, long maturity), developmental aspects and social considerations, and private financing (private return). To manage the reluctance of fund managers and trustees to invest in long-term projects because of liquidity constraints, schemes in which governments (supported by development banks) would finance greenfield investments and pension funds would invest in brownfield investments (for example, once the revenues from the greenfield investments are generated) could be considered. Regional development banks are also uniquely placed to coordinate regional projects given their expertise in their regions of interest.

Regional capital markets and financial integration. Supporting the establishment of regionally integrated financial and capital markets, improving market infrastructure and the payment system, and allowing cross-border investments from pension funds can help broaden the investor base for infrastructure investment. The regional work of the African Financial Markets Initiative could be strengthened to help countries develop their local capital markets and integrate them regionally. Regional efforts should also include capacity building for pension fund managers—for instance, in collaboration with the Africa Pension Funds Network.

Strengthening capacity. Regional technical assistance from multilateral institutions is increasingly addressing the challenges specific to Africa. In addition to existing programs on macroeconomic policy and debt management, it will be useful to develop programs tailored to African capital market development, pension fund reform, and pension fund supervision and management. In addition, timely data on African infrastructure and pension funds are difficult to obtain, and multilateral institutions should include these in their effort to support the data revolution. More generally, countries' investment climates should be improved through adequate policies with respect to openness to investors, transparency, predictability, rule of law, and respect for contracts. The Policy Framework for Investment, a voluntary process guided by the Organization for Economic Cooperation and Development, can help countries improve issues such as the coherence of the investment framework, risk mitigation, pricing, financing, inclusiveness, and responsible conduct.

Complementing domestic pension investment through cofinancing and innovative policies. Coinvestment with international investors can be a useful tool for alleviating international investors' fear of policy reversal. Partnership with local funds that have higher stakes (and need to earn more than the inflation rate) can help attract foreign financing. The issuance and listing of infrastructure bonds in some countries can be replicated in the rest of the continent, and domestic pension funds can cofinance with their own government and with other institutions that are investing in African infrastructure. Indeed, regional and international investors, including pension funds from more developed economies (including South Africa), infrastructure funds (often backed by multilaterals), and multilateral and national development banks are increasingly investing in African infrastructure.

A holistic approach will be important to leverage African pension funds for infrastructure development. The potential of African pension funds to finance infrastructure will be exploited fully only with the support of all stakeholders in identifying bottlenecks and in elaborating solutions.

In summary, pension reform driven by strong political leadership and ownership by all stakeholders can help improve the performance of African pension systems and develop pension assets. However, pension reform should be carefully designed so as to learn from the lessons of the mixed results of earlier experiences in Latin America, notably in Chile, as well as in central and eastern European countries. Improvements to the governance, regulation, and supervision of pension funds can help pension funds invest in infrastructure in a manner consistent with their primary goal of ensuring old-age income security. Even when sufficient pension assets are available and asset allocation to infrastructure investments is made, African countries will still need to develop domestic financial and capital market instruments for infrastructure investment. Finally, given the large scale of infrastructure investment, African countries will need to consider the net benefits of complementing domestic pension assets with foreign and multilateral investments through cofinancing and innovative policies.

9

Conclusion

Why Africa? Well, to start, Africans care about their continent. All over the continent, a young and growing population of increasingly urbanized men and women are seeking a better future, just like their peers in other parts of the world. At the policy level, the African Union's Agenda 2063 embodies the vision of a prosperous and equitable continent as seen by its people. But people outside Africa should also care about the continent, not the least because a more peaceful and prosperous Africa is in their interest because it would create more opportunities for trade and investments, more jobs, and more security for all. Such an Africa will yield large global public goods. Reducing the continent solely to an aid recipient, a security risk, a giant oilfield, or the next Chinese bridgehead does not give a picture clear enough to guide meaningful policies for Africa. Instead, adding an economic lens to the typical ones normally used to view Africa is not only useful but unavoidable for those interested in realizing the vision of Africa as a global public good.

How Africa? Think about your last visit to your optometrist, when she selected a combination of lenses that worked best for you. One of the advantages of using an economic lens is that it forces the debate about the continent to be based on facts, however limited they may be, rather than opinions. Facts about micro- and macroeconomic as well as financial market variables are the best way to go beyond hardwired, preconceived opinions and start a meaningful discussion about the priorities of the continent. Investing in data collection, including qualitative surveys, case studies, and meta-analysis, will yield great dividends for stakeholders inside and outside Africa. Interestingly, some of the best analysis on Africa these days comes from the financial press.

Using an economic lens helps go beyond the oft-quoted averages and understand the diversity of the continent. Focusing the lens to understand differences among countries and even within a country is often worth the effort if policies are to be effective.

A healthy debate about drivers of economic growth and ways to make it more inclusive will help guide policies. Recent discoveries of oil and gas in many countries, coupled with the continent being resource rich, provide an opportunity for nongovernment actors to build on a large body of economic studies and country experiences and engage with policymakers.

Not using an economic lens exposes Africa observers and actors to the risk of overlooking the strong undercurrents that are shaping the future of the continent. For instance, it is critical to think ahead about how the rapid adoption of mobile technology and, more generally, innovation, robust demographic trends, and fast-paced urbanization will influence the continent and the rest of the world. The challenge is to take the right policy measures now so as to leverage these trends to the benefit of the African population.

There is no doubt that Africa is changing, in many aspects more rapidly that one can sense. We have the opportunity to not only be part of this change but also to shape it for the common good. To finish, let me borrow a concept from social psychology. One of the few lessons from my psychology course (taken in the last century) that struck a chord with me is that *attitudes* are defined as "feelings, often influenced by our beliefs, that predispose our reactions to objects, people, and events." The stakes are very high for the more than 1 billion Africans and for the next generations of Africans. The world owes it to them and to itself to at least revisit the current attitudes toward the continent. A sentence with words such as *innovation*, *growth*, or *employment* together with *Africa* should not present an oxymoron. I hope that the discussion in this book helps to show that this is indeed not only possible, but that positive attitudes on the continent are being followed by actions. According to Myers (2012, p. 556), "the traffic between our attitudes and our actions is two-way. Our attitudes affect our actions. And our actions affect our attitudes." This finding implies that once attitudes toward Africa improve and are followed by positive actions, then a virtuous circle can be unlocked for the benefits of future generations of Africans and their partners. Investing in African tech firms would not only be seen as a possible business opportunity but would also be followed by investments in such firms, which in turn would reinforce the belief that such investment should be seriously considered.

REFERENCES

Adam, Christopher S., and Sebastien E. J. Walker. 2015. "Mobile Money and Monetary Policy in East African Countries." University of Oxford (www.sbs.ox.ac.uk/sites/default/files/research-projects/mobile-money/Monetary-policy-paper.pdf).

Adams, Paul. 2015. "Africa Debt Rising." Africa Research Institute, January 22 (www.africaresearchinstitute.org/publications/africa-debt-rising-2/).

Africa-EU Partnership. 2007. "The Africa-EU Strategic Partnership: A Joint Africa-EU Strategy" (www.africa-eu-partnership.org/sites/default/ files/documents/eas2007_joint_strategy_en.pdf).

———. 2014. "Fourth EU-Africa Summit: Roadmap 2014–2017" (www.consilium.europa.eu/uedocs/cms_Data/docs/pressdata/en/ec/142094.pdf).

Africa Growth Initiative. 2016. "Growth in Sub-Saharan Africa: The Role of External Factors." Policy Brief. Brookings Global Economy and Development, April 14 (www.brookings.edu/wp-content/uploads/2016/04/growth-sub-saharan-africa-external-factors.pdf).

African Center for Economic Transformation (ACET). 2014. "Growth with DEPTH—2014 African Transformation Report." Accra (http://acetforafrica.org/).

African Development Bank. 2011. "Africa's Middle Class Triples to More than 310m over Past 30 Years due to Economic Growth and Rising Job Culture, Reports AfDB." May 10 (www.afdb.org/en/news-and-events/article/africas-middle-class-triples-to-more-than-310m-over-past-30-years-due-to-economic-growth-and-rising-job-culture-reports-afdb-7986/).

———. 2013a. "At the Center of Africa's Transformation Strategy for 2013–2022" (www.afdb.org/fileadmin/uploads/afdb/Documents/Policy-Documents/AfDB_Strategy_for_2013%E2%80%932022_-_At_the_Center_of_Africa%E2%80%99s_Transformation.pdf).

———. 2013b. "Economic Integration in WAEMU: Will the Multilateral Monitoring Mechanism Lead to Growth and Welfare Convergence?" (www.afdb.org/uploads/tx_llafdbpapers/Economic_Integration_in_WAEMU.pdf).

African Development Bank and World Bank. 2011. *Handbook on Infrastructure Statistics* (www.afdb.org/fileadmin/uploads/afdb/Documents/Publications/AfDB%20Infrastructure_web.pdf).

African Union Commission. 2015. "Framework Document: The Africa We Want." September (www.un.org/en/africa/osaa/pdf/au/agenda2063-framework.pdf).

Africa Progress Panel. 2015. *Power, People, Planet: Seizing Africa's Energy and Climate Opportunities* (www.africaprogresspanel.org/wp-content/uploads/2015/06/APP_REPORT_2015_FINAL_low1.pdf).

Afrika, Jean-Guy K., and Gerald Ajumbo. 2012. "Informal Cross Border Trade in Africa: Implications and Policy Recommendations." *Africa Economic Brief* 3, no. 10 (www.afdb.org/fileadmin/uploads/afdb/Documents/Publications/Economic%20Brief%20-%20Informal%20Cross%20Border%20Trade%20in%20Africa%20Implications%20and%20Policy%20Recommendations%20-%20Volume%203.pdf).

Alessi, Christopher, and Stephanie Hanson. 2012. "Combating Maritime Piracy." New York: Council on Foreign Relations (www.cfr.org/piracy/combating-maritime-piracy/p18376).

Alexander, Harriet. 2013. "Where Are the World's Major Military Bases?" *Telegraph*, July 11 (www.telegraph.co.uk/news/ uknews/defence/10173740/Where-are-the-worlds-major-military-bases.html).

Andriamananjara, Soamiely, and Amadou Sy. 2015. "AGOA and Dutch Disease: The Case of Madagascar." Brookings Institution, February 18 (www.brookings.edu/blog/africa-in-focus/2015/02/18/agoa-and-dutch-disease-the-case-of-madagascar/).

Arezki, Rabah, Patrick Bolton, Sanjay Peters, Frédéric Samama, and Joseph Stiglitz. 2017. "From Global Savings Glut to Financing Infrastructure." *Economic Policy* 32, no. 90 (1 April), pp. 221–261 (https://doi.org/10.1093/epolic/eix005).

Arezki, Rabah, Klaus Deininger, and Harris Selod. 2012. "Global Land Rush." *Finance and Development* 49, no. 1 (www.imf.org/external/pubs/ft/fandd/2012/03/arezki.htm).

Arezki, Rabah, Thorvaldur Gylfason, and Amadou Sy, eds. 2011. "Beyond the Curse: Policies to Harness the Power of Natural Resources." Washington, D.C.: International Monetary Fund.

Armendáriz de Aghion, B. 1999. "Development Banking." *Journal of Development Economics* 58, pp. 83–100.

Ashiagor, David, Nadiya Satyamurthy, Mike Casey, and Joevas Asare. 2014. "Pension Funds and Private Equity: Unlocking Africa's Potential." Commonwealth Secretariat (www.avca-africa.org/media/1329/pension_funds_and_private_equity_2014.pdf).

Aziz, Zeti Akhtar. 2013. "Governor's Speech at the Brunei Darussalam Islamic Investment Summit 2013: 'Regulatory and Governance for Islamic Finance.'" Bank Negara Malaysia, June 19 (www.bnm.gov.my/index.php?ch=en_speech&pg=en_speech&ac=469&lang=en).

Balthasar, Dominik, and Cristina Barrios. 2014. "Africa: The EU-US Security-Economy Nexus." Paris: European Union Institute for Security Studies, July (www.iss.europa.eu/sites/default/files/EUISSFiles/Alert_34_Africa.pdf).

Bhushan, Aniket, Yiagadeesen Samy, and Kemi Medu. 2013. "Financing the Post-2015 Development Agenda: Domestic Revenue Mobilization in Africa." Research Report. Ottawa: North-South Institute.

Brautigam, Deborah. 2015. *Will Africa Feed China?* Oxford University Press.

British Petroleum. 2014. *BP Energy Outlook 2035* (www.bp.com/content/dam/bp/pdf/energy-economics/energy-outlook-2016/bp-energy-outlook-2014.pdf).

Brookings Institution. 2015. "Brookings Financial and Digital Inclusion Project Report" (www.brookings.edu/~/media/Research/Files/Reports/2015/08/financial-digital-inclusion-2015-villasenor-west-lewis/fdip_countries.pdf?la=en).

Brooks, Karen Mcconnell, Deon P. Filmer, M. Louise Fox, Aparajita Goyal, Taye Alemu Mengistae, Patrick Premand, Dena Ringold, Siddharth Sharma, and Sergiy Zorya. 2014. *Youth Employment in Sub-Saharan Africa*. Washington, D.C.: World Bank Group (http://documents.worldbank.org/curated/en/424011468192529027/Full-report).

Buhari, Muhammadu. 2016. "The Three Changes Nigeria Needs." *Wall Street Journal*, June 13.

Calderón, César. 2009. "Infrastructure and Growth in Africa." Policy Research Working Paper 3. Washington, D.C.: World Bank Group.

Center for Global Development and the African Population and Health Research Center. 2014. "Delivering on the Data Revolution in Sub-Saharan Africa—Final Report of the Data for African Development Working Group" (www.cgdev.org/sites/default/files/CGD14-01%20complete%20for%20web%200710.pdf).

Centers for Disease Control and Prevention. 2016. "Cost of the Ebola Epidemic" (www.cdc.gov/vhf/ebola/pdf/cost-response.pdf).

Chandy, Laurence, Veronika Penciakova, and Natasha Ledlie. 2013. "Africa's Challenge to End Extreme Poverty by 2030: Too Slow or Too Far Behind?" Washington, D.C.: Brookings Institution, April (www.brookings.edu/blog/up-front/2013/05/29/africas-challenge-to-end-extreme-poverty-by-2030-too-slow-or-too-far-behind/).

Chilosi, Thierry, Damien Dugauquier, Geraldinde Lambe, and Michimaru Onizuka. 2013. "African Payments: Insights into African Transaction Flows." SWIFT White Paper (www.swift.com/node/14411).

"China to Expand Cooperation with Africa in Infrastructure Construction." 2014. CNTV, May 9 (http://english.cntv.cn/2014/05/09/VIDE1399589761933797.shtml).

CitiesAlliance. 2010. "World Statistics Day: A Look at Urbanisation" (www.citiesalliance.org/node/2195).

Copley, Amy, Fenohasina Maret Rakotondrazaka, and Amadou Sy. 2014. "The U.S.-Africa Leaders Summit: A Focus on Foreign Direct Investment." *Africa in Focus* (blog), Brookings Institution, July 11 (www.brookings.edu/blog/africa-in-focus/2014/07/11/the-u-s-africa-leaders-summit-a-focus-on-foreign-direct-investment/#ftnte3).

Derviş, Kemal. 2014. "The 'Expectation Revolution' Is Rattling Chile, Turkey, and Brazil." *Huffington Post* (www.huffingtonpost.com/kemal-dervis/the-expectation-revolutio_b_4603712.html).

Dollar, David. 2015. "Chinese Economy Doing Fine, No Basis for Large Devaluation." Brookings Global Economy and Development, August 14 (www.brookings.edu/research/interviews/2015/08/14-chinese-economy-devaluation-dollar).

Donohue, Tom, and Jay Timmons. 2014. "Ex-Im Bank Levels the Playing Field for U.S. Exporters." *Wall Street Journal*, June 13 (www.wsj.com/articles/ex-im-bank-levels-playing-field-for-u-s-exporter-1402695738).

Dosso, Zoom. 2014. "Ebola Infections Set to Soar in Liberia: WHO." Yahoo!, September 8 (http://news.yahoo.com/african-union-calls-ebola-travel-bans-lifted-163924718.html).

Drummond, Paulo, and Estelle Xue Liu. 2014. "If China Sneezes, Africa Can Now Catch a Cold." *IMFBlog*, March 20 (http://blog-imfdirect.imf.org/2014/03/20/if-china-sneezes-africa-can-now-catch-a-cold/).

Eagle, William. 2014. "Ebola Claims Another Victim—Economic Growth." *VOA News*, September 1 (www.voanews.com/content/ebola-claims-another-victim-economic-growth/2434979.html).

Economist. 2000. "The Hopeless Continent." May 13 (www.economist.com/printedition/2000-05-13).

———. 2011. "Africa Rising." December 3 (www.economist.com/node/21541015).

Erlanger, Steven. 2016. "'Brexit': Explaining Britain's Vote on European Union Membership." *New York Times*, October 27 (www.nytimes.com/interactive/2016/world/europe/britain-european-union-brexit.html?_r=0).

Ernst & Young. 2015. "Africa Attractiveness Program: Making Choices" (www.ey.com/Publication/vwLUAssets/EY-africa-attractiveness-survey-2015-making-choices/$FILE/EY-africa-attractiveness-survey-2015-making-choices.pdf).

———. 2016. "Africa Attractiveness Program: Navigating Africa's Current Uncertainties" (www.ey.com/za/en/issues/business-environment/ey-africa-attractiveness-program-2016).

European Commission. 2014. "Africa-EU Peace and Security Partnership." Brussels: European Commission (http://ec.europa.eu/europeaid/what/development-policies/intervention-areas/peace-and-security/africa-eu-peace-security-partnership_en.htm).

European External Action Service. 2014. "Ongoing Missions and Operations." Brussels: European External Action Service (www.eeas.europa.eu/csdp/missions-and-operations/).

Evans, Mathew. 2015. "We Can't Ignore the Air Pollution Crisis in Africa's Fast-Growing Megacities." *The Conversation*, August 24 (http://theconversation.com/we-cant-ignore-the-air-pollution-crisis-in-africas-fast-growing-megacities-46305).

Export-Import Bank of the United States. 2013. *2013 Annual Report*. Washington, D.C.: Export-Import Bank of the United States.

———. 2017. *2017 Annual Report*. Washington, D.C.: Export-Import Bank of the United States.

Faria, Andre, and Paolo Mauro. 2009. "Institutions and the External Capital Structure of Countries." *Journal of International Money and Finance* 28, no. 3, pp. 367–391.

Fay, Marianne, Michael Toman, Daniel Benitez, and Stefan Csordas. 2011. "Infrastructure and Sustainable Development," in *Post-crisis Growth and Development*, edited by Shahrokh Fardoust, Yongbeom Kim, and Claudia Sepulveda (Washington, D.C.: World Bank) (http://siteresources.worldbank.org/DEC/Resources/ PCGD_Consolidated.pdf).

Felbab-Brown, Vanda. 2011. "Paying Off Somali Pirates: Still the Least Bad Option?" Brookings, March 4 (www.brookings.edu/opinions/paying-off-somali-pirates-still-the-least-bad-option/).

Fetzer, Thiemo, and Amadou Sy. 2015. "Big Data and Sustainable Development: Evidence from the Dakar Metropolitan Area in Senegal." Brookings Institution, April 23 (www.brookings.edu/blog/africa-in-focus/2015/04/23/big-data-and-sustainable-development-evidence-from-the-dakar-metropolitan-area-in-senegal/).

Filmer, Deon, and Louise Fox. 2014. *Youth Employment in Sub-Saharan Africa*. Washington, D.C.: World Bank (https://openknowledge.worldbank.org/bitstream/handle/10986/16608/9781464801075.pdf).

Finnan, Daniel. 2016. "Brexit Best for UK-Africa Ties, British Africa Minister Claims." Radio France International, June 5 (http://en.rfi.fr/africa/20160605-uk-africa-brexit-european-union-james-duddridge-united-kingdom).

Foster, Vivien, and Cecilia Briceño-Garmendia, eds. 2009. *Africa's Infrastructure: A Time for Transformation*. Washington, D.C.: World Bank (http://

documents.worldbank.org/curated/en/2009/01/11487313/africas-infra structure-time-transformation).

Frankel, Jeffrey A., and Andrew K. Rose. 2000. "Estimating the Effect of Currency Unions on Trade and Output." NBER Working Paper 7857. Cambridge, Mass.: National Bureau of Economic Research, August (www.nber.org/papers/w7857).

Fundira, Taku. 2017. "Africa's Food Trade: Trade Data Overview." Tralac (Trade Law Centre) (www.tralac.org/resources/our-resources/12129-africa-s-food-trade-overview.html).

Gettleman, Jeffery. 2016. "'Africa Rising'? 'Africa Reeling' May Be More Fitting Now." *New York Times*, October 17.

Glick, Reuven, and Andrew K. Rose. 2001. "Does a Currency Union Affect Trade? The Time Series Evidence." NBER Working Paper 8396. Cambridge, Mass.: National Bureau of Economic Research, July (www.nber.org/papers/w8396).

GSM Association. 2017. *The Mobile Economy: Sub-Saharan Africa 2017* (www.gsmaintelligence.com/research/?file=7bf3592e6d750144e58d9dcfac6adfab&download).

Gutman, Jeffrey. 2015. "Foresight Africa 2015: Infrastructure Requires More than Raising Money." Brookings Institution, January 22 (www.brookings.edu/blog/africa-in-focus/2015/01/22/foresight-africa-2015-infrastructure-requires-more-than-raising-money/#ftnte2).

Gutman, Jeffrey, Amadou Sy, and Soumya Chattopadhyay. 2015. "Financing African Infrastructure: Can the World Deliver?" Brookings Global Economy and Development, March (www.brookings.edu/wp-content/uploads/2016/07/AGIFinancingAfricanInfrastructure_FinalWebv2.pdf).

Hansen, Andrew. 2008. "The French Military in Africa." *Council on Foreign Relations* (blog), February 8 (www.cfr.org/ france/french-military-africa/p12578#p4).

Henckel, Tim, and Warwick McKibbin. 2010. "The Economics of Infrastructure in a Globalized World: Issues, Lessons and Future Challenges." Brookings Institution, June 4 (www.brookings.edu/research/the-economics-of-in frastructure-in-a-globalized-world-issues-lessons-and-future-challenges/).

Henderson, J. Vernon, Adam Storeygard, and David N. Weil. 2012. "Measuring Economic Growth from Outer Space." *American Economic Review* 102, no. 2, pp. 994–1028 (www.aeaweb.org/articles.php?doi=10.1257/aer.102.2.994).

Heritage Foundation. 2015. "2015 Index of Economic Freedom Promoting Economic Opportunity and Prosperity" (www.heritage.org/index/pdf/2015/book/index_2015.pdf).

Hüttl, Pia, and Silvia Merler. 2016. "Leaving the EU Would Mean Renegotiating More than 100 Trade Agreements." London School of Economics and

Political Science, March 4 (blogs.lse.ac.uk/brexit/2016/03/04/leaving-the-eu-would-mean-renegotiating-more-than-100-trade-agreements/).

Inderst, Georg, and Fiona Stewart. 2014. *Institutional Investment in Infrastructure in Emerging Markets and Developing Economies*. Washington, D.C.: World Bank.

Infrastructure Consortium for Africa (ICA). 2014. *Infrastructure Financing Trends in Africa: ICA Report 2013*. Tunis, Tunisia: ICA Secretariat, African Development Bank (www.icafrica.org/fileadmin/ documents/Annual_Reports/ICA-2013-INFRA-FIN-TRENDS-AFRICA-2013-FINAL-WEB.pdf).

Ingram, George. 2014. "The U.S.-Africa Leaders Summit: Africa's Dramatic Development Story." *Africa in Focus* (blog), Brookings Institution, July 28 (www.brookings.edu/blogs/africa-in-focus/posts/2014/07/28-us-africa-leaders-summit-development-ingram).

Ingram, George, and Steve Rocker. 2013. "U.S. Development Assistance and Sub-Saharan Africa: Opportunities for Engagement," in *Top Five Reasons Why Africa Should Be a Priority for the United States* (Washington, D.C.: Brookings Institution) (www.brookings.edu/research/reports/2013/04/us-development-assistance-engagement-africa-ingram0).

Institute of International Finance. 2011. "Financial Investment in Commodities Markets: Potential Impact on Commodity Prices and Volatility." Washington, D.C. (www.eia.gov/finance/markets/reports_presentations/2012PaperFinancialInvestment.pdf).

Intermedia. 2014. "Financial Inclusion Insights: Nigeria" (http://finclusion.org/uploads/file/reports/2014%20InterMedia%20FII%20NIGERIA%20QuickSights%20Summary%20Report.pdf).

International Labour Organization. 2014. *Global Employment Trends 2014* (www.ilo.org/global/research/global-reports/global-employment-trends/2014/lang—en/index.htm).

International Monetary Fund (IMF). 2013. *World Economic Outlook: Transitions and Tensions*. October. Washington, D.C.: International Monetary Fund (www.imf.org/external/pubs/ft/weo/2013/02/index.htm).

———. 2014a. *Regional Economic Outlook: Sub-Saharan Africa—Fostering Durable and Inclusive Growth*. April. Washington, D.C.: International Monetary Fund.

———. 2014b. *Regional Economic Outlook: Sub-Saharan Africa—Staying the Course*. October. Washington, D.C.: International Monetary Fund.

———. 2014c. *World Economic Outlook*. October. Washington, D.C.: International Monetary Fund.

———. 2015a. "Making Public Investment More Efficient." International Monetary Fund Staff Report. Washington, D.C.: International Monetary Fund.

———. 2015b. *Regional Economic Outlook—Sub-Saharan Africa—Navigating Headwinds*. April 15. Washington, D.C.: International Monetary Fund (www.imf.org/external/pubs/ft/reo/2015/afr/eng/pdf/sreo0415.pdf).

———. 2015c. "West African Economic and Monetary Union Common Policies of Member Countries—Staff Report; Press Release; and Statement by the Executive Director." April. Washington, D.C.: International Monetary Fund (www.imf.org/external/pubs/ft/scr/2015/cr15100.pdf).

———. 2015d. *World Economic Outlook*. April. Washington, D.C.: International Monetary Fund.

———. 2016. *World Economic Outlook: Subdued Demands: Symptoms and Remedies*. October. Washington, D.C.: International Monetary Fund (www.imf.org/external/pubs/ft/weo/2016/02/pdf/text.pdf).

———. 2017a. *Regional Economic Outlook: Fiscal Adjustment and Economic Diversification*. October. Washington, D.C.: International Monetary Fund (www.imf.org/en/Publications/REO/SSA/Issues/2017/10/19/sreo1017).

———. 2017b. *Regional Economic Outlook: Sub-Saharan Africa: Restarting the Growth Engine*. May. Washington, D.C.: International Monetary Fund (www.imf.org/en/Publications/REO/SSA/Issues/2017/05/03/sreo0517).

Izquierdo, Romero, Randall Romero, and Ernesto Talvi. 2008. "Booms and Busts in Latin America: The Role of External Factors." Inter-American Development Bank Working Paper #631, February (https://publications.iadb.org/bitstream/handle/11319/1612/Booms%20and%20Busts%20in%20Latin%20America%3a%20The%20Role%20of%20External%20Factors%20.pdf?sequence=1&isAllowed=y).

Japanese Ministry of Foreign Affairs. 2013. "Japan's International Cooperation." Japan's Official Development Assistance, White Paper 2012 (www.mofa.go.jp/policy/oda/white/2012/html/index.html).

Jerven, Morten. 2013. "Why We Need to Invest in African Development Statistics: From a Diagnosis of Africa's Statistical Tragedy towards a Statistical Renaissance." African Arguments, September 26 (http://africanarguments.org/2013/09/26/why-we-need-to-invest-in-african-development-statistics-from-a-diagnosis-of-africas-statistical-tragedy-towards-a-statistical-renaissance-by-morten-jerven/).

Johnson, Chloe, and Kellan Howell. 2014. "White House, Private Groups Move to Save Ex-Im Bank." *Washington Times*, June 23 (www.washingtontimes.com/news/2014/jun/23/white-house-private-groups-move-to-save-ex-im-bank/).

Joselow, Gabe. 2013. "Somali Diaspora Drawn Back to Mogadishu." Voice of America, October 14 (www.voanews.com/a/somali-diaspora-drawn-back-to-mogadishu/1769185.html).

Kaberuka, Donald. 2014. "To Prevent Pandemic of Fear, Isolate Ebola, not the Countries." *The East African*, September 6 (www.theeastafrican.co.ke/oped

/comment/isolate-Ebola-not-the-countries/434750-2443414-efaghx/index .html).

Kaufman, Daniel, Aart Kraay, and Massimo Mastruzzi. 2011. "The Worldwide Governance Indicators: Methodology and Analytical Issues." *Hague Journal on the Rule of Law* 3, no. 2 (June), pp. 220–246.

Kenya National Bureau of Statistics. 2014. "Information on the Revised National Accounts" (www.knbs.or.ke/highlights-of-the-revision-of-national -accounts/).

Kharas, Homi. 2017. "The Unprecedented Expansion of the Global Middle Class: An Update." Global Economy & Development Working Paper 100. Washington, D.C.: Brookings Institution.

Kimenyi, Mwangi S. 2013. "U.S.-Africa Leaders Summit: Seizing the Opportunity to Reposition Africa-U.S. Relations." Brookings Institution, January 23 (www.brookings.edu/blog/africa-in-focus/2014/01/23/u-s-africa-leaders -summit-seizing-the-opportunity-to-reposition-africa-u-s-relations/).

KMPG and ACCA. 2017. *Balancing Rules and Flexibility for Growth: A Study of Corporate Governance Requirements across Global Markets, Phase 2—Africa.* London: ACCA Global (www.accaglobal.com/content/dam /ACCA_Global/Technical/Governance/Corporate_Governance_in_Africa /Balancing%20rules%20and%20flexibility%20for%20growth%20in%20 Africa.pdf).

Larivé, Maxime. 2014. "Welcome to France's New War on Terror in Africa: Operation Barkhane." *National Interest*, August 7 (http://nationalinterest .org/feature/welcome-frances-new-war-terror-africa-operation-barkhane -11029).

Lefebvre, Ben. 2013. "What Uses More Electricity: Liberia, or Cowboys Stadium on Game Day?" *Wall Street Journal*, September 13 (https://blogs.wsj .com/corporate-intelligence/2013/09/13/what-uses-more-electricity-liberia -or-cowboys-stadium-on-game-day/).

Leke, Acha, Susan Lund, Charles Roxburgh, and Arend van Wamelen. 2010. "What's Driving Africa's Growth." McKinsey, June (www.mckinsey.com /global-themes/middle-east-and-africa/whats-driving-africas-growth).

Leo, Benjamin. 2014. "Why Can't America Do Investment Promotion in Africa Like China (or Canada)?" Center for Global Development (www.cgdev.org /blog/why-can%E2%80%99t-america-do-investment-promotion-africa -china-or-canada).

Lesser, Ian, Karim El Aynaoui, Memory Dube, Peter Draper, Eckart Woertz, Kristine Berzina, Andrés Serbín, Amadou Sy, Adriana Erthal Abdenur, Esther Brimmer, and Karim El Mokri. 2014. "Atlantic Currents: An Annual Report on Wider Atlantic Perspectives and Patterns." German Marshall Fund of the United States and OCP Policy Center, October 17 (www.gmfus .org/publications/atlantic-currents-annual-report-wider-atlantic-perspectives -and-patterns).

Levine, Ross. 2005. "Finance and Growth: Theory and Evidence," in *Handbook of Economic Growth*, vol. 1A, edited by Philippe Aghion and Steven N. Durlauf (Amsterdam: North-Holland), pp. 865–934.

Levitt, Arthur. 2000. "Speech by SEC Chairman: Remarks before the Conference on the Rise and Effectiveness of New Corporate Governance Standards." New York: U.S. Securities & Exchange Commission, Federal Reserve Bank of New York, December 12.

Lubold, Gordon. 2014. "Has the White House Bungled a Historic Africa Summit?" *Foreign Policy*, July 9 (http://foreignpolicy.com/2014/07/09/has-the-white-house-bungled-a-historic-africa-summit/).

Madu, Uzo. 2016. "Brexit, EU, Trade: What's in It for Africa?" Borderlex, May 19 (www.borderlex.eu/brexit-eu-trade-policy-whats-africa/).

Mancuso, Dan, and David Vinco. 2014. "Providing Support for SMEs," in *Berne Union Yearbook 2014*, pp. 78–80 (www.berneunion.org/Publications).

Masse, Jean Marie. 2013. "Medium and Long-Term Credit Risk Guarantees in Africa: Potential for Expansion of Support for Energy Projects." In *Africa Energy Yearbook 2013*. Africa Energy Forum.

Mbu, John. 2016. "Why Eurobonds Are an Important Source of Finance for Africa." The World Economic Forum (www.weforum.org/agenda/2016/02/overview-of-the-sub-saharan-african-eurobond-market/).

McArthur, John, and Jessica Pugliese. 2013. "How to Create Economic Opportunities and Jobs for Youth in 2014." Brookings Institution, December 23 (www.brookings.edu/blog/africa-in-focus/2013/12/23/how-to-create-economic-opportunities-and-jobs-for-youth-in-2014/).

McMillan, Margaret, and Ken Harttgen. 2014. "What Is Driving the Africa Growth Miracle?" NBER Working Paper 20077. Cambridge, Mass.: National Bureau of Economic Research, April (www.nber.org/papers/w20077).

Mo Ibrahim Foundation. 2014. *Regional Integration: Uniting to Compete*. London: Mo Ibrahim Foundation (http://mo.ibrahim.foundation/news/2014/2014-regional-integration-uniting-to-compete-revised-and-updated-facts-figures-report-available-now-for-download/).

———. 2015. "The 2015 Ibrahim Index of African Governance: Key Findings" (http://mo.ibrahim.foundation/news/2015/the-2015-ibrahim-index-of-african-governance-key-findings/).

Myers, David. 2012. *Social Psychology*, 12th ed. New York: McGraw-Hill Education.

New Partnership for Africa's Development. 2014. "The Dakar Agenda for Action (DAA): Moving Forward Financing for Africa's Infrastructure" (www.afdb.org/fileadmin/uploads/afdb/Documents/Generic-Documents/The_Dakar_Agenda_for_Action__DAA__-_Moving_Forward_Financing_for_Africa%E2%80%99s_Infrastructure.pdf).

Obama, Barack. 2009. "Remarks by the President to the Ghanaian Parliament." White House, Office of the Press Secretary, July 11 (https://obamawhitehouse.archives.gov/the-press-office/remarks-president-ghanaian-parliament).

O'Hanlon, Mike, and David Petraeus. 2014. "Export-Import Bank an Easy Call." *USA Today*, September 5 (www.brookings.edu/opinions/export-import-bank-an-easy-call/).

ONE. 2013. "The 2013 Data Report: Special Report Tracking Development Assistance, European Union." Washington, D.C.: The One Campaign (http://one.org.s3.amazonaws.com/pdfs/data_report_2013_tracking_development_assistance_eu.pdf).

Organization for Economic Cooperation and Development (OECD). 2012. *Multilateral Aid Report* (www.oecd.org/dac/aid-architecture/DCD_DAC(2012)33_FINAL.pdf).

———. 2013. "G20/OECD High-Level Principles of Long-Term Investment Financing by Institutional Investors" (www.oecd.org/daf/fin/private-pensions/G20-OECD-Principles-LTI-Financing.pdf).

———. 2014. *Development Aid at a Glance: Statistics by Region, Africa* (www.iri.edu.ar/publicaciones_iri/anuario/anuario_2015/cooperacion/109.pdf).

Pew Research Center. 2011. "The Future of the Global Muslim Population." January 27 (www.pewforum.org/2011/01/27/the-future-of-the-global-muslim-population/).

———. 2014. "Global Opposition to U.S. Surveillance and Drones, but Limited Harm to America's Image." July 14 (www.pewglobal.org/files/2014/07/2014-07-14-Balance-of-Power.pdf).

PricewaterhouseCoopers. 2015. "Africa Risk in Review 2015" (www.pwc.co.za/en/assets/pdf/africa-risk-in-review-2015.pdf).

Pritchett, Lant, and Lawrence Summers. 2014. "Growth Slowdowns: Middle-Income Trap vs. Regression to the Mean." Vox, December 11 (http://voxeu.org/article/growth-slowdowns-middle-income-trap-vs-regression-mean).

Ravallion, Martin, Shaohua Chen, and Prem Sangraula. 2008. "New Evidence on the Urbanization of Global Poverty." Development Research Group, World Bank (http://siteresources.worldbank.org/INTWDR2008/Resources/2795087-1191427986785/RavallionMEtAl_UrbanizationOfGlobalPoverty.pdf).

Rodrik, Dani. 2013. "Africa's Structural Transformation Challenge." Project Syndicate, December 12 (www.project-syndicate.org/commentary/dani-rodrik-shows-why-sub-saharan-africa-s-impressive-economic-performance-is-not-sustainable#DXLC5Bq5yAoAZX2R.99).

———. 2014. "An African Growth Miracle?" NBER Working Paper 20188. Cambridge, Mass.: National Bureau of Economic Research, June (www.nber.org/papers/w20188).

Schneidman, Witney, and Zenia Lewis. 2014. "The U.S.-Africa Leaders Summit: Deepening Trade and Commercial Ties." *Africa in Focus* (blog), Brookings Institution, July 24 (www.brookings.edu/blogs/africa-in-focus/posts/2014/07/24-deeping-trade-commercial-ties).

Schueneman, Tom. 2015. "Latest Round of Climate Talk in Bonn Conclude with (Some) Progress on Loss and Damage." The Energy Collective, September 8 (www.theenergycollective.com/globalwarmingisreal/2269209/latest-round-climate-talk-bonn-conclude-some-progress-loss-and-damage).

Sheets, Nathan. 2014. "Remarks of Under Secretary Sheets at the National Press Club, Event Hosted by Brookings Institution, December 3, 2014" (www.treasury.gov/press-center/press-releases/Pages/jl9710.aspx).

Simpasa, Anthony, and Daniel Gurara. 2012. "Inflation Dynamics in Selected East African Countries: Ethiopia, Kenya, Tanzania and Uganda." African Development Bank Brief (www.afdb.org/fileadmin/uploads/afdb/Documents/Publications/07022012Inflation%20East%20Africa%20-%20ENG%20-%20Internal.pdf).

Specter, Michael. 2014. "Ebola and the Cost of Fear." *New Yorker*, September 19 (www.newyorker.com/news/daily-comment/ebola-cost-fear).

Sy, Amadou. 2013a. "Financing Africa's Infrastructure Gap." Brookings Institution, October 9 (www.brookings.edu/blog/up-front/2013/10/09/financing-africas-infrastructure-gap/).

———. 2013b. "Post-2015 Millennium Development Goals: More and Better Finance Will Not Be Enough." Brookings Global Economy and Development, December 3 (www.brookings.edu/blog/africa-in-focus/2013/12/03/post-2015-millennium-development-goals-more-and-better-finance-will-not-be-enough/).

———. 2014a. "Is Africa at a Historical Crossroads to Convergence?," in Think Tank 20, "Growth, Convergence and Income Distribution: The Road from the Brisbane G-20 Summit." Brookings Institution, October, pp. 11–21 (www.brookings.edu/wp-content/uploads/2016/07/tt20-africa-convergence-sy.pdf).

———. 2014b. "Which African Countries Are at Risk from the Current Market Turmoil?" Brookings Institution, February 7 (www.brookings.edu/blog/africa-in-focus/2014/02/07/which-african-countries-are-at-risk-from-the-current-market-turmoil/).

———. 2015a. "Are African Countries Rebasing GDP in 2014 Finding Evidence of Structural Transformation?" Brookings Global Economy and Development, March 3 (www.brookings.edu/blog/africa-in-focus/2015/03/03/are-african-countries-rebasing-gdp-in-2014-finding-evidence-of-structural-transformation/#ftnte1).

———. 2015b. "Chinese Yuan Devaluation Is Not the Real Concern for Africa: A Weakened Chinese Economy Is!" Brookings Global Economy and Development, August 21 (www.brookings.edu/blog/africa-in-focus/2015/08/21/chinese-yuan-devaluation-is-not-the-real-concern-for-africa-a-weakened-chinese-economy-is/).

———. 2015c. "Trends and Developments in African Frontier Bond Markets." Brookings Global Economy and Development, March (www.brookings.edu/wp-content/uploads/2015/03/global_20160810_african_frontier_bond_markets.pdf).

———. 2016. "Impediment to Growth." *Finance and Development* 53, no. 2 (June) (www.imf.org/external/pubs/ft/fandd/2016/06/sy.htm).

———. 2017. "Leveraging African Pension Funds for Financing Infrastructure Development, March (www.brookings.edu/wp-content/uploads/2017/03/global_20170314_african-pension-funds.pdf).

Sy, Amadou, and Fenohasina Maret Rakotondrazaka. 2015. "Private Capital Flows, Official Development Assistance, and Remittances to Africa: Who Gets What?" Brookings Global Economy and Development, May (www.brookings.edu/research/private-capital-flows-official-development-assistance-and-remittances-to-africa-who-gets-what/).

Sy, Amadou. and Jessica Smith. 2013. "Captain Phillips and the Drivers of Piracy in East Africa and Somalia." Brookings Institution, October 18 (www.brookings.edu/blog/africa-in-focus/2013/10/18/captain-phillips-and-the-drivers-of-piracy-in-east-africa-and-somalia/).

Sy, Amadou, and Ernesto Talvi. 2016. "How Much of Sub-Saharan Africa's Growth Slowdown Is Being Driven by External Factors?" Brookings Global Economy and Development, April 21 (www.brookings.edu/blog/africa-in-focus/2016/04/21/how-much-of-sub-saharan-africas-growth-slowdown-is-being-driven-by-external-factors/).

Sy, Amadou N. R., and Mariama Sow. 2016a. "Domestic Resource Mobilization and External Financing: When Does Governance Matter? Evidence from Sub-Saharan Africa." Working Paper 19. Africa Growth Initiative. Brookings Global Economy and Development (www.brookings.edu/wp-content/uploads/2016/12/global_122116_governance.pdf).

———. 2016b. "Four Questions on the State of the West African Economic and Monetary Union and Implications for Other Regional Economic Communities." *Africa in Focus* (blog), Brookings Institution, March 15 (www.brookings.edu/blogs/africa-in-focus/posts/2016/03/15-west-africa-economic-monetary-union-sy-sow).

Tang, Ke, and Wei Xiong. 2010. "The Financialisation of Commodities." Vox, November 30 (www.voxeu.org/article/financialisation-commodities).

Tardy, Thierry. 2013. "Funding Peace Operations: Better Value for EU Money." Paris: European Institute for Security Studies (www.iss.europa.eu/content/funding-peace-operations-better-value-eu-money).

Taylor, Adam. 2014. "MAP: The U.S. Military Currently Has Troops in These African Countries." *Washington Post*, May 21 (www.washingtonpost.com/blogs/worldviews/wp/2014/05/21/map-the-u-s-currently-has-troops-in-these-african-countries/).

TheCityUK. 2013. "UK, the Leading Western Centre for Sovereign Wealth Funds." Financial Markets Series, June (www.thecityuk.com/assets/2015/Reports-PDF/Sovereign-Wealth-Funds-2015.pdf).

Tsangarides Charalambos, Pierre Ewenczyk, and Michal Hulej. 2006. "Stylized Facts on Bilateral Trade and. Currency Unions: Implications for Africa."

IMF Working Paper WP/06/31. Washington, D.C.: International Monetary Fund.

Tyson, Judith. 2015. "Sub-Saharan Africa International Sovereign Bonds." International Economic Development Group (www.odi.org/publications/9205-sub-saharan-africa-international-sovereign-bonds).

United Nations. 2014a. *A World That Counts: Mobilising a Data Revolution for Sustainable Development* (www.undatarevolution.org/wp-content/uploads/2014/11/A-World-That-Counts.pdf).

———. 2014b. *World Urbanization Prospects.* New York: Department of Economic and Social Affairs (http://esa.un.org/unpd/wup/highlights/wup2014-highlights.pdf).

———. 2015a. "Scale of Assessments for the Apportionment of the Expenses of United Nations Peacekeeping Operations" (www.un.org/en/ga/search/view_doc.asp?symbol=A/70/331/Add.1).

———. 2015b. "Transforming Our World: The 2030 Agenda for Sustainable Development." Resolution adopted by the General Assembly on September 25, 2015. A/RES/70/1 (www.un.org/ga/search/view_doc.asp?symbol=A/RES/70/1&Lang=E).

United Nations Conference on Trade and Development (UNCTAD). 2013. *World Investment Report 2013.* New York: United Nations.

———. 2014a. "Bilateral FDI Statistics." New York: United Nations.

———. 2014b. *World Investment Report 2014.* New York: United Nations.

———. 2016. "World Investment Report 2016: Investor Nationality-Policy Challenges." United Nations (http://unctad.org/en/PublicationsLibrary/wir2016_en.pdf).

United Nations Economic Commission for Africa (UNECA). 2012. "The Impact of the European Debt Crisis on Africa's Economy: A Background Paper." Addis Ababa: African Union Commission (https://www.uneca.org/sites/default/files/uploaded-documents/CoM/cfm2012/com12-theimpact-of-theeuropeandebtcrisis-onafricaeconomya-backgroundpaper_en_0.pdf).

———. 2013. "Making the Most of Africa's Commodities: Industrializing for Growth, Jobs and Economic Transformation" (www.uneca.org/sites/default/files/PublicationFiles/unera_report_eng_final_web.pdf).

United Nations Environment Programme. 2012. *Cities and Carbon Finance: A Feasibility Study on an Urban Clean Development Mechanism* (http://staging.unep.org/urban_environment/PDFs/UNEP_UrbanCDMreport.pdf).

———. 2013. *Africa's Adaptation Gap Technical Report: Climate-Change Impacts, Adaptation Challenges and Costs for Africa* (https://reliefweb.int/sites/reliefweb.int/files/resources/AfricaAdapatationGapreport.pdf).

United Nations Office on Drugs and Crime. 2013. "Transnational Organized Crime in Eastern Africa: A Threat Assessment." September (www.unodc.org/documents/data-and-analysis/Studies/TOC_East_Africa_2013.pdf).

United Nations Security Council. 2011. *Report of the Secretary-General on the Protection of Somali Natural Resources and Waters*. S/2011/661. October 25 (www.securitycouncilreport.org/un-documents/document/somalia-s-2011-661.php).

Vanguard Media. 2017. "IMF Forecasts 0.8% Economic Growth for Nigeria." August 3 (www.vanguardngr.com/2017/08/imf-forecasts-0-8-economic-growth-nigeria/).

Vollgraaff, Rene. 2016. "Brexit May Cut S. Africa GDP Growth by 0.1 Percentage Point." Bloomberg, June 16 (www.bloomberg.com/news/articles/2016-06-16/brexit-could-shave-0-1ppt-from-s-africa-gdp-growth-study-says).

Walsh, Jim. 2013. "Does Feel-Good 'Captain Phillips' Film Unfairly Depict Somali Plight?" *MinnPost*, October 16.

Watkins, Kevin. 2016. "What Would a Brexit Mean for EU Development Assistance?" Devex, June 6 (www.devex.com/news/what-would-a-brexit-mean-for-eu-development-assistance-88265).

Weil, David, Isaac Mbiti, and Francis Mwega, 2012. "The Implications of Innovations in the Financial Sector on the Conduct of Monetary Policy in East Africa." Working Paper, International Growth Centre.

White House. Office of the Press Secretary. 2014a. "Fact Sheet: U.S.-EU Counterterrorism Cooperation." White House Press Release, March 26 (www.whitehouse.gov/the-press-office/2014/03/26/fact-sheet-us-eu-counterterrorism-cooperation).

———. 2014b. "Fact Sheet: U.S. Support for Peacekeeping in Africa." White House Press Release, August 6 (www.whitehouse.gov/the-press-office/2014/08/06/fact-sheet-us-support-peacekeeping-africa).

———. 2014c. "Statement by the Chair of the U.S.-Africa Leaders Summit." White House Press Release, August 6 (www.whitehouse.gov/the-press-office/2014/08/06/statement-chair-us-africa-leaders-summit).

———. 2015. Office of the Press Secretary. "Fact Sheet: The Export-Import Bank: Supporting American Exports and American Workers in Every State across the Country." June 30 (https://obamawhitehouse.archives.gov/the-press-office/2015/06/30/fact-sheet-export-import-bank-supporting-american-exports-and-american).

World Bank. 2014a. "African Cities: Stronger Local Capital Markets Needed to Finance Sustainable Development." April 18 (www.worldbank.org/en/news/feature/2014/04/18/africa-local-capital-markets-to-finance-sustainable-development).

———. 2014b. "Ebola: Economic Impact Already Serious; Could Be 'Catastrophic' without Swift Response." September 17 (www.worldbank.org/en/news/press-release/2014/09/17/ebola-economic-impact-serious-catastrophic-swift-response-countries-international-community-world-bank).

———. 2014c. *The Economic Impact of the 2014 Ebola Epidemic: Short and Medium Term Estimates for West Africa*. Washington, D.C.: World Bank

Group (http://documents.worldbank.org/curated/en/524521468141287875/pdf/912190WP0see0a00070385314B00PUBLIC0.pdf).

———. 2014d. "Prioritizing Projects to Enhance Development Impact." Note prepared by the World Bank Staff for the G20 Investment and Infrastructure Working Group and the G20 Development Working Group, Washington, D.C., June (www.g20.utoronto.ca/2014/6%20Prioritizing%20Projects%20to%20Enhance%20Development%20Impact.pdf).

———. 2015a. *Africa's Pulse.* Volume 11, April. Washington, D.C.: World Bank Group.

———. 2015b. *Africa's Pulse.* Volume 12, October. Washington, D.C.: World Bank Group.

———. 2016a. *Africa's Pulse.* Volume 14, October. Washington, D.C.: World Bank Group.

———. 2016b. *World Bank Development Indicators.* 2016. Washington, D.C.: World Bank Group (https://openknowledge.worldbank.org/bitstream/handle/10986/23969/9781464806834.pdf).

———. 2017a. *Africa's Pulse.* Volume 15, April. Washington, D.C.: World Bank Group.

———. 2017b. "Remittance Prices Worldwide" (www.remittanceprices.worldbank.org).

World Economic Forum. 2015. *Africa Competitiveness Report 2015* (www3.weforum.org/docs/WEF_ACR_2015/Africa_Competitiveness_Report_2015.pdf).

World Health Organization. 2010. "Hidden Cities: Unmasking and Overcoming Health Inequities in Urban Settings." Kobe, Japan: WHO Centre for Health Development (www.who.int/kobe_centre/publications/hiddencities_media/who_un_habitat_hidden_cities_web.pdf).

INDEX

Abe, Shinzo, 28, 163, 213–14
Accountants and auditors, 225
Adams, Paul, 45
Addis Ababa Action Agenda (2015), 12, 106, 226
Adesina, Akinwumi, 222
AfDB. *See* African Development Bank
Africa: African Common Position, 113; China, perception of, 208–09; China-Africa Development Fund, 89; climate change and, 110–13; Common African Position on the Post-2015 Development Agenda, 72; data revolution in, 17; economic boom (2004–11), 30–39; EU-Africa Business Forums, 203; Forum on China-Africa Cooperation (2015), 102; free trade agreements in, 11, 126, 150; industrialization of, 16, 55, 223; Standby Force of, 202; U.S.-Africa Business Forum (2016), 180–84; U.S.-Africa Civil Society Forum (2014), 164; U.S. political and policy lenses for, 1; World Governance Indicators on, 145, 170, 227. *See also* Current state of Africa; Goals for Africa; Partnerships of Africa; U.S.-Africa Leaders Summit; *specific countries and regions*
Africa Corporate Governance Network, 224
"Africa Debt Rising" (Adams), 45
Africa50 Infrastructure Fund, 89, 222, 234
Africa Global Partnership Platform, 233
Africa Growth Initiative (AGI, Brookings Institution): on economic influence of external factors, 35; on financing for development, 65; on foreign direct investment, 166; review of Africa summits, 159; U.S.-Africa Leaders Summit participation, 176–77; on U.S. policy toward Africa, 147
Africa Infrastructure Country Diagnostic (AICD), 234
Africa Investment Initiative of the New Partnership for Africa's Development, 173
African Charter on Democracy, Elections, and Governance, 202

African Development Bank (AfDB): Africa50 Infrastructure Fund, 89, 222, 234; Africa Infrastructure Country Diagnostic (AICD), 234; climate change adaptation and mitigation efforts, 115; energy infrastructure financing coordination, 72, 89; highway project in Senegal and, 132; Infrastructure Project Preparation Facility (IPPF), 90; on middle class, 32; New Deal on Energy for Africa, 234–35; presidential policies of, 221–23; U.S. Department of Commerce operations in, 182
African Financial Markets Initiative, 239
African Group of Negotiators, 113
African Ministerial Conference on the Environment, 113
African Union (AU): African Peace and Security Architecture, 202, 204; Agenda 2063 of, 3–5, 229–30, 241; Ebola crisis, response to, 137–39, 222–23; EU summit attendance and, 161; infrastructure support, 232–33; Made in Africa Foundation, 89; peacekeeping missions of, 199; Support to Ebola Outbreak in West Africa mission, 139; tourism, Ebola outbreak and, 137–38; U.S.-Africa Leaders Summit and, 161–64
African Union Mission, 109, 199
Africa Pension Funds Network, 239
Africa Progress Panel, 111–12, 115
Africa's Pulse (World Bank), 8–9, 48–49
Aghion, Armedáriz de, 85
AGI. *See* Africa Growth Initiative
AGOA. *See* U.S. African Growth and Opportunity Act
Agricultural sector: Agenda 2063 goals for, 4; agroprocessing, 13; Brexit effect on, 110; Chinese investment in, 209–11; climate change and, 111, 116; competition in, 110; corruption and, 210; Ebola outbreak and, 136; economic reliance on, 15–16, 209; employment in, 33, 55–56; food deficit and, 210; foreign direct investment potential for, 29, 33; GDP rebasing and, 20–22; growth of, 12; infrastructure for, 88, 229; innovation in, 140–41; land grabs in, 209–11; policy recommendations for, 212; poverty rates and, 111; productivity increases in, 130; staple food crops and, 56, 136; subsidies for, 110. *See also specific countries and regions*
AICD (Africa Infrastructure Country Diagnostic), 234
Aid. *See* Foreign aid
AIG, 193
Al-Shabab, 30
Andriamananjara, Soamiely, 185
Angola: Chinese relations with, 47, 100, 208; commodity exports of, 11, 12, 26, 51; credit rating downgrade of, 104; export diversification, lack of, 9; foreign direct investment in, 28; GDP of, 208; infrastructure investments in, 73, 79, 93, 96; U.S. relations with, 181
Antimoney laundering (AML) rules, 70, 157
Arcelor Mittal, 137
Arezki, Rabah, 209, 211–12
Ashegoda wind farm (Ethiopia), 125
Asia: financial crisis (1997–98), 40; industrial sector in, 16; manufacturing sector in, 223–24. *See also specific countries*
Asian Infrastructure Investment Bank, 235
Association of Southeast Asian Nations (ASEAN) intraregional trade, 128
Aziz, Zeti Akhtar, 93

Ban Ki-moon, 118, 234
Banking sector. *See* Financial and banking sector
Basel Committee on Banking Supervision, 70, 86, 192
al-Bashir, Omar, 163–64
Batthacharya, Amar, 62
Belgium: foreign direct investment of, 166; piracy in Somalia and, 61

Benchmarks: for African summits, 164–65; for big data, 133; China as, 27; for EU countries, 129; for government instruments, 238; for revised GDP, 20–23; for WAEMU countries' ease of doing business, 129
Berne Union, 90, 189, 192–93
Big data, 3, 130–34, 143
Bilateral investment treaties (BITs), 171–73, 203
Bill and Melinda Gates Foundation, 69
Biometric identification technology, 142
Bitcoin, 145
Blended financing, 155, 173
Blockchain technology, 145
BNP Paribas, 70
Boko Haram, 30
Border relations. *See* Cross-border relations
Botswana: governance performance in, 170; pension funds in, 84, 235
BP Energy Outlook 2035, 26–27
Brackett, Bob, 91
Brautigam, Deborah, 209–12
Brazil, trade with Africa, 27
Bribery, 224. *See also* Corruption
Briceno-Garmendia, Cecilia, 76, 88
BRICS (Brazil, Russia, India, China, and South Africa) countries: development bank of, 157, 235; economic development of Africa and, 68; foreign direct investment of, 31
BRICS Development Bank, 157, 235
Brookings Institution: Financial and Digital Inclusion Project (FDIP), 119–21; Global Findex report (2014), 122. *See also* Africa Growth Initiative
Brooks, Karen Mcconnell, 57
Brownfield infrastructure projects, 87, 238
Buhari, Muhammadu, 51, 148
Burkina Faso: democracy in, 9; foreign direct investment in, 28; natural resources in, 34, 123
Burundi: conflict in, 11; railway in, 207
Business sector. *See* Private sector
Canadian Pension Plan, 84
Cape Verde: budget reforms in, 220; independence of, 5; infrastructure investments in, 73, 75
Capital markets, 144, 224, 237–39
Captain Phillips (movie), 58, 61
Cell phones. *See* Mobile phones
Cement production, 12
Centers for Disease Control and Prevention, 139
Central African Economic and Monetary Community, 68
Central African Republic: aid from Japan, 214; conflict in, 11, 29–30, 34, 218; International Support Mission in, 199; security operations in, 198–99, 204; U.S.-Africa Leaders Summit exclusion and, 161–64
Central Bank of Kenya, 143
Central Bank of Nigeria, 121
Central Bank of West African States, 92, 127
CFT (combating the financing of terrorism) rules, 70, 157
Chad: infrastructure investments in, 79; security operations in, 199
Chattopadhyay, Soumya, 81
Child mortality rate, 11
China: African perception of, 208–09; agricultural sector of Africa and, 209–11; aid given by, 27–28, 206; bilateral investment treaties of, 172; climate change and, 110–12, 114; currency devaluation in, 46–50; Ebola outbreak and, 139; economic development of Africa and, 27–28, 68, 77–78, 89, 206–07; economic effect on Africa, 10–11, 36–37, 48; economic slowdown in, 11, 47–50, 99–100, 123; foreign direct investment of, 27–28, 31, 72, 166–69, 207–08; Forum on China-Africa Cooperation, 102, 159–61, 163–65, 174; GDP of, 48; natural resources, demand for, 26; trade with Africa, 27, 157
China-Africa Development Fund, 89
China Development Bank, 89

China Union, 137
Chinese Africa Development Fund, 206
Climate change: adaptation and mitigation for, 110–15; agricultural sector and, 111, 116; Climate Change Conference in Paris (COP21), 12, 112–14, 118; as economic threat, 99; financing for low-carbon technology and, 156–58; foreign aid to combat, 71; Green Climate Fund, 113, 115, 156; renewable energy resources and, 112, 125, 141–42, 157; urbanization and, 115–18
Climate financing, 156
Clinton, Bill, 185
Coca-Cola, 183
Coinvestments, 239
Collier, Paul, 211
Combating the financing of terrorism (CFT) rules, 70, 157
Commercial Bank of Africa, 121
Commercial fishing, 58–60
Commission on Growth and Development, 158
Commodities: dependence on, 220; diversification of, 9, 12, 123–25, 151; as driver of growth, 26; financialization of, 124; reduction in value of, 10–11, 36–39, 98–99, 123, 183, 219; stewardship of, 13. *See also specific commodities*
Compact of Mayors, 118
Competition: for African trade, 174; agricultural sector and, 110; currency appreciation and depreciation, 46–47, 186; Ex-Im Bank and, 188, 190; exchange rates and, 129–30; financial sector development and, 143; infrastructure and, 106, 222, 229; natural resource dependence and, 15; non-oil economy and, 101; remittance costs and, 156; structural transformation for, 130; transportation costs and, 230; U.S. trade and, 152–53
Conflict. *See* Violence
Connected Farmer program, 141
Continental Business Network High-Level Leader's Dialogue (2016), 233
Continental Free Trade Area, 11, 126, 223
Convergence, 14–15, 129
Corporate governance, 223–25
Corruption: agricultural sector and, 210; combating, 201; corporate governance, effect on, 224; credibility and, 52; development financing, effect on, 228; as drain on resources, 221; financial sector and, 145–46; illicit financial flows and, 71, 173, 201; International Chamber of Commerce Rules on Combating Corruption, 171
Cost of living, 32
Côte d'Ivoire: agriculture in, 12, 130, 210; conflict in, 28, 34; debt servicing in, 42–44; Ebola outbreak, impact on, 136; GDP of, 9; infrastructure investments in, 93; security operations in, 199
Credit ratings, 104
Credit risk assessments, 143
Cross-border relations: conflicts and, 11; flows and remittances, 143–44; infrastructure projects, 222; trade procedures, 128
Cryptocurrencies, 144–45
Cuba, assistance in Ebola outbreak, 139
Currencies: Chinese yuan, weakening of, 46–50; common, 30, 126–28; competition and, 46–47, 186; cryptocurrencies, 144–45; debt servicing and, 40–46; devaluations of, 11–12, 40–46, 49, 99, 128; Dutch disease and, 186–88; of EAC, 30; intraregional trade and, 157; of Nigeria, 52; unions for, 126, 129; of West Africa, 126–29
Current state of Africa, 8–25; agriculture, natural resources, and services, 15–16; convergence or divergence, 14–15; GDP, rebasing of, 17–18; industrial sector, 16; narrative of, 9–13; positive trends, 11; services subsector, 22–25; sustainable growth, drivers of, 18–22
Customs unions, 30, 128

Dakar Agenda (2014), 233
Dakar Diamniadio Toll Highway (Senegal), 131–34
Decade of Sustainable Energy for All (2014–24), 234
Deindustrialization, 55, 223–24
Deininger, Klaus, 209, 211–12
Democracy: in Burkina Faso, 9; and demographic dividend, 27; in Eritrea, 163; and human rights, 175; and Roadmap for the Joint Strategy, 202
Democratic Republic of the Congo (DRC): Chinese relations with, 100; coltan trade ban from, 171; conflict in, 9, 11, 30; Ebola outbreak, assistance for, 139; governance performance in, 170; Kerry's visit to, 175; security operations in, 198
Demographics. *See* Population demographics
Derviş, Kemal, 56
Development. *See* Financing for development; Infrastructure
Diaspora bonds, 90, 96
Digital payment systems, 11, 12, 141
Diouf, Abdou, 5
Doha Declaration (2008), 63, 68
Dollar, David, 48
Dollars, bond repayments in, 40–42, 44–46
Domestic bond markets, 29, 69, 104
Domestic budget spending on infrastructure, 74–75, 80
Domestic private financing, 155
Domestic revenue sources, 75. *See also* Tax revenues
DRC. *See* Democratic Republic of the Congo
Drummond, Paul, 48
Duddridge, James, 109–10
Dutch disease, 186–88
Dutch-Moroccan Foreign Fighter Project, 200

East Africa: agricultural sector in, 33, 141; financial inclusion in, 142; financial technology in, 145; highways in, 12; oil discoveries in, 34; piracy in, 58–61; railway projects in, 207; regional integration of, 150. *See also specific countries*
East African Community (EAC): common currency for, 30; economic growth of, 18; foreign direct investment in, 28; U.S. cooperation agreement with, 181
East Africa Trade and Investment Hub, 184, 195
East Asia, manufacturing sector in, 223–24
Ebola crisis: AfDB's response to, 222–23; agricultural sector and, 136; effects of, 135–39; financial and banking sector and, 137; foreign aid for, 138–39; global economic policymaking and, 138, 154, 158; health infrastructure and, 6, 135–39; media coverage of, 177–80; mining sector and, 136–37; mobile wallet innovation and, 141; tax revenues and, 137; tourism and, 137–38; transportation and, 136–38
Ebola Response Fund, 222–23
ECAs (export credit agencies), 189
Economic boom (2004–11): benefits of, 32–33; external sources and, 36–39; fiscal sustainability and, 37–38; foreign investment growth and, 30–31; foreign investment sustainability and, 33–34; middle class and, 31–32
Economic Community of Central African States, 199
Economic Community of West African States, 126, 195
Economic integration. *See* Regional economic integration
Economic Partnership Agreements (EPAs), 195, 203, 205
Economist, on hopelessness of Africa, 8
Education: infrastructure technology and, 142; investments in, 221; as soft infrastructure, 130; U.S. support for, 202; for workforce development, 13, 32–33. *See also* Knowledge and skills transfer

Emefiele, Godwin, 50
Employment: in agricultural sector, 33, 55–56; automation and, 13; challenges in, 56–57; creation of, U.S. relations and, 183–84; female labor force and, 13; foreign direct investment and, 32; in manufacturing sector, 16, 55–56; pension fund performance and, 236; piracy, deterrence of, 60; policy recommendations for, 56–57; in Senegal, 6; in small and medium enterprises, 184; in sub-Saharan Africa, 53–57; youth labor force and, 11, 13, 53–54, 56. *See also* Informal sector; Unemployment
Energy: AfDB support for, 72, 89, 234–35; climate change and, 112; cost for consumers of, 32; Decade of Sustainable Energy for All (2014–24), 234; financing for, 2, 68–69, 71–72, 74, 77, 80; foreign direct investment in, 34; Global Covenant of Mayors for Climate and Energy, 118; International Energy Agency, 112, 156–57; New Deal on Energy for Africa, 234–35; potential for generation of, 12; renewable technology for, 112, 125, 141–42, 156–58; for rural areas, technology for, 141–42; subsidies for, 220; Transformative Partnership on Energy for Africa, 234; urbanization and, 116; U.S.-Africa Clean Energy Development and Finance Center, 191; U.S. Electrify Africa Act and, 181; U.S. energy boom, 124–25, 182. *See also* Power Africa; *specific sectors*
Energy Information Administration, 124–25
EPAs (Economic Partnership Agreements), 195, 203, 205
Equity market investments, 29, 34, 124
Eritrea: infrastructure investments in, 79; U.S.-Africa Leaders Summit exclusion and, 161–63
Ernst & Young Africa Attractiveness Survey, 152, 183
Ethiopia: Chinese relations with, 47; climate change and, 111–12; conflict in, 8; corporate governance in, 224; economic growth of, 12; energy resources in, 125; famine relief in, 5; financial inclusion in, 119–20; foreign direct investment in, 28, 34; GDP of, 9, 208; infrastructure financing in, 96; mobile services in, 120; natural resources in, 123; security operations in, 200; U.S. relations with, 182
EU-Africa Business Forums, 203
Eurobonds, 12, 29, 93–96
Europe and European Union (EU): Accounting and Transparency Directive, 171; African Peace Facility, 199; aid given by, 196–97; bilateral investment treaties of, 172; Brexit and, 107–10; climate change and, 110–11; Common Agricultural Policy, 110; Common Security and Defense Policy, 198; debt crisis in, 196; EU-Africa Summits of Heads of State, 159–61, 163–65; European Development Fund of, 108–09; financial crisis in, 40; foreign direct investment of, 166–69; industrial sector growth in, 16; intraregional trade in, 128; security in Africa, 198–200; strategies for Africa, 202–03; trade with Africa, 109–10, 194; U.S. competition for trade in Africa, 194–96; U.S. cooperation in Africa, 203–05. *See also specific countries*
EU–Southern African Development Community Economic Partnership Agreement, 109–10
Exchange rate systems, 128–30, 220–21
Export credit agencies (ECAs), 189, 192–93. *See also* Export-Import Bank of the United States
Export-Import Bank of China, 207
Export-Import Bank of the United States (Ex-Im Bank): private sector replacing, 191–93; reauthorization

of, 188, 193–94; sub-Saharan Africa and, 190–91; U.S. businesses in sub-Saharan Africa and, 188–90
External financing. *See* Foreign aid; Foreign direct investment
External sustainability, 38–39
Extractive Industries Transparency Initiative, 149, 171, 205

FDI. *See* Foreign direct investment
FDIP (Financial and Digital Inclusion Project), 119–21
Felbab-Brown, Vanda, 60
Fetzer, Thiemo, 131
Filmer, Deon P., 30
Financial and banking sector: access to, 143, 154–56, 224; borrowing costs, 220; building, 63; competition and efficiency in, 143; development of, 144; domestic debt markets, 45–46; Ebola outbreak and, 137; entrepreneurship, encouragement of, 70; foreign direct investment in, 29, 32; global financial regulation and, 70, 86, 157, 192; governance and corruption in, 145; illicit financial flows and, 70–71, 173, 201; inclusion through expanded services in, 118–22, 140, 142; infrastructure financing of, 86; macroeconomic issues and, 145–46; mobile payments for, 11, 120, 140–42; of Nigeria, 50–52; remittances and cross-border relations, 143–44. *See also specific banks*
Financial and Digital Inclusion Project (FDIP), 119–21
Financial literacy, 144
Financing for development, 62–96; capital inflow requirements and, 154–55; capital markets for, 155–56; concerns for, 81–82; corruption, effect of, 228; development finance institutions, 155; Eurobonds and, 93–96; external financial flows to sub-Saharan Africa, 65–68; infrastructure inadequacy and, 72–76; Islamic Sukuk financing, 91–93; in Liberia, 87–91; long-term investing for, 83–87; priorities in, 68–72; recommendations for, 82–83; sovereign bonds for, 40–46; Sustainable Development Goals, 62–65; trends in, 76–80; urbanization and, 118. *See also* Export-Import Bank of the United States; Foreign direct investment
Financing for Development Meeting (2015), 65
Fiscal sustainability, 37–38, 46, 221
Fishing industry, 58–60
Foreign aid: Brexit and, 108–09; from China, 27–28, 206; for development assistance, 33; for Ebola crisis, 138–39; from European Union, 196–97; fishery programs and, 60; health infrastructure and, 197, 201, 204; increase in, 31; from Japan, 213–14; top contributors of, 196; total for 2012, 196; from United States, 196–97. *See also* Official development assistance
Foreign direct investment (FDI): in agricultural sector, 29, 33; bilateral investment treaties and, 171–72; dependence on, 220; economic and trade integration for, 30; employment and, 32; in energy, 34; in financial and banking sector, 29, 32; GDP growth attracting, 18; global, Africa's share of, 224; governance and, 64, 170–71, 227–28; increase in, 31–32, 65–66, 69; in industrial sector, 34; in information and communications technology, 2, 29, 73–74, 77; for infrastructure, 29, 231, 239; key countries for, 28; in mining sector, 168; in mobile phone technology, 32; for natural gas sector, 28; in natural resources, 64, 122–23, 168; for oil sector, 28, 168; policy recommendations in, 172–73; in small and medium enterprises, 32–33; in sub-Saharan Africa, 64–68; sustainability of, 33–34; trends in, 166–73. *See also* Official development assistance; *specific countries*

Foreign exchange, 40–46, 49–52, 105, 127
Foreign Policy (Lubold), 174
Forum on China-Africa Cooperation (2015), 102
Foster, Vivien, 76, 88
Fox, M. Louise, 30
France: aid given by, 196–97; bilateral investment treaties of, 172; foreign direct investment of, 29, 166, 170; security operations in Africa, 199, 204; WAEMU, institutional agreement with, 127
Fraud, 224. *See also* Corruption
Free trade agreements: continental, 11, 126, 150; regional integration and, 30, 150. *See also specific agreements*
French Development Agency, 132
Frontier markets, 65

G-8 (Group of 8), 107–08, 156
G-20 (Group of 20), 154
"G20/OECD High-Level Principles of Long-Term Investment Financing by Institutional Investors," 85–86
G-77 (Group of 77), 113
Gabon: credit rating downgrade of, 104; debt servicing in, 42–43; infrastructure investments in, 93
Gambia: Chinese relations with, 100; currency in, 91
GDP (gross domestic product): Agenda 2063 goals for, 4; expected growth in, 9; FDI, attracting, 18; manufacturing sector and, 21–22, 223; mining sector and, 21–22; rebasing of, 17–22; remittances as percentage of, 155; service sector and, 18–25; Sustainable Development Goals and, 219; World Bank forecast for, 230. *See also specific countries*
GE, 29
Geothermal energy production, 125
Germany: aid given by, 196; bilateral investment treaties of, 172; foreign direct investment of, 166
Gettleman, Jeffery, 8
Ghana: capital flow reversal in, 216–17; commodity exports and, 26; currency devaluation in, 40, 43; debt servicing in, 45–46; Ebola outbreak, assistance for, 139; Ex-Im Bank project authorizations in, 190; employment in, 55; fiscal position, deterioration of, 11; foreign borrowing of, 104; foreign direct investment in, 28; IMF program of, 104; infrastructure investments in, 93; Obama's speech to parliament, 176; pension funds in, 144; renewable energy projects in, 157; security operations in, 200
Global Counterterrorism Forum, 200
Global Covenant of Mayors for Climate and Energy, 118
Global Employment Trends 2014 (ILO), 53–55
Global Entrepreneurship summit (2015), 184
Global financial crisis (2008–09), 86, 98, 100, 128, 196
Global Findex (2014), 122
"Global Land Rush" (Arezki, Deininger, and Selod), 211
Global poverty, 14–15
Global value chains, 71, 130, 220, 229, 231
Global warming. *See* Climate change
Goals for Africa, 226–40; governance and development, 226–28; infrastructure financing, 228–36; national level recommendations, 236–38; regional level recommendations, 238–40; U.S. assistance in economic development, 148–53
Google, 29, 33
Governance: climate change and, 114–15; corporate governance, benefit to, 224; development financing and, 226–27; economic, improvement in, 150; EU assistance for, 202; financial sector and, 145–46; foreign direct investment and, 64, 170–71, 227–28; institutional quality and, 10–11; intraregional

trade barriers and, 128; public financing and domestic markets, 69, 75; resource management and, 27; tax revenue management and, 33, 51–52, 106, 226–27; U.S. assistance for, 150, 201; World Governance Indicators, 145, 170
Grand Renaissance Dam, Ethiopia, 125
Green Climate Fund, 113, 115, 156
Greenfield infrastructure projects, 86–87, 152, 183, 238
Gross domestic product. *See* GDP
Group of Five (Indonesia, Malaysia, Saudi Arabia, Thailand, and United Arab Emirates), trade with sub-Saharan Africa, 27
Growth Commission, 125
GSM Association, 119
Guinea: agriculture in, 136; conflict in, 11; Ebola outbreak in, 135–36; GDP of, 135
Guinea-Bissau: conflict in, 11; independence of, 5
Gulf of Aden, commercial fishing in, 58
Gulf of Guinea, piracy in, 11, 30
Gutman, Jeffrey, 81
Gutsche Family Investment, 183

H1N1 flu epidemic (2009), 138
Hassan, Mohamed Abdi, 61
Health infrastructure: Ebola crisis and, 6, 135–39; foreign aid and, 197, 201, 204; mobile payments and, 141
Heritage Foundation, 149–50
Highways, 12, 131–34, 229
Hijackings and hostage-takings, 58–61
HIV/AIDS, 197
Horn of Africa Region and Sahel Region Capacity-Building Working Groups, 200, 204
Huawai, 29, 33
Human capital, 221. *See also* Education
Human Development Index, 5, 8, 11
Humanitarian aid, 197
Human mobility, 116, 132–34. *See also* Transportation
Human rights issues, 175, 202

"Ibrahim Index of African Governance," 8, 150
Identification systems, 142
Illicit financial flows, 70–71, 173, 201
ILO (International Labour Organization), 53–55
IMF. *See* International Monetary Fund
"Index on Economic Freedom" (Heritage Foundation), 149–50
India: climate change and, 111; foreign direct investment of, 166, 215–16; growth of, 50; raw material imports of, 215; trade with, 27, 214–15
India African Forum Summit (2015), 214
Indian Ocean, maritime training missions in, 198
Indonesia: piracy and, 60; trade with sub-Saharan Africa, 27
Industrial sector: deindustrialization and, 55, 223–24; employment in, 55; foreign direct investment in, 34; GDP rebasing and, 20–22; global value chains and, 71, 130; structural transformation and, 16. *See also* Manufacturing sector
Informal sector: economic reliance on, 15; financial technology and, 146; GDP rebasing and, 18–20; industrial sector and, 16; piracy and, 58; productivity and, 13; tax revenues, effect on, 118
Information and communications technology: financing for, 80, 229–30; foreign direct investment in, 2, 29, 73–74, 77; GDP rebasing and, 20; policymaker support for, 24; regional integration and, 222; trade, effect on, 229. *See also* Mobile phones
Infrastructure: AfDB's support of, 222, 234–35; for agroprocessing and manufacturing, 13, 33; brownfield projects, 87, 238; capital inflow requirements for, 154–55; capital markets for, 155–56; competitiveness and, 106, 222, 229; Eurobonds for, 12; foreign direct investment for, 29, 231, 239; greenfield

Infrastructure (cont.)
projects, 86–87, 152, 183, 238; international financing for, 156; pension funds for, 235–38; private financing of, 2; programs for, 228–35; technology improvements and, 141–42; total spending needs for, 88. *See also* Energy; Financing for development; Transportation; Urbanization
Infrastructure bonds, 90, 238
Infrastructure Consortium for Africa, 222
Infrastructure Project Preparation Facility (IPPF), 90
Innovations: in agriculture, 140–41; in financial technology, 141; in financing, 89–90, 140; in health sector, 141; in infrastructure, 141–42, 238
Institute of International Finance, 124
Insurance companies, 144, 193
Intermedia survey, 121
International Chamber of Commerce, 171, 205
International Conference on Financing for Development (2015), 63, 68, 113–14, 156. *See also* Addis Ababa Action Agenda
International Energy Agency, 112, 156–57
International Labour Organization (ILO), 53–55
International Maritime Organization, 59
International Monetary Fund (IMF): debt management assistance from, 45; Direction of Trade Statistics, 182; Ebola outbreak and, 139; on EU trade with Africa, 196; growth estimates for sub-Saharan Africa, 34–35, 98; growth estimates for West Africa, 135; on infrastructure needs, 72, 231–32; on oil-dependent nations, 104–05; on public investments, inefficiencies of, 75; *Regional Economic Outlook* on sub-Saharan Africa, 9–10, 48–49, 98; U.S. Treasury's global economic agenda and, 153; World Bank–IMF Spring Meetings, 216, 218–21; *World Economic Outlook*, 45
International private financing, 155
International Tropical Timber Organization, 171, 205
Intraregional trade, 126–29, 151, 157, 229–30
IPPF (Infrastructure Project Preparation Facility), 90
Islamic Corporation for the Development of the Private Sector, 92
Islamic financing for infrastructure, 91–93

Japan: aid given by, 213–14; bilateral investment treaties of, 172; foreign direct investment of, 28, 166–69, 213–14; Tokyo International Conference on African Development, 159–61, 163–65, 213–14
Japanese Overseas Cooperation Volunteers (JOCV), 213
Japan International Cooperation Agency (JICA), 213

Kaberuka, Donald, 221–23
Karti, Ali Ahmed, 163–64
Kaufman, Daniel, 170, 227
Kenya: Chinese relations with, 47; commodity imports, success of, 12; energy resources in, 125; financial inclusion in, 119–21; GDP of, 9, 17–23; Global Entrepreneurship summit in, 184; government securities in, 144; infrastructure investments in, 73, 75, 90, 96; mobile services in, 120, 140–42; natural resources in, 123; pension funds in, 84, 235; railway construction in, 207; retail sector in, 32; security operations in, 199–200
Kenyatta, Uhuru, 207
Kerry, John, 175
Kharas, Homi, 31–32
Kim, Jim Yong, 217
Kimberley Process, 171
Kimenyi, Mwangi, 176

Kituyi, Mukhisa, 62
Knowledge and skills transfer, 64, 71, 173
Know-your-customer regulations, 142, 157, 192
Kraay, Aart, 170, 227

Lake Chad basin, conflict in, 11
Lake Turkana wind farm (Kenya), 125
Land grabs, 209–11
Latin America, foreign direct investment of, 166
Leo, Benjamin, 172
Lesotho: infrastructure investments in, 73; mobile payments in, 144
Levitt, Arthur, 224
Liberia: agriculture in, 136; Ebola outbreak in, 135–37; financial technology in, 141; financing for development in, 87–91; GDP of, 135; infrastructure investments in, 79, 87–91; recovery of, 29, 88, 135
Libya, security operations in, 198
Life expectancy, 27
Li Keqiang, 206–07
Liu, Estelle, 48
Long-term investing for development financing, 34, 83–87. *See also* Foreign direct investment
Lubold, Gordon, 174

Macroeconomic challenges, 130, 145–46, 221
Madagascar, U.S. African Growth and Opportunity Act and, 185–88
M-Akiba (mobile banking), 140
Malacca Strait area, piracy in, 60
Malawi, infrastructure investments in, 79
Malaysia: Islamic sukuk use in, 92; piracy and, 60; trade with sub-Saharan Africa, 27
Mali: conflict in, 30, 34; International Support Mission in, 199; security operations in, 198, 204
Mandela Washington Fellowship, 201–02
Manuel, Trevor, 108
Manufacturing sector: in Asia, 223–24; employment in, 16, 55–56; GDP contributions to, 223; GDP rebasing and, 21–22; infrastructure and, 230; intermediate goods, increase in exports of, 151; technology and, 13. *See also* Industrial sector
Maritime law, 59
Maritime training missions, 198
Mastruzzi, Massimo, 170, 227
Mauritania: Chinese relations with, 100; EU relations with, 195
Mauritius: foreign direct investment of, 166, 168, 173, 215–16; governance performance in, 170
McArthur, John, 56–57
MDBs. *See* Multilateral development banks
Megacities, 116
Metal: decrease in global prices for, 98–99, 135; gold production, 123. *See also* Mining sector
Microfinance, 120–21, 142, 192
Microsoft, 29, 33
Middle class: consumer spending and, 29, 168, 170; convergence among countries and, 14; defined, 31–32; increase in, 11, 27, 31–32; of sub-Saharan Africa, 56
Millennium Challenge Corporation, 150, 181
Millennium Development Goals, 62–65. *See also* Sustainable Development Goals
Mining sector: "blood diamonds" and, 171; Ebola outbreak and, 136–37; employment and, 32; foreign direct investment for, 168; GDP rebasing and, 21–22
M-Kopa Solar (mobile banking), 141
Mobile phones: big data and, 131–34; data for transportation projects and, 3; financial inclusion and, 119–22, 140, 142; foreign direct investment in, 32; increase in use of, 119; microfinance and, 142; for mobile payments, 11, 120, 140–42

Mo Ibrahim Foundation, 8, 150, 195
Mongolia, exports of, 123
Monterrey Consensus (2002), 63–64, 68
Morgan Stanley Capital International African Frontier Market, 29
Morocco: Dutch-Moroccan Foreign Fighter Project, 200; energy resources in, 125; EU summit attendance and, 161
Mozambique: Chinese relations with, 47; corporate governance in, 224; debts of, 11; gas discoveries in, 34; GDP of, 208; Japanese foreign investment in, 214; Japanese relations with, 28; natural resources in, 123; U.S. relations with, 182
M-Pesa (mobile banking), 11, 120, 140
M-Shwari (mobile banking), 121, 140
Mugabe, Robert, 161
Multilateral development banks (MDBs), 85–86, 115, 132, 155. *See also specific organizations*
Municipal bonds, 69
MV *Maersk Alabama,* 58
Myers, David, 243

Namibia: infrastructure investments in, 93; pension funds in, 84, 235
Natural gas sector: employment in, 55; foreign direct investment for, 28; global production and, 26–27; technological innovation and, 123; U.S. energy boom and, 124–25
Natural resources: demand from emerging markets, 26; economic reliance on, 15–16; employment and, 32; foreign direct investment for, 64, 122–23, 168; global trends for, 122–26; governance of, 27. *See also specific resources*
NEPAD (New Partnership for Africa's Development), 232–33
"NEPAD Continental Business Network (CBN) Report on De-Risking Infrastructure and PIDA Projects in Africa," 233
Netherlands, Dutch-Moroccan Foreign Fighter Project, 200
NetMob conference (2015), 131
New Deal on Energy for Africa, 234–35
New Partnership for Africa's Development (NEPAD), 90, 232–33
Niger: climate change adaptations of, 112; security operations in, 198, 204
Niger Delta Avengers, 51
Nigeria: agriculture in, 136; capital flow reversal in, 216–17; Central Bank of Nigeria (CBN), 50, 52; commodity exports of, 11, 12, 26, 51, 123–24; conflict in, 6; currency devaluation in, 12, 40, 43, 49, 128; Ebola outbreak in, 135–36; Ex-Im Bank project authorizations in, 190; export diversification, lack of, 9; financial inclusion in, 119, 121; foreign direct investment in, 28, 168; GDP of, 17–23, 50, 101, 219; industries in, 16, 20, 24; infrastructure investments in, 73–74, 79, 91–93, 96; mobile services in, 121, 140; pension funds in, 84, 235; policy and economic management in, 50–52; railway project in, 207; remittances to, 33, 70; slow growth of, 99; terrorism in, 30, 204; U.S. relations with, 182
Njoroge, Patrick, 107

Obama, Barack: AGOA Extension and Enhancement Act, 181; economic development goals for Africa, 148–53; speech to Ghanaian parliament, 176. *See also* Power Africa; U.S.-Africa Leaders Summit
Ocean preservation, 71
ODI (Overseas Development Institute), 40, 43
OECD. *See* Organization for Economic Cooperation and Development
Official development assistance (ODA): EU-U.S. cooperation in, 204; good governance attracting, 228; increase in, 69; infrastructure gap and, 72, 78–80; from Japan, 213–14; remittances and FDI vs., 65–68; total for 2012, 196

O'Hanlon, Mike, 188
Oil sector: attacks on, 51; China, exports to, 48; commodities as driver of growth in, 26; decrease in global oil prices and, 10–11, 98–100, 102–06, 219; diversification, lack of, 9, 12; employment in, 32, 55; fiscal reforms for, 221; foreign direct investment for, 28, 168; as global percentage, 26–27; international reserves for, 104; sub-Saharan Africa and, 102–07; technological innovation and, 28, 123; U.S. energy boom and, 124–25, 182
Open Government Partnership, 149
Opportunities. *See* Risks and opportunities
Organization for Economic Cooperation and Development (OECD), 85, 173, 196, 239
Organization of Petroleum Exporting Countries (OPEC), 12
Organized crime, 71, 202. *See also* Piracy
Overseas Development Institute (ODI), 40, 43

Paris Conference of Parties (2015), 12, 112–14, 118
Partnerships of Africa, 147–225; EU strategies and, 202–03; EU-U.S. cooperation and, 203–04; EU vs. U.S. engagement strategies, 194–201; Ex-Im Bank, 188–94; foreign direct investment trends, 166–73; Kaberuka on development, 221–23; multilateral institutions, 216–21; private sector role and, 223–25; U.S.-Africa Business Forum, 180–84; U.S.-Africa Leaders Summit, 158–66, 174–80; U.S. African Growth and Opportunity Act and, 185–88; U.S. goals for Africa, 148–53; U.S. strategies and, 201–02; U.S. Treasury's global agenda, 153–58. *See also specific countries*
Peacekeeping Rapid Response Partnership, 201
Pension funds, 235–40; financial technology and, 144; for infrastructure investments, 75–76, 84, 235–38; management of, 237; national support for, 236–38; regional support for, 238–40; SWFs vs., 84
Per capita incomes, 14–15
Petraeus, David, 188
Pew Research Center, on African public opinion of China, 208
PIDA (Program for Infrastructure Development in Africa), 86, 222, 232–33
Piracy: in East Africa and Somalia, 58–61; in Gulf of Guinea, 11, 30
Policy Framework for Investment, 239
Policy recommendations: agricultural sector and, 212; capacity strengthening, 239; Chinese economic slowdown and, 49; economic environment, supporting, 236; employment and, 56–57; fiscal sustainability, 37–38; foreign direct investment governance and, 64, 172–73; global commitments and, 12; global financial regulations and, 70; infrastructure investment, 28, 68, 89, 95–96, 229, 237–38; innovation, 238–39; for Nigeria, 50–52; oil-dependent economies and, 103; pension systems and, 237, 240; political leadership and, 236; regional financing and capital markets, 238–39; services sector, support for, 13, 15–16, 24; tax revenues, 75
Pollution, 58, 60, 71, 116. *See also* Climate change
Population demographics: growth of, 13, 230; life expectancy and, 27; urbanization and, 116; youth, increase in, 11, 13, 30, 56, 218
Poverty rates: agricultural sector and, 111; climate change and, 117; decrease in, 14, 98; financial inclusion and, 122; global poverty and, 14–15; infrastructure and, 230; per capita incomes and, 14–15; social protection programs and, 100, 106–07

Power Africa (U.S. initiative): benefits of, 152–53; business community and, 148; Ex-Im Bank and, 191; infrastructure finance and, 156; purpose of, 175; renewable energy and, 125; Swedish investment in, 71–72; U.S. Electrify Africa Act and, 181
Presidential Infrastructure Champion Initiative, 233
PricewaterhouseCoopers, 224
Pritchett, Lant, 24
Pritzker, Penny, 175
Private capital flows, 65–66, 68, 77, 224
Private equity firms, 29
Private payment networks, 145
Private sector: blended financing and, 155, 173; bottlenecks for, 231; corruption and, 70; Ebola Response Fund, 222; employment in, 32–33; information and communication investments of, 2; infrastructure investments of, 88–89, 101, 148, 158, 175, 203, 233; Islamic securities, 91–93; knowledge and skills transfers to, 64; oil exports and, 106; pension systems and, 236; role of, 2–3, 77–78, 223–25; Ex-Im Bank and, 188–89, 191–93. *See also* Foreign direct investment; Official development assistance
Program for Infrastructure Development in Africa (PIDA), 86, 222, 232–33
Public investment, 230, 232
Public-private partnerships, 83, 156–57, 213, 232–33
Public sector, 88, 91, 175, 224. *See also* Governance; Pension funds; Tax revenues
Pugliese, Jessica, 56–57

Qaddafi, Muammar, 5

Race, financial services access and, 122
Railroads, 207, 229
Rakotondrazaka, Fenohasina Maret, 65
Ransom payments, 58–59
Raw materials, 34, 151, 215
Regional development banks, 115, 238
Regional economic integration: EU promotion of, 203; improvement in, 11; infrastructure projects and, 222; trade benefits of, 30; U.S. promotion of, 150–51; West African Economic and Monetary Union and, 126–29
Regional Economic Outlook (IMF), 9–10, 48–49, 98
Regional Infrastructure Development Master Plan (RIDMP), 233–34
Remittances: cost of, 70, 144, 156; dependence on, 33; financial sector and, 143–44; as GDP percentage, 155; increase in, 66–67, 70; in middle-income countries, 68
Renewable energy resources, 112, 125, 141–42, 156–58
Repressed economies, 149–50
Republic of the Congo: Chinese relations with, 100; credit rating downgrade of, 104; infrastructure investments in, 79
Research and development, 29, 212
Retail sector, 12, 29, 32
RIDMP (Regional Infrastructure Development Master Plan), 233–34
Risks and opportunities, 97–146; big data and, 130–34; Brexit and, 107–10; climate change and, 110–15; Ebola outbreak, effects of, 135–39; financial and digital inclusion and, 118–22; financial sector development and, 142–46; innovation and, 140–42; macroeconomic stability and, 130; natural resources and, 122–26; regional economic communities and, 126–29; in sub-Saharan Africa, 98–102; sub-Saharan Africa's oil exporters and, 102–07; urbanization and sustainability, 115–18
Rodrik, Dani, 23, 27, 56, 223
Rural areas: employment in, 56; energy technology for, 141–42; health clinics in, 141; infrastructure for, 130–31, 141–42, 229, 231; land tenure systems, 101; migration to urban

areas, 116; mobile payments and, 141; poverty in, 111
Russia, climate change and, 111
Rwanda: climate change adaptations of, 112; corporate governance in, 224; GDP of, 28, 208; health innovations in, 141; infrastructure investments in, 93; mobile services in, 140; natural resources in, 123; railway in, 207; recovery of, 29; security operations in, 200; U.S. relations with, 182

SABMiller, 183
Sachs, Jeffrey, 63
Safaricom, 121
Sahel: conflict in, 1, 11; Horn of Africa Region and Sahel Region Capacity-Building Working Groups, 200, 204; security operations in, 199, 204
Samaritan's Purse, 179
Sanitation systems, 69, 78
Sapiro, Miriam, 189–90
SARS epidemic (2002–04), 138
Saudi Arabia, trade with sub-Saharan Africa, 27
Sawyer, Patrick, 179
SDGs. *See* Sustainable Development Goals
Security: EU assistance in, 202, 204; as piracy deterrent, 59–61; U.K. assistance in, 109; U.S. assistance in, 176, 199, 201, 204
Security Governance Initiative, 201, 204
Seko, Mobutu Sese, 5
Selod, Harris, 209, 211–12
Senegal: agriculture in, 210; Dakar Integrated Special Economic Zone, 132; debt servicing in, 42–43; employment in, 6; foreign direct investment in, 28; GDP of, 9; independence of, 5; infrastructure investments in, 92, 93; municipal bonds in, 69; presidential elections in, 6; remittances to, 70; security operations in, 200; toll highway in, 3, 131–34
Senghor, Léopold Sédar, 5
Service sector: economic reliance on, 15, 18; GDP rebasing and, 18–25; governance needs in, 13; growth in, 15, 16; structural transformation and, 130
Seychelles, infrastructure investments in, 93
Sheets, Nathan, 153–56
Sierra Leone: agriculture in, 136; Chinese relations with, 100; Ebola outbreak in, 135–37, 141; financial technology in, 141; GDP of, 135; infrastructure investments in, 79; recovery of, 29; security operations in, 199–200
Silk Road Infrastructure Fund, 235
Singapore: foreign direct investment of, 166; piracy and, 60
Sirleaf, Ellen Johnson, 87
Slums, 117
Small and medium enterprises (SMEs): access to finance, 143, 146, 155; defined, 192; Ex-Im Bank and, 190–93; employment in, 184; foreign direct investment in, 32–33
Smart contracts, 145
Soft infrastructure, 130. *See also* Education; Technology
Solar power, 125, 141–42
Somalia: African Union Mission, 109, 199; governance in, 60–61; piracy in, 58–61; remittances to, 70; security operations in, 198
Somali Basin, commercial fishing in, 58
South Africa: apartheid in, 5; capital flow reversal in, 216–17; Chinese relations with, 47, 100; currency devaluation in, 128; deindustrialization in, 223; Ebola outbreak, assistance for, 139; Ex-Im Bank project authorizations in, 190; EU summit boycott and, 161; financial inclusion in, 119, 121–22; foreign borrowing of, 104; foreign direct investment in, 28, 168, 170; GDP of, 219–20; governance performance in, 170; infrastructure investments in, 73–74, 75, 79; mobile services in, 121–22; pension funds in, 84, 235; renewable energy projects in, 157; slow growth of, 11, 99

South America, foreign direct investment of, 166
Southern African Development Community, 109–10, 127, 195, 233–34
Southern Africa Trade Hub, 184, 195
South–South cooperation and investment, 33, 166
South Sudan: aid from Japan, 214; civil war in, 8, 11, 29–30, 34, 218; infrastructure investments in, 73, 79; railway in, 207
Sovereign bonds, 29, 40–46, 75, 92
Sovereign wealth funds (SWFs), 83–86
Sow, Mariama, 127, 226
Spence, Michael, 125
Staple food crops, 56, 136
Stock and bond markets, 124
Structural transformation: convergence and divergence, 13–15; economic growth and, 24; GDP rebasing and, 17; industrialization and, 16; macroeconomic stability and, 130; need for, 220; in sub-Saharan Africa, 56; urbanization and, 116
Sub-Saharan Africa: bilateral investment treaties in, 172; commodities as driver of growth in, 26; convergence in, 14–15; debt servicing in, 40–42; employment in, 54–56; energy resources in, 125; Eurobond use in, 93–94; external factors influencing growth in, 35–39, 48; financial inclusion in, 118–22, 140, 142; foreign direct investment in, 64–68, 166–73; GDP of, 9–10, 17–18, 34–35, 54, 98, 176, 219, 230; infrastructure needs of, 72–75; innovation in, 140–42; middle class in, 31–32; Muslim population in, 92; oil exports of, 102–07; per capita income in, 6; regional economic integration and, 126–29; renewable energy projects in, 157; repressed economies in, 149; risks and opportunities in, 98–102; trade partners of, 27; U.S. relations with, 148–53, 181–82. *See also specific countries*
Subsidies: for agriculture, 110; budget issues and, 220; electronic payments, 146; for fuel, 49, 100; reducing, 220
Sudan: EU summit and, 161, 164–65; U.S.-Africa Leaders Summit exclusion and, 161–63
Sukuk financing, 91–93
Summers, Lawrence, 24
Sustainability of economic prosperity, 26–52; China's role in development, 27–28; Chinese yuan devaluation and, 46–50; external factors' influence on growth, 34–39; foreign exchange risk of sovereign bonds, 40–46; foreign investment and, 30–34; fragile countries and, 29–30; growth prospects and, 26–27; Nigeria, case study on, 50–51; opportunity areas for, 29; prosperous countries and, 28; tax revenues and public services, 63
Sustainable Development Goals (SDGs): big data and, 130–31; Common African Position on the Post-2015 Development Agenda, 72; creation of, 62; domestic revenue mobilization for, 226–27; as driver of growth, 12, 98; financing for, 62–65; GDP growth rates and, 219; infrastructure improvements and, 88; oil-dependent economies and, 103; urbanization and, 117
Swaziland, infrastructure investments in, 75
Sweden, Power Africa initiative and, 72
SWFs (sovereign wealth funds), 83–86
SWIFT, 157
Sy, Amadou, 81, 127

Tang, Ke, 124
Tanzania: agriculture in, 140–41; foreign direct investment in, 28, 173; GDP of, 17, 19–23; infrastructure investments in, 75; mobile services in,

140; natural resources in, 123; security operations in, 200; U.S. relations with, 182
Tariffs, 128, 185
Tax revenues: domestic base for, 63; Ebola outbreak and, 137; evasion of taxes and, 221, 225; financial technology for collection of, 141; illicit financial flows and tax evasion, 70–71, 173; increasing, 100–101, 106; informal sector, effect of, 118; infrastructure spending and, 74–75, 80; management of, 33, 51–52, 106, 226–27; rate of, 220; system strength for, 63; value added tax and, 49, 51, 100, 106–07, 221
Technology: for biometric identification, 142; employment and, 13; financial, 141–42, 144–45; foreign direct investment for, 29, 64; for governance, corruption, and trust, 145; natural resource extraction and, 28, 123; for pension reform, 238; for renewable energy resources, 112, 125, 141–42, 156–58. *See also* Information and communications technology; Mobile phones
Terms-of-trade, 10, 51
Terrorism: combating the financing of terrorism (CFT) rules, 70, 157; economic growth, effect on, 30; French military presence to deter, 199, 204; Global Counterterrorism Forum, 200; oil sector, attacks on, 51; U.S. military presence to deter, 176
Textile industry, 185–88
Thailand, trade with Africa, 27
Third International Conference on Financing for Development (2015), 12
Tigo Kilimo, 140–41
Togo, infrastructure investments in, 79
Tourism, Ebola outbreak and, 137–38
Trade: bans on, 170–71; border procedures and, 128; competition in, 174; global, reduction in, 182–83; information and communications technology and, 229; intraregional, 126–29, 151, 157, 229–30; regional economic integration and, 30, 127, 144; terms of trade, 10, 51; transportation for increase in, 12; U.S.-EU competition for, 194–96; U.S. relations and, 149–58. *See also* Free trade agreements; Transaction costs; *specific countries*
Trade Africa (U.S. initiative), 150, 181, 195
Trade Winds Business Forum, 182
Transaction costs: banking regulations as, 157; economic and trade integration to reduce, 30, 127, 144; payment system integration and, 69; small and medium enterprises and, 192
Transformative Partnership on Energy for Africa, 234
Transparency: Africa summits and, 164–65, 183; capital markets and, 238; Chinese financing and, 208–09; climate change mitigation and, 118; corporate governance and, 225; economic governance and, 150; EU strategies for, 202; Extractive Industries Transparency Initiative, 149, 171, 205; in natural resource sector, 228
Transportation: to boost trade, 12; costs of, 230–31; domestic financing for, 80; Ebola outbreak and, 136–38; financing for, 2, 69, 78; health innovations and, 141; highways, 12, 131–34, 229; intraregional trade barriers and, 128; railroads, 207, 229; regional integration and, 222
Tripartite Free Trade Area, 150
Twitter, 179
Tyson, Judith, 40, 43–45

Uganda: Ebola outbreak, assistance for, 139; GDP of, 17, 19, 21–23; infrastructure investments in, 75, 125; mobile services in, 140; natural resources in, 123; railway in, 207; security operations in, 200

Unemployment: contrasted with economic growth, 8, 32; piracy and, 58; in sub-Saharan African, 55; youth population and, 54, 56
United Arab Emirates, trade with sub-Saharan Africa, 27
United Kingdom: aid given by, 196–97; bilateral investment treaties of, 172; Brexit and, 107–10; Department for International Development, 109; foreign direct investment of, 166; security operations in Africa, 199–200
United Nations (UN): Climate Change Conference in Paris (COP21), 12, 112–14, 118; Conference on Trade and Development (UNCTAD), 166, 168, 171, 173; Data Innovation for Policy Makers conference (2014), 131; Ebola outbreak and, 138–39; Economic Commission on Africa, 222–24; Environmental Programme, 112; fishermen-pirates, assessment on, 58–60; Framework Convention on Climate Change, 115; Global Compact, 65; High-Level Panel on the Post-2015 Development Agenda, 63; illicit financial flows, discouragement of, 71; Meeting on Climate Change (2015), 113; Mission for Emergency Ebola Response, 139; peacekeeping missions, 198, 200–01, 204. *See also* Sustainable Development Goals
United Nations General Assembly, 62, 234
United Nations Security Council, 60, 199
United States: aid given by, 196–97; bilateral investment treaties of, 172–73; Chinese currency devaluation and, 47; climate change and, 110–11, 113; Dodd-Frank Act, 170; Doing Business in Africa campaign, 152, 182, 184, 191, 195; EAC cooperation agreement, 181; Ebola outbreak and, 139; economic development goals for Africa, 148–53; energy boom in, 124–25, 182; EU competition for trade in Africa, 194–96; EU cooperation in Africa, 203–05; exports, decline in, 182; foreign direct investment of, 166–69; global economic and financial policy, 153–58; interest rates in, 46, 94, 99; Office of African Nations, 150; Office of Technical Assistance, 45; policy recommendations for, 172–73; President's Emergency Plan for AIDS Relief (PEPFAR), 197; renewable energy resources and, 34, 125; security operations in Africa, 176, 198–200; strategies for Africa, 201–02; Strategy toward Sub-Saharan Africa (2012), 148, 152; trade with Africa, 50, 151, 194–95. *See also* Power Africa; *entries starting with U.S.*
Urbanization: challenges of, 3; climate change and, 115–18; consumer spending and, 29; economic effect of, 11, 27; infrastructure financing, 68–69, 73; rural to urban migration, 116
U.S.-Africa Business Forum (2016), 180–84
U.S.-Africa Civil Society Forum (2014), 164
U.S.-Africa Clean Energy Development and Finance Center, 191
U.S.-Africa Leaders Summit (2014): African Peacekeeping Rapid Response Partnership, 200, 204; bilateral meetings and format of, 174; business forum, 175; competition for trade and, 174–75; design features and recommendations, 159–66; Ebola outbreak and, 138, 158; human rights issues and, 175; media coverage trends and, 177–80; strategies for, 148, 158–59, 201–02; successes of, 176–77

U.S. African Growth and Opportunity Act (AGOA): AGOA Extension and Enhancement Act, 181; conflicting agenda with EU, 205; coverage of, 159–60; Ex-Im Bank and, 193; Madagascar and, 185–88; outcome of, 176; overview of, 185; purpose of, 151; strengthening, 153; trade promotion of, 203

Violence: climactic events linked to, 111; countries experiencing, 11, 29–30, 34; countries recovering from, 29; decrease in, 27; foreign direct investment and, 34. *See also* Piracy; Security; Terrorism
Voice of America, 137

Walmart, 29
Water subsidies, 220
Watkins, Kevin, 108–09
Weather events, vulnerability to, 114, 117
West Africa: foreign direct investment in, 28; highways in, 12, 131–34; regional integration of, 126. *See also* Ebola crisis; *specific countries*
West African Economic and Monetary Union (WAEMU): Ebola outbreak, assistance for, 139; economic integration and, 126–29; infrastructure financing in, 95–96; macroeconomic stability in, 130; private capital flows and, 68–69
West Africa Trade and Investment Hub, 184, 195
Will Africa Feed China? (Brautigam), 209, 212
Wind farms, 125, 157
Women: access to credit, 143; employment and entrepreneurship, 13, 201, 236; financial services, access to, 119–20, 122; international summits, inclusion in, 164
World Bank: Africa Infrastructure Country Diagnostic (AICD), 234; *Africa's Pulse,* 8–9, 48–49; big data and, 131; climate change adaptation and mitigation efforts, 115; debt management assistance from, 45; on Ebola outbreak impact, 136–39; Global Financial Inclusion Index (Findex), 120; Global Infrastructure Fund, 234; highway project in Senegal and, 132; increased loans from, 217–18; on infrastructure needs, 72–73; infrastructure plan, 231; International Development Association, 196, 217; on Kenya, 18; on middle class, 32; Multiple Finance Self-Assessment exercise, 117; private investment, catalyzing, 155; on public-private partnerships, 157; on service sector in Africa, 18; on urbanization and poverty reduction, 117; U.S. Treasury's global economic agenda and, 153; weather events, losses due to, 114; World Bank–IMF Spring Meetings, 216, 218–21; *Youth Employment in Sub-Saharan Africa,* 53
World Bank Group, 89, 108
World Economic Forum (2014), 206
World Economic Outlook (IMF), 48
World Governance Indicators, 145, 170, 227
World Investment Report 2014 (UNCTAD), 168, 173
World Urbanization Prospects (UN), 116

Xi Jinping, 207
Xiong, Wei, 124

Young African Leaders Initiative, 201
Youth: employment of, 11, 13, 53–54, 56; leadership, encouraging, 201–02; population increase of, 11, 13, 30, 56, 218
Youth Employment in Sub-Saharan Africa (World Bank), 53

Zambia: capital flow reversal in, 216–17; Chinese relations with, 47, 100; commodity exports and, 11; currency devaluation in, 43; GDP of, 17, 19, 21–23; infrastructure investments in, 93
Zenawi, Meles, 108
Zimbabwe: EU summit boycott and, 161; governance performance in, 170; U.S.-Africa Leaders Summit exclusion and, 161–63
Zipline (drone company), 141
Zuma, Jacob, 161
Zurich Global Corporate, 193